Praise for Fountain Creek

"*Fountain Creek* takes us on a fascinating tour of an abused and unassuming stream, fed by the effluent of cities and carrying with it centuries of human history. Jim O'Donnell reminds us that—even within earshot of the interstate's roar—water still flows and wildness persists."

—ZAK PODMORE, *Life After Dead Pool*

"A beautifully told story about an essential body of water and the options for its future as the West gets hotter and drier."

—BETSY GAINES QUAMMEN, *True West*

"O'Donnell steps cautiously and curiously into Fountain Creek and encourages us all to love our home rivers, even when we're afraid of what we might find."

—LAURA PASKUS, *Water Bodies*

"*Fountain Creek* is a meticulous, heartfelt ode to a chronically mistreated watershed. Every stream in the American West deserves a biographer as affectionate, thorough, and lyrical as O'Donnell. May this book help us find the wisdom to restore Fountain Creek and many other waterways like it."

—BEN GOLDFARB, *Crossings*

"O'Donnell's compassion for the roaming watercourse is evident with his knowledge of the past and firsthand observations. Through sharp examination and expressive writing, *Fountain Creek* gives readers deeper respect and understanding of why Fountain Creek is a crucial and vital resource which can not and should not be discounted or ignored."

-JEFFERY PAYNE, Poor Richard's Books

"In his affecting, prismatic, and beautifully-wrought exploration of the past, present, and possible future of Fountain Creek, O'Donnell reminds us that we have a chance at healing the world at large, if only we look first to places closest to home."

—AMY BRADY, *Ice*

"What might still flow through these damned-up and dried-out days of ours? *Fountain Creek* is lovingly navigated and tenderly told by O'Donnell and becomes a baptismal stream for the Anthropocene. This book *swims*."

—TIM DEE, *Four Fields*

"*Fountain Creek* shows how myths of place and belonging influence our interactions with the natural world."

—STERLING SHALLBETTER, Old Firehouse Books

"A quietly beautiful exercise in the glory of natural spaces, O'Donnell's *Fountain Creek* is a panacea for and an acknowledgement of the hurts and injustices done to the wild world on behalf of humanity's irrepressible 'progress.'"

—MOLLY IMBER, Maria's Bookshop

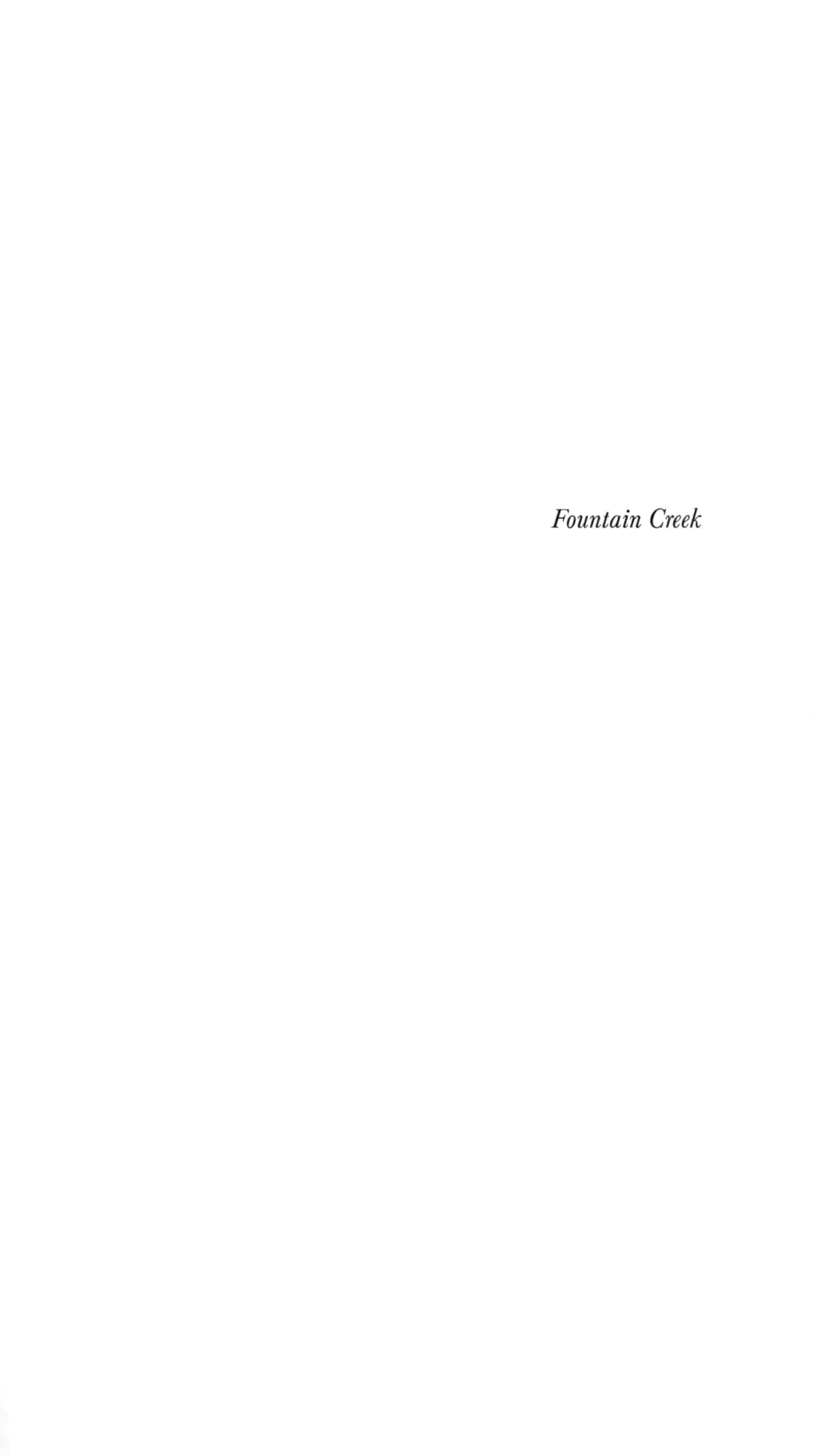

Fountain Creek

FOUNTAIN CREEK

Big Lessons From a Little River

Jim O'Donnell

TORREY HOUSE PRESS

Salt Lake City • Torrey

First Torrey House Press Edition, November 2024

Published by Torrey House Press
Salt Lake City, Utah
www.torreyhouse.org

International Standard Book Number: 979-8-89092-011-9
E-book ISBN: 979-8-89092-012-6
Library of Congress Control Number: 2023952235

Cover design by Kathleen Metcalf
Interior design by Gray Buck-Cockayne
Distributed to the trade by Consortium Book Sales and Distribution

Torrey House Press offices in Salt Lake City sit on the homelands of Ute, Goshute, Shoshone, and Paiute nations. Offices in Torrey are on the homelands of Southern Paiute, Ute, and Navajo nations.

For my grandchildren, my great-grandchildren,
and my great-great grandchildren.

We live for the other, only.

TABLE OF CONTENTS

NOTE

Throughout this book, I have chosen to use the Indigenous names for the nations and people that inhabited or utilized the Fountain watershed and continue to call it home. I've done this for two reasons. First, calling people by the names they've chosen to call themselves is basic human to human respect. Second, there is currently a movement to return many landscape feature names in Colorado to their original, pre-colonial labels. It is my opinion that this move is far past due, and I hope to see this movement gain speed. These names may challenge your tongue and your brain a bit—and that's a good thing.

Before making this choice, I spoke with numerous Indigenous friends and acquaintances and found my desire to utilize the pre-colonial names to have widespread support.

Finally, note that there is no one agreed upon spelling for these names and so I've chosen to use the spellings preferred by tribal governments.

Nuuchiu (Ute)
Tin-ne-ah (Apache)
Numunuu (Comanche)
Hinono'eino (Arapahoe)
Tsistsistas (Cheyenne)
Ka'igwu (Kiowa)

"...a river is a peculiar and insidious affair that is not always what it seems and...it slides into other dimensions in lovely and mysterious ways."

–Ann Zwinger, Run, River, Run

"People don't pay attention. And then one day there's an accounting.
And after that, nothing is the same."

–Cormac McCarthy, No Country for Old Men

FOUNTAIN CREEK

City

Peak

Rivers

Interstate

U.S. Route

State Highway

Watershed Boundary

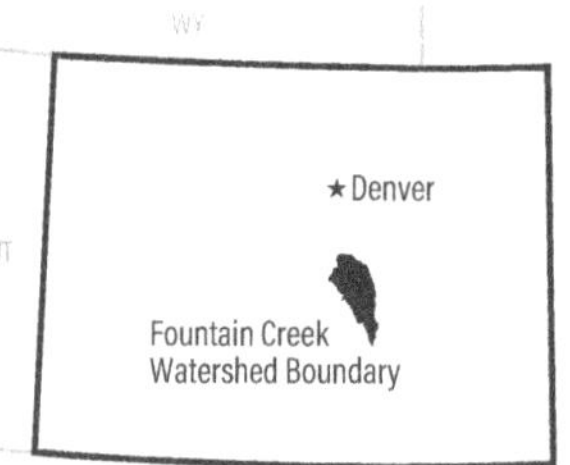

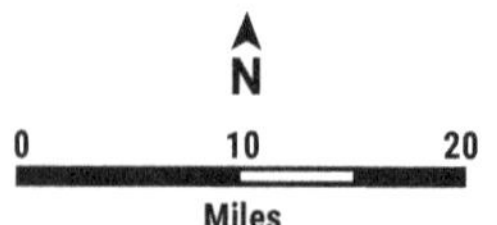

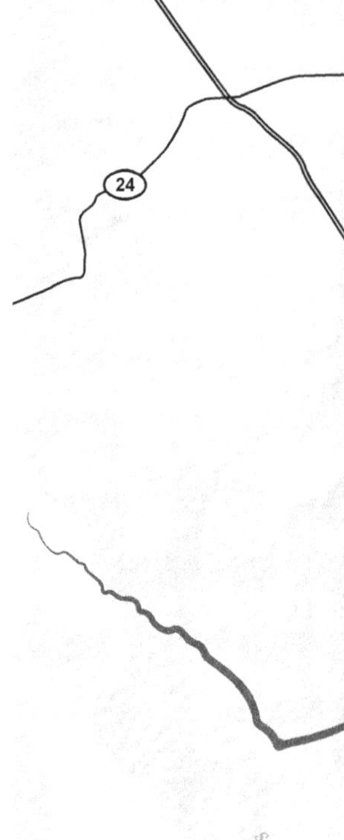

Vanessa Holz, Designer
Zach Scribner, GIS Analyst & Archaeologist

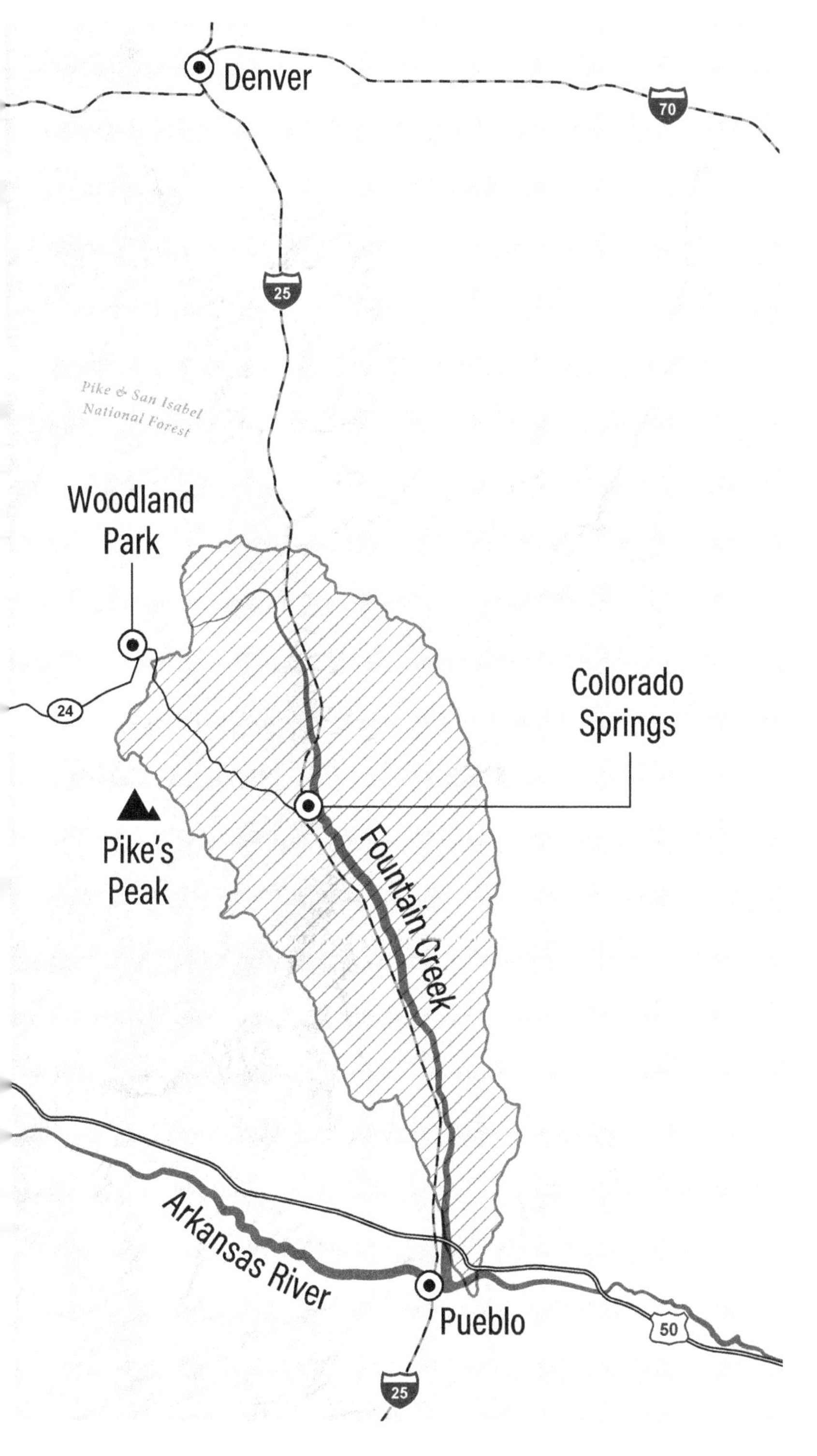
Denver
70
25
Pike & San Isabel
National Forest
Woodland
Park
24
Colorado
Springs
Pike's
Peak
Fountain Creek
Arkansas River
Pueblo
50
25

THE CREEK

Three geese scooted the creek then veered toward a mass of cattails. A coyote slipped into the tamarisk, reappeared upstream, then vanished. Deer prints tracked feeble smears of snow edging the ice. I came to the bridge just after dawn. Along the creek, the forest was all faded yellows and shades of gray.

I walked up from the Fountain trailing the ghost whinny of a woodpecker. It moved ahead, elusive, always beyond sight. The sky, a cold indifferent blue, pushed to the rim of the mountains where gloomy clouds crowded the peaks and ridges. Ponds, frozen in Januarys past, held thin, spherical lips of ice bordering the shore and the base of cattails. A nuthatch called, a nasally wah-wah-wah. I stopped, but as with the woodpecker, I couldn't locate the bird.

For several hours I moved north, pushing through the creekside forest. I came to a cement barrier where an irrigation canal siphoned a significant portion of the creek's flow. The water tumbled over a rock ledge into a frothy pool. A blue heron stood where the flow eddied. Several hooded mergansers bobbed in the froth alongside a plastic shopping bag, bits of blue plastic, and an old Gatorade bottle. A mallard shouted, rose and turned north.

The heron, barely a body length away, just across the flow, focused on a school of pinky-sized silver chub and minnows crowding the pool. She waited, betraying nothing. Then, she stabbed, pulling two minnows into her beak. She gulped and returned to her statuesque hunting position.

I plopped to the ground, opened my pack, and poured a cupful of coffee from my thermos. I added a generous splash of whiskey, closed my eyes, pulled a deep breath, and listened to the soothing chorus of the creek.

There was a place along that section of Colorado's Fountain Creek where a beaver had constructed a dam. The structure grew at the confluence of the Fountain and a brook cascading from the forest. The beaver's pond was long, skinny, and deep, snaking from the dam through an elven copse of elms, willows, and sheltering cottonwoods. The aquatic rodent had cleared dozens of trees, creating a wide, open meadow filled with water, a rich wetland ecosystem in the middle of the forest.

I had seen snowy egrets fish the pond while teals and wood ducks dabbled. I had counted sora at the pond. Sora, Virginia rail, sandpiper, and, once, a white ibis, a coastal bird from the southeast, rarely seen in the mountain west. One summer afternoon, I'd sat at the edge of the pond breathing the rich, wet scents. Duckweed blanketed the water, turning the forest a glowing green. The beaver surfaced, a yard distant, her head crowned in a ring of duckweed. Another day, midwinter, the beaver had pushed through a film of ice and studied me over, eyes and nose just breaking the surface. She watched me for what felt like a century, then slipped beneath the black waters.

The beaver dam and pond were my goal that day.

At some point, the path led through a collapse of elms. The trees had been toppled by an unprecedented windstorm that battered the Front Range of the Rocky Mountains six weeks earlier. Meteorologists described the blow as "ludicrous" for its intensity. Climate-change-driven temperature differences between the poles and the equator had forced the jet stream more southerly. The peaks increased the high-altitude turbulence, and the wind crashed into the foothills and prairies of eastern Colorado with hurricane-force winds, throwing countless trees to the ground and driving a grass-fed wildfire that burned through communities northwest of Denver. Nearly two thousand homes turned to ash in less than an hour.

I crawled over and under the downed trees, leaves and dry grasses rustling and crunching under my boots. West, across the creek, the blinking billboard of a hotel flashed in the gloam. The hotel stood next to the crowded Interstate 25, a massive north-south highway running the length of Colorado's Front Range. A whale-like military aircraft banked then cut east. A shopping cart lay in the mud collecting trash from upstream: plastic bags, plastic water bottles, bits of clothing, and a diaper. Mallards flushed from the bank. Two kingfishers raced for a willow. The sky darkened and a perfume of snow fringed the wind. I shivered.

The path I followed runs for several miles along Fountain Creek, just south of the city of Colorado Springs.

We call the Fountain a "creek" because once upon a time, it actually was a creek: a thirsty, ephemeral waterway, a tributary to the Arkansas River, prone to occasional dramatic floods. Today, the Fountain runs full and swift the entire year.

The Fountain trickles from snows blanketing the slopes of the 14,115-foot-high mountain most Americans know as Pike's Peak. The original people of the region, the Tabeguache Ute—Nuuchiu in their own language—know the peak as Tavá Kaa-vi, "Sun Mountain," and the waters birthed from Tavá flow seventy-four-and-a-half miles to its confluence with the Arkansas River at 4,695 feet in my hometown of Pueblo, Colorado.

Tavá Kaa-vi has many names in many languages—Nuuchiu, Hinono'eino, Ka'igwu, Numunuu, Tin-ne-ah, English, French, Spanish—and there is some controversy as to how we should refer to the massive pile of pinkish granite. To me, it's just The Peak.

—

In middle school, I biked with my friend Scott Grant to the creek. We rode through a shadowed cottonwood gallery—populated, so we had been told, with drug dealers and Satan-worshippers—to the creek's edge, where we sought arrowheads in the shifting, pink sands of the dry bed. In high school, another friend, Dave Atencio, and I fished from a bridge at the confluence. We sipped at cans of Coors pulled from an ice-filled Styrofoam cooler we'd liberated from his father's garage. Nearly frozen was the only way I could stomach Coors. It was true then, and it is even more true today. Atencio and I took mostly trout and a few bass, then scrambled down to the sandbar east of the bridge to build a fire, cook, eat, and make up stories about things that hadn't happened to us yet. We drank well into the night. In the fall, we hunted, illegally, for pheasant and quail in the sloughs and river bottom forests north of the city. In the winter, Atencio and I returned, exploring the artless red sands for bankside Pleistocene reliquaries, the sediments iced and prickly on our bare, digging fingers.

Scott is dead. A bullet took his head apart while at a party in high school. Atencio is also dead. He, at least, made it into his early forties before a heart attack took him after a softball game. For me, the Fountain carries ghosts.

Fountain Creek is one of the most human-dominated water systems in the American West—and that's saying something.

Over the years, the Fountain has been dammed, diverted, poisoned, rerouted, mapped, named, channelized, filled with physical and human debris, reduced, augmented, confused, litigated, studied, stolen, replaced, piped, known, unknown, forgotten, remembered, misunderstood, blamed, monitored, sampled, screened, and very nearly tamed. More than anything else, humans have altered the very nature of the Fountain, pumping water from Colorado's western slope into the Fountain's watershed, making what was once an occasional creek into a full-time river. Across the American West, climate change driven droughts and altered precipitation cycles collide with overconsumption, drying up "real" rivers. The creation of a "new" river, then, is more than a bit mind-bending.

To the west, the storm tumbled down the mountains, draping the blue in a turbulent gray. At the edge of the ridge, you could see that it was snowing. The temperature plummeted. The wind kicked up. The song of the blow in the treetops swirled with that of the water rushing over the gravel in the creek. Soon I could not distinguish one from the other.

I counted fifteen crows huddled in a cottonwood, clicking, rattling, and croaking. I imagined them discussing the impending storm. I followed a hole through a crowd of willows back to the water, passing over ancient sediments held in place by the roots of trees and grasses, and onto the shifting deposits bordering the creek.

The alluvial sands of the Fountain are varying shades of pink, red, and orange. They are tracked in prints of heron, geese, ducks, fox, coyote, skunk, porcupine, beaver, deer, squirrels, and the occasional elk, bear, and mountain lion. And, of course, people. Nearly a million people live within the Fountain watershed. When the creek rises, it washes the sediments free of prints. When the flow drops, tracks reappear within hours. With each step, I added my prints to the ephemeral tapestry of life along the creek.

But the beaver's dam was gone. The pond drained. The water-loving rodent that had eyed me the previous summer was nowhere to be found. The dam, the pond, the beaver—they had all been there just one month earlier. There hadn't been enough moisture for a flood to wash the dam away. Even more confusing, logs from the dam were scattered upstream along the gravel, some of the larger chunks of wood resting twenty to thirty feet from where the dam had been. I circled back through the willows to what had been the top of the pond, scouring the area for evidence.

Without the dam, the wetland drained. Only small pools remained, the briefly stilled waters glistening under the gray. The brook bubbled, rippling the surface, stirring tufts of bent, yellow grasses, while the moss-covered rocks shone neon green against the black and yellow canvas.

I made my way back to where the dam had been, completing a circle. On the gravel beach, the light had shifted. In the sand, among the prints of geese, coyotes, and anglers, I made out the faint track of a machine, a tracked Bobcat or, perhaps, a Kubota excavator. The beaver dam had been deliberately dismantled, the pond purposefully drained, the beaver possibly killed or, at best, driven off.

There had been no reason, at least none that I could see, for tearing the dam apart. It hadn't threatened any road, trail, farm, building, or other human prize. It had simply been there, filtering sediments and pollutants, slowing the flow, replenishing the aquifer and hosting a diverse ecosystem.

I kicked at the tracks in the sand.

If there's a specific word that describes a special place in nature harmed or violated by human beings, I haven't found it. "Desecration" comes close but doesn't quite fit. If there isn't such a word, there ought to be, for it is an all-too-common occurrence. The fact that there may not be a word for such a thing suggests we accept such violations as normal.

I sat again, poured more coffee, splashed in the whiskey, and watched snow tumble to the water. The oversized flakes were puffy and light. Across the Fountain, a man finished a fresh wooden fence. He had set the posts in concrete and shoveled sand and gravel across the cement to protect it from the coming freeze. Behind the man, I-25 roared, packed with rush-hour commuters. Another military transport circled overhead. A helicopter, another plane, a quad drone, then sirens.

I tell myself, or more accurately, I try to teach myself not to collapse into anger and despair with every slight to the land and waters. They are too many, too often, and if you take it all to heart—which I tend to—functioning in this age of this world becomes impossible.

I pushed myself out of the sand and gathered the logs, branches, and sticks that had once made up the beaver's dam. Some were the size of my leg and heavy. Most were forearm sized. I carried these in bundles. I piled the wood next to the creek, tore off my gloves and coat, rolled up my sleeves, and set about rebuilding the dam.

First, I forced a dozen or more smaller sticks vertically into the bed of the brook. The water filled my boots and soaked my pants. My feet numbed. Next, I cut willow with a knife my son had given me for Christmas and wove the branches through the vertical supports. I placed the larger logs horizontally behind the structure and packed it all with mud.

I knew full well this was a useless gesture. I was acting out, trying to make myself feel better, as if by taking some sort of action I might have influence yet. I could never construct a dam as well as a beaver could. My dam would conform in no way to what the beaver or the creek wanted or needed. My dam, I knew, wouldn't survive the first of the heavy spring flows in the brook, and anyway, the creek will win out. It always has and it always will. Water always wins. The Fountain will remain. A beaver will build a fresh structure. An egret will fish among the duckweed. A rust-colored coyote will prowl the woods. The creek will survive. The river knows what it knows. The story does not end. The story never ends.

But what of my children? My grandchildren? What about you? What about me? My existence in this world has felt like

I am a man with hands chained behind his back, working to untangle a knotted ball of yarn, strings, cables, ropes, cords, and threads. Life in the age of climate change—fatherhood in the age of climate change—confounded and, far too frequently, depressed me. More often than not, it seems I am faking my way through an existence that doesn't quite work for me, and I just don't understand what to do about it all. I scramble for purchase. I scramble for purpose. Many days I don't know where I'm headed.

This book, then, is an imperfect attempt at finding the truth of something. Not all the truth and certainly not the truth of everything. But a truth about something. This is the story of how we've learned everything there is to know about a creek and how we've learned so little about ourselves; it aims to bear witness, to grieve, to offer gratitude, and to uncover something essential about this moment, about us as a people, the Fountain, and the future of water in the American West.

By the time the snow arrived, I had a dam that slowed and pooled water while not halting the flow. The water backed up, the pond grew. It was nearly dark and the wind shifted, driving the snow horizontal into my face, stinging in a thousand unique pricks. I was soaked, sweating, and caked in mud. The temperature plummeted and a deep shiver took hold, the kind of relentless shuddering that tells you you might soon be in a whole heap of trouble. I worried that my wife, Rasa, might be anxious about me.

I pulled on my coat and gloves. I finished the whiskey, took up my pack, hopped the brook, and scrambled up the embankment.

A great V of geese passed overhead, pushing up the Fountain, into the storm.

ORIGINS

"Years of drought and famine come and years of flood and famine come, and the climate is not changed with dance, libation, or prayer."

–John Wesley Powell

It all began with a flood.

At midnight on June 17th, 1965, James Osnowitz cleared his desk and departed the offices of *The Pueblo Chieftain*, where he interned as a reporter. Word was the Fountain was to flood, and Osnowitz hoped to watch the waters rise near a crossing just north of the City of Pueblo. He made for home, changed clothes, and scrawled a message for his parents across a blackboard in the kitchen. "Driving north," he wrote, and promised to call from Colorado Springs. Osnowitz dropped into the local bar hoping to convince a friend or two to join him on the adventure. No one took him up and he set out alone into the rain.

Around the same time, my father was also on the road, pushing north into the storm. At midnight, he had completed his own work shift assembling car pistons at the Triplex plant near the Pueblo airport. Like Osnowitz, my father went home to clean up and change clothes. He was expected at court in Boulder early the following morning for a speeding ticket that he insists was not deserved. He crossed the Fourth Street bridge and noticed the creek was unusually high. But he didn't think much of it and, about an hour ahead of Osnowitz, he made his way north.

That same night, Ronnie White, a recent graduate of Widefield High School near Colorado Springs, drove his 1950 Plymouth to meet with friends. He'd also promised to check in with his mom at the local grocery store where she worked.

My father, twenty-five years old at the time, survived the harrowing journey to Boulder. Osnowitz, twenty-two, did not. Eighteen-year-old White disappeared.

"The storm, awesome and ugly, vented its anger capriciously," wrote Associated Press reporter David Cook. Another journalist called it "freaky weather" while, "Wind, Rain, Hail Batter Colorado" ran as a headline in *The Pueblo Chieftain* on June 16th, 1965.

That spring had been unusually wet. Rain fell nearly every day since May 22nd, and the soil along the Front Range was saturated. The National Weather Service described the rain on June fourteenth as "heavy," "light" on the fifteenth but "torrential" on the sixteenth, and "tremendous" on June seventeenth—the night the Fountain flooded Pueblo, the night my father crept north, trailing a bulldozer that cleared the road ahead, the night White's Plymouth was swept from B Street in a wall of water, and the night Osnowitz drove his car off a bridge, collapsed by the storm, and into the flood just north of Colorado Springs, drowning in the surge.

In early summer 1965, unstable atmospheric conditions pulled wild amounts of moisture from the Gulf of Mexico. Heat lifted the humid air to where it collided with cool Pacific Northwest currents near the peaks. Odd, early morning thunderstorms developed along the mountain chain between Pueblo and Denver. That reliable wind from the west never showed. Instead, a light breeze blew from the east and the storms stuck to the top of the watershed, dumping torrents of rain and hail, and kicking off several tornados.

In Pueblo, the Fountain spilled from the channel, ripping metal structures from their foundations north of the Sweeney Feed Mill, smashing them into east Fourth Street Bridge. Water poured over the bridge and into the neighborhoods beyond, inundating fifty-three city blocks with water eight to ten feet deep.

Seventeen-year-old Diana Maes watched the waters rise, but she could not convince her father to escape. Years later, she told an interviewer how her father simply refused to believe the Fountain could flood. It simply was not that kind of river, he insisted. It was not until the flood waters lapped at the feet of his chair that they raced from the house.

Nearby, Casilda Rodriguez hurriedly packed her most important things in a suitcase. Her husband and brother-in-law had gone down to the bridge to watch the flood, and, as the waters filled her house, she panicked. "I was crying, excited, and nervous," she told a reporter in 1988. "We had been working on our home for three years remodeling. Then we had to leave for four days and when we returned, we had to live upstairs and cook on the grill; everything was destroyed. Three feet of water filled the house. We should have moved, but we couldn't because of our finances." It was two days before her husband returned.

More than one thousand Puebloans evacuated to Risley Junior High School. Hundreds were trapped in their homes, in trees, or on small islands. Twenty-four hours later, when the waters began to recede, Puebloans found a good portion of the city had become a muddy mess.

When it was all said and done, two dozen Coloradoans were dead, more than six hundred injured; some five thousand homes were destroyed along with nearly seven thousand small businesses. The destruction spread from Denver to Colorado Springs to Pueblo and east, nearly to the Kansas border. Damages totaled $550 million, $5.1 billion in 2023 dollars.

If you plop down at the keyboard and search up "deadliest train wrecks in American history," you'll find a list that begins with Malbone Street, 102 dead. That tragedy is followed by Nashville, 101 dead, Ashtabula, 98 dead, and Wellington, 96 dead. For some reason, the Eden disaster never tops the list. It may seem a tad audacious to dispute the mighty search engines, but the deadliest train wreck in American history in fact occurred along the banks of the Fountain.

About six miles north of Pueblo, Porter Draw meets Fountain Creek. Porter drains an extensive, mostly treeless spread of low hills dotted with grasses, sage, prickly pear, cholla, and, since the 1990s, a sprawl of cheap looking, oversized homes. It enters the Fountain from the west, or the right bank.

When we talk about "left" or "right" banks of a river, imagine yourself standing in the middle of the water facing downstream. The right bank is on your right and the left bank is on your left. This may seem a little confusing at first, but it is actually rather useful as a descriptor since rivers rarely run strictly north-south or east-west.

In 1904, Porter was known as Dry Gulch or Hogan's Gulch, a parched, crumbly, twenty- to thirty-foot-deep erosional cut named for the family that ranched the land bisected by the draw. At the time, a wooden trestle known as 110-B bridged Dry Gulch, facilitating heavy train traffic between Denver and Pueblo.

Around 5 p.m. on Sunday August 7th, 1904, just prior to leaving Denver, engineer Henry S. Hinman was handed a "bulletin order." The Missouri Pacific's No. 11 Flyer, making the daily run from Denver to St. Louis via Pueblo and Kansas City, was to proceed cautiously. Heavy rain, the bulletin warned, was falling between Colorado Springs and Pueblo. Slow down. Watch for water.

The No. 11 and its six cars rumbled south at normal speed to Palmer Lake, where Herbert R. Graves, manager of the Pueblo Plumbing Company, boarded the train. Graves had spent the weekend with his wife in the high country, where she retreated each summer to avoid the hay fever that burdened her life in Pueblo. Jacob Emrich also boarded at Palmer Lake. The head cashier for the Pueblo Zinc Smelter left his wife, Addie, and their youngest children at their summer home while he returned to Pueblo to deal with business issues.

Graves and Emrich weren't the only ones. In those days, Pueblo's industrial, bourgeoisie elite regularly escaped the summer heat of the polluted, buggy city, migrating to higher elevations where many maintained second homes. As the No. 11 departed, Graves, Emrich, and their clique settled in for dinner, expecting the reliably smooth passage to Pueblo.

By all accounts, engineer Hinman took the bulletin order warning seriously. A northbound train crossed the 110-B at 7:15 p.m., reporting no issues. When the rain set in south of Colorado Springs, Hinman slowed the locomotive from sixty miles per hour to twenty, then to fifteen, as the rain grew to a downpour, the evening light faded, and visibility dropped to almost zero. The acetylene headlight projected a scant two hundred feet in front of the engine. Some passengers complained about the slow speeds. They had schedules to keep, appointments to meet, family waiting. Hinman, however, proceeded with caution as ordered, watching for water. The No. 11 arrived at Dry Gulch at 8:15 p.m.

According to Ione Miller, writing in 1999, David Mayfield, fireman for the No. 11, was the first to realize there was a problem.

Hogan's Gulch—Dry Gulch—was at flood, and the once reliably dry arroyo tore into the Fountain, dislodging a rickety county road bridge along the way, smashing it into the 110-B. In a later inquiry, Mayfield, the only surviving member of the locomotive's crew, testified that as the train crossed the 110-B he was horrified by a sickening "side-to-side" sway of the bridge. He described the sound as similar to pipes breaking—the stomach-wrenching bending of steel and the shattering of wood. Mayfield hit the throttle, increasing speed in hope of landing the 298,640-pound engine on the opposite bank before the trestle collapsed.

Dow Helmers, in *Tragedy at Eden*, recounts how the front end of the No. 11 reached the south bank of the gulch but that behind the engine, the bridge collapsed. The tender, baggage car, coach, and smoking car pulled the locomotive backwards into the roiling waters. The engine landed on its side. The flood tumbled the passenger cars end over end before they came to rest some 1,500 feet downstream.

Somehow, Mayfield either leapt or was thrown from the cab window before the engine fell. He crashed to the embankment. A surge of water washed him into the torrent. Pushed tens of yards downstream, he scrambled from the flood and raced back to the engine searching for Hinman, the crew, and the passengers. But the engine was gone, sunk. Lightning crashed around him. Between the thunderclaps came a horrifying sound: the screams of the injured, the trapped, the drowning. Injured himself and helpless to save anyone, Mayfield set off down the track for help, seeking the Eden depot a mile distant.

Passenger Richard Brunazzi pulled himself from the floor of one of the Pullman sleeping cars, checked his family, and, finding them shaken but unharmed, jumped from the halted car. Thanks to a recently installed automatic braking system, the two Pullmans and the dining car had decoupled from the rest of the train and jerked to a halt on the north edge of the gulch, throwing the passengers but leaving them mostly uninjured. Brunazzi made his way forward in the dark downpour until he realized the front half of the train was gone. The roar before him was the flood, the night pierced by thunder, rending metal, and screams for help.

Ninety-seven bodies were pulled from the wreck, fifty-two of them prominent Puebloans. Fourteen were never found. Some estimates of the missing claim twenty to thirty bringing the overall death toll to somewhere between 111 and 125. The conductor's list of passengers likewise drowned in the Fountain and bodies disappeared into the quicksand. For years after, human remains that turned up along the sandy banks of the Fountain or the lower Arkansas River were presumed victims of the Eden disaster.

If Colorado's Fountain Creek is reliable for any one single thing, it is its extraordinary unreliability. The Fountain floods and floods often—and violently. How often? I could not find a complete list of inundations so I set to creating my own, pulling from the work of other researchers, USGS publications, old newspaper accounts, and old timey traveler's journals. For a time, I grew obsessed with finding flood mentions that predate 1826, but that search hit dead end after dead end, though I presume a sedimentologist or hydrologist might piece together a deeper history through sediment cores, satellite data, and other remote sensing tools. As far as I know, this is the most comprehensive list of Fountain floods that exists.

Spring 1826: Major flood, details unknown.
Spring 1844: "Four feet of snow fell over the valley and lay there for three moons. The flood waters reached from bluff to bluff."
Spring 1859: Details unknown.
June 18, 1864: "But about 4 o'clock a heavy cloud came up over Cheyenne Mountain and the sky gathered darkness until nearly sundown, when rain and hail began to fall in tremendous

torrents . . . the rain came down, not in drops, but in floods . . . the country was flooded as if a vast lake . . . a wide torrent, covering all the low country adjacent to the creek . . . for a month or more it was impossible to ford the Fountain below Colorado City."

May 21-22, 1876: Snowmelt from The Peak drove the Fountain to flood.

May 1878: "Monument and Fountain creeks swept out bridges, El Paso County losses very heavy, caused by cloudburst near Divide followed by hail."

June 1884: "The Fountain at Pueblo was wide, swift and deep on Thursday [June 26] and swept away both the wagon bridge on Fifth Street and the Denver and Rio Grande Railroad bridge."

July 25, 1885: A severe cloudburst north of Colorado Springs drove a "sharp flood" on the Monument, a tributary to the Fountain.

May 30, 1894: "The flood has done great damage at this place . . . the Fountain, which flows through this town [Colorado City], has been very high for the past twenty-four hours . . . early this morning the north approach of West First Street bridge was carried away . . . at 7:30 this evening a two-room house . . . was carried away."

May 31, 1894: "Rain has been falling steadily all day, making a continuous fall of fifty hours . . . the Fountain has been tearing away stone walls and foundations and bridges [in Manitou Springs] all day."

June 2, 1894: "The damage caused by the stream [in Pueblo] cannot be estimated." (It was later estimated at $2 million in property damage.)

May 27, 1902: ". . . a sudden flood on Fountain Creek . . . the flood moved the depot from the west side of the tracks to the east side . . . wall of water ten feet high . . . destroyed everything in the lowlands of Fountain Creek."

August 1904: Eden disaster.

May 18, 1914: "Cloudbursts just south of Colorado Springs contributed to the wall of water said to be fifteen to twenty feet in height that came roaring into town [Pueblo] . . . the immense dredge and steam shovel used by the Pueblo Sand Company . . . floated downstream and were practically covered in sand."

June 1921: "The flood on Fountain Creek overflowed the valley from Colorado Springs to the mouth of the creek at Pueblo, destroying bridges and damaging agricultural land."

July 27-30, 1932: ". . . a wall of water swept through Templeton Gap . . . flooding Papetown mining settlements . . . and most of the northern part of the city [Colorado Springs] . . . torrential rains near Fountain . . . 200 foot section on the Denver and Rio Grande washed to a depth of about six feet."

May 30, 1935: "Dozens of houses in the low-lying areas were lifted from their foundations . . . all the bridges across Monument and Fountain Creeks in the city [Colorado Springs] except one were destroyed."

June 17, 1965, May 1995, June 1997 . . .

April 29, 1999: "Heavy rains swelled Fountain Creek . . . prompting flooding . . . in Pueblo, city crews worked to keep the Fountain from washing away the riverbank behind the Target store . . . many people are homeless due to the flooding . . ."

June 2005, May 2007, September 2013, May 2023 . . .

The Fountain is home to a multitude of ghosts. People lost their lives in nearly every one of these floods. How many is guesswork. Five were believed lost in the 1894 flood. Officially, eighteen died in 1935. These tolls are surely undercounts. It was common in those days for the working poor, the unhoused, immigrants, and ethnic minorities to settle along the river and creek banks because those areas were typically considered unattractive or unhealthy by wealthier, white Coloradoans. These creek side communities were essentially unknown to authorities.

Or ignored. The people undocumented, uncounted, many being single men who had come from across the world to work at John D. Rockefeller's Colorado Fuel and Iron Company (CF&I).

As with the 1965 flood, the 1921 inundation, one of the deadliest and most destructive in American history, sits within family memory. My maternal grandmother, six years old at the time, recalled scrambling into the attic of her auntie's home in Pueblo's East Side neighborhood, her brother, sisters, and cousins pulling her to safety.

The 1921 flood spread throughout the entire Arkansas River basin causing $25 million in damages, over $415 million in 2023 dollars, in Pueblo alone. Officially, 120 to 250 individuals lost their lives in 1921, but a 2020 master's thesis on the Great Pueblo Flood by Harvard scholar Jonathan Cohen suggests a more severe toll, reaching upwards of 1,500 with 600 being the low-end estimate. Cohen notes that most of the victims were poor or recent immigrants whose names were, and remain, unknown to authorities.

Bodies from the 1921 flood turned up downstream for decades. In the late 1950s, the battered remains of a woman fell from a cutbank dozens of miles east of Pueblo. The bits and pieces of clothing and jewelry that remained indicated she might have been a victim of the '21 flood.

In 1998, three children playing in debris along a dry creek bed in Colorado Springs stumbled across the skeleton of Ronnie White. For all those years, Ruby Heatherly had sought her son Ronnie in the faces of strangers, in stores, or at events, desperate to somehow stumble upon her lost son. "I had asked God," she said after White's skeleton was recovered, "that I would like to find closure in my lifetime. After thirty-two years, it's here."

If it all begins with a flood, it also ends with a flood. And then it begins again.

In December 1939, when the Kremlin sent waves of young men to die in the frozen forests of Finland, Tove Jansson, dismayed by the imperial war brought to her country, sat to pen a story with the type of happy ending she hoped for her own nation. "I suddenly felt an urge to write down something that was to begin with 'once upon a time,'" she wrote years later. With Soviet bombs falling on the cities of Helsinki, Turku, and Oulu, and young Finnish men dying in the snow-covered taiga fighting in defense of their homeland, a happy ending seemed elusive at best. The result of Jansson's efforts was *The Moomins and the Great Flood*.

Two of my three children are half-Finnish. Their mother, my first and hopefully only ex-wife, hails from the Swedish-speaking island chain off the southwest Finnish coast. The Moomins are a family of white, round trolls—somewhat resembling a hippopotamus—and central characters in picture books and comic strips created by Jansson. They are incredibly popular in Scandinavia and they were a staple in our single-father run household. On one trip to Finland to visit relatives, I gathered up every Swedish-language Moomin book I could get my hands on and brought them home. I was committed to the bilingualism of my kids and, although I spoke some Finnish, I needed to up my Swedish skills.

"Papa, you don't pronounce it like that," my daughter told me multiple times during each reading. My son also hounded me on my tragic Swedish. "You'd better learn to read then," I told them, and they did.

In Jansson's once upon a time, Moominpappa set off on an adventure with the Hattifattners and was late for dinner. Moominmamma and Moomintroll left to find him, entering a frightening forest, travelling through imposing mountains, and finally getting caught out in a multi-day downpour. When the rain ended, the world was flooded. The pair set sail in an armchair. A message in a bottle informs them that Moominpappa is safe but trapped in a tree where he sought refuge from the rising waters.

A stork helped them locate the hungry, stranded adventurer, and they headed for home only to find the flood had washed their house to a new location: a dreamy, idyllic basin they named Moominvalley. The family settled into their new life with their new friends to live, yes, happily ever after.

A happily-ever-after tale born of wartime trauma. History may not repeat itself but it certainly does echo. What fresh stories and visions will be born of Russia's latest colonial war, the unprovoked attack on Ukraine, a situation strikingly similar to Finland's Winter War?

Flood stories pervade human cultures. Everyone it seems, no matter what continent they inhabit, has a flood story.

In Finnish mythology, the hero Väinämöinen suffers a nasty wound while out doing the heroic things heroes do. The Haava rune of the *Kalevala* recounts how blood poured from the wound like a river at flood, drowning the whole world. There was "no high mountain that was not flooded."

A flood. A boat. A healing. Creation. A primordial Goldeneye cures Väinämöinen's knee by building a nest in the wound and laying the World-Egg from which a whole new existence emerged.

The story of Väinämöinen's wound and the flood do not appear in Elias Lönnrot's well-known collected version of the *Kalevala* but does turn up in the accounts collected from Finland's west coast by the Aurora Society in the early 1800's. The Finnish myth of Väinämöinen's flood may have emerged from Finns' Proto-Indo-European ancestors who'd migrated west from the Volga and surely knew stories of what had happened in the Black Sea.

In the late 1990s, archaeologists uncovered the remains of an eight-thousand-year-old village three hundred feet under the Black Sea about twelve miles off the northern coast of Turkey.

Drowned prehistoric settlements were not unheard of in the region. Bulgarian archaeologists had surveyed and excavated several sites along their own coastline since the 1970s. What made the Turkish finds so special was both their age and depth.

Oceanographers Bill Ryan and Walter Pittman of Colombia University were unsurprised by these finds. Their own research indicated that the Black Sea was once a large freshwater lake fed by the ancestral rivers of today's Dnipro, Dnister, Danube, and Kuban. These rivers coursed through a broad, fertile plain dotted with farming communities.

These were the waning years of the last ice age. As the glaciers covering northern Europe melted, rising seas rushed into the Mediterranean, filling it like a bathtub. At some point, the Bosporus ridge overtopped, and a wall of water crashed into the Black Sea basin with a force estimated to be two hundred times greater than Niagara Falls. The rush of water "roared and surged at full spate for at least three hundred days," Ryan and Pittman wrote in their book *Noah's Flood*. The water inundated a mile or more of the basin each day.

For the farmers and pastoralists of the basin, this was an unmitigated disaster. Imagine rising water creeping dozens of yards toward your house each day, eating up the forest, your fields and, before long, your home. The people of the basin scattered, spreading throughout the region—refugees of the Great Flood—some arriving among the Proto-Finns along the Volga, and others to Mesopotamia, where their stories were recorded on clay tablets in cuneiform runes.

The story of the Black Sea flood made its way from Nippur into the Akkadian *Atra-Hasis* and later into the *Epic of Gilgamesh,* where the god Enlil destroys obnoxious humanity with a flood. Later, the Hebrews took the flood story, using it as the basis for the myth of Noah and the Ark. Stories of the Black Sea flood may also be the basis of Plato's Atlantis allegory and may have eventually made it as far north as Finland.

Maybe. This is all speculation. It is informed speculation buoyed by an abundance of research across a number of disciplines, but it remains speculation.

The Ryan-Pittman hypothesis is controversial. Many geologists theorize that the Black Sea filled over a longer period of time or in a series of less dramatic surges. Some archaeologists believe the flood myths populating Mesopotamian cultures during the Old Babylonian Period instead refer to the flooding of the Persian Gulf about nine thousand years ago.

The Noah story pervades Western culture. Yet it is far from the only flood myth. In fact, flood stories are so globally ubiquitous that a pseudoscientific movement has developed to push the idea that these stories combine to support the idea of the global Biblical flood. This is, of course, pure folly akin to *Ancient Aliens*.

What do these stories tell us and what do they not tell us? Not to put too hard a point on it, but they do not confirm the Biblical flood. While there are some similarities among these stories, there are major differences pointing to unique, localized, geologic, and landscape processes.

Flood legends are extremely common among Indigenous people of North America. In these stories, rain swells rivers, glacial lakes burst, inundating the landscape, the sea rises. In one story, a woman builds a fire at the edge of the water to cook her catch of fish, but each day she must move her camp further back up the shore. Each day, a little more. These are clearly stories dating to the end of the last glaciations some ten thousand years ago.

Certain clans of the desert dwelling Hopi people of Arizona tell how they arrived in reed boats after floods inundated the world. Flood stories exist even among the landlocked Nuuchiu of the Fountain watershed. In one story, a powerful leader, bereaved at the loss of his wife, sets out to find her in the

Spirit World. With the help of Rabbit, the two are momentarily reunited before being driven apart again by a great flood that carves the canyons of Colorado.

In another narrative, the water grows angry. As the flood approaches, Rabbit, Wolf, and Coyote run from the rising waters, climbing high into the mountains as the torrent licks at their heels. Eventually they stop, exhausted, hungry, and thirsty. They drink from the water. Instead of salty, undrinkable seawater the floodwaters are fresh and clean. A wave dashes them against a rock and Rabbit, frustrated, takes out his bow and fires an arrow into the water. The flood explodes, flying into the sky as millions of raindrops that fall in torrents throughout the world. The heroes find fruits and vegetables but instead of eating, they save the seeds and scatter them across the land to regrow the world.

Yet another Nuuchiu story tells of the formation of Garden of the Gods at the base of The Peak. The origin of the story is unclear and there are several versions, but it is most likely from the Tabeguache band that lived on and around The Peak. It too tells that, at one time, a flood covered the world, leaving only The Peak above water. Thousands upon thousands of animals drowned and the creator turned the carcasses to sandstone. As the floodwaters retreated, the sandstone carcasses created what we know now as Garden of the Gods, an otherworldly landscape of three-hundred-foot-tall rock that was once been sand dunes and is now a crowded urban park.

The fact that the floodwaters in the Nuuchiu stories are fresh and not salty suggests floodwaters from ancient glacial lakes or even the melting of the Laurentide ice sheet. Perhaps, some of these are ancient stories of flooding along the Fountain.

Anatomically, modern humans were born on the dry savannahs of eastern Africa. Pervasive flood myths, however, suggest that socially, and perhaps even spiritually, we were born of flood. Or, more accurately, floods.

We ignore myths at our peril. These aren't just the stories

of birth, they are stories of rebirth. A common theme among nearly all of the world's flood stories is that creation is a process that never ends. The apocalypse isn't coming, it's here now. The world is ending each and every day, and each and every day, it is born anew.

Craig Childs calls this the "Everending Earth." In *Apocalyptic Planet*, Childs makes clear what should be evident to us all: our planet is an unstable one, the world is anything but reliable, and we should hold no expectation that it will ever be reliable. Ours is a planet of disasters and extremes, and if we can let that reality sink in, Childs says, we can accept our home for what it is. We can stop grasping for a control that we will never attain. If we can manage that, we might begin to imagine a future brighter than any we could construct now.

The apparent unreliability of the world, however, is more often than not, a human failing—not a failing of Mother Nature. We assume floods just happen. They do. However, the destruction caused by flooding rivers is a human choice.

Two or perhaps three years prior to the June 1965 floods, someone at the Gotula Trucking Company in Pueblo bulldozed a large gravel platform into the Fountain's floodplain. Intended for new office space, the platform dramatically narrowed the creek's channel between Eighth and Fourth streets. Around the same time, someone else emptied several dump truck loads of dirt and construction debris into the creek bed near Second Street. The result, a narrowed channel in both locations, removed the ability of the Fountain to manage itself. If the creek had been left alone, it could have carried up to 75 percent more flood water suggested the Director of the Pueblo Regional Planning Commission, C. Allen Blomquist, several weeks after the 1965 flood. "The narrowing greatly contributed" to the flooding of homes and businesses, he told *The Pueblo Chieftain*.

In 1965 an unusual weather pattern dropped bizarre amounts of rain into the Fountain watershed, but a century of mining, timber harvesting, overgrazing, and urbanization had rendered the ground and soil unable to absorb the water as they once had. Add in the removal of thousands of beaver and beaver dams from the region, and there was nothing to slow the waters. Channel constriction in a number of places along the Fountain forced more water downstream faster than it would normally travel. Add to these human created vulnerabilities such as the construction of homes and businesses in the floodplain, and you have a major problem.

What was true in 1965 was probably true in 1904. Severe overgrazing in the upper areas of the Hogan's Gulch drainage resulted in a hardpan landscape devoid of grasses, shrubs, and most other vegetation. Take a glass of water and pour it on a patch of grass. What happens? Now, take that same glass of water and pour it on a cement driveway. By 1904, the Hogan's Gulch watershed had become similar to the cement driveway. The land could no longer soak up the water and it raced off, gouging the soil, carrying it away into the Fountain then the Arkansas. The gulch itself had eroded to the depth it had due to the overgrazing and tree cutting.

It can be hard to accept our role in these disasters. Just weeks after the 1965 flood, in an astounding case of hubris blended with a healthy dose of sheer dishonesty, newspaper editor Ralph C. Taylor conjectured that someone else was to blame for the flood. "Maybe the Indians displeased the Great Spirit Manitou many moons ago and the river that comes from the boiling springs is unhappy with the people," he wrote.

"There is no such thing as a natural disaster," Andrew Digmore, a physical geographer at the University of Edinburgh once told me, "only natural hazards and human vulnerabilities." I'd called Digmore when I was on a deep dive, learning about past cultures and societies that had adapted to a changing climate versus those that could not, or would not. What could we learn, I wondered, from history that could be applied to today? I asked Digmore about the apparent "collapse" of centuries-old Norse settlements in Greenland in the 1400s, and how Jared Diamond was wrong about pretty much everything, always. "Even if you perfect the things you've always done, the outside world is always changing. The goal posts shift," Digmore said. "We create most of our own problems."

Along the road, searching for Moominpappa, Moominmamma and Moomintroll find aid and comfort from a number of supernatural creatures—stand-ins for community members. The pair is faced with hardships they must overcome, and yet they can't overcome those struggles alone. It is only in community—and in this case community and relationships means both the tangible and the ethereal—that they succeed, rescuing Moominpappa and finding their way to a new way of being. In the Moomin world, things we define as "real" are as important as those things that reside beyond the scope of our immediate understanding. *The Moomins and the Great Flood* is an allegory of resilience.

For Jansson, the great flood may have been intended as a stand-in for invasion and war, but stories of floods have something to teach us about how we might unwrap resilience and survive the age of climate change. The world changes, floods happen, get out of the way, be flexible, find strength in community, build relationships, be kind, and don't make your own problems worse.

Early on a cool spring morning, I drove to the eastern edge of Pueblo to pick up my father. The Peak remained locked in snow and a shivering breeze blew from the northwest. It wasn't a wind, but that kind of trickling movement of air that seeps its way through the weave of your clothing.

My father's wife, my stepmother, was dying. One of the most kind and generous people I have ever known, Sylvia had contracted cancer. The cure proved far more destructive than the disease. The medications ate at her brain, rendering a talented, fun, intelligent person to a confused, angry, and sorrowful wraith. I sat with her, stumbling my way through attempted jokes. Sylvia looked at me, not comprehending. My father had been her loving, ever-present caretaker, and the years of effort had worn him to a nub. He needed a break, and I had invited him out for the day to explore the upper reaches of the Fountain. We were both unmoored.

We drove north, contributing to the forever traffic jam that is I-25. To the right, broad, open ranchland spread east to the cottonwoods marking the edge of the creek. For most of its path, the Fountain flows through a wide and shallow prairie valley sunk between low mesas to the east and rolling grass-covered hills that give way to mountains to the west. A classic plains creek. It is only above Colorado Springs that the Fountain is a mountain stream.

"I never thought much about where the Fountain begins," my father pondered.

"Well, let's go find it," I said.

In the summer of 2020, a fire burned west of Taos, New Mexico, where I raised my kids. On my birthday, my teenage daughter created a watercolor. She draped oranges, reds, yellows, and pinks across a sky that leaked into the purple mountains of our homeland. At the center of the watercolor, an enormous plume of thick, black smoke rose into the fiery sky. I hung the painting on my office wall above a world map. I printed a large, color map of the Fountain Creek watershed and hung it on my wall below the watercolor covering the world map. Then I sat and stared.

On the map, the Fountain watershed appeared as a solitary lung ridged in purple. The creek and its tributaries coursed the lung as blue veins, arteries feeding the life organ. Which of these blue veins was the source of the Fountain?

For scientists and watershed managers the answer is simple. The Peak is the birthplace of the Fountain, the highest point in the watershed. That's decided. Still, other values come into play. For some, the source of a river is the tributary that begins the farthest away from the mouth of the river. The point furthest from the mouth of the Fountain, as far as I could tell, was Mt. Deception, the headwaters of Monument Creek, the Fountain's primary tributary. One hydrologist insisted that the true source of the Fountain is indeed Monument Creek and that the Fountain's rightful name was the Monument or, he said, "Whatever the Ute called it." Another man told me the true source of the Fountain begins above Palmer Lake, on the West Fork of the Monument to be specific. Dirty Woman Creek was another contender. So too was Ruxton, which flows from the snows on The Peak. For me, however, the exact origins of the Fountain remain inconsequential. A river, or in this case a creek, is also a journey, a dream of a journey or a journey looking to find its own way. It begins at the source and it returns to the source. The source is always metaphorical. A river, or a creek, means something different to everyone who touches it.

"The true source of the Fountain is behind the Safeway in Woodland Park," my friend Summer Lajoie said. She was a forest bather, a bird watcher, and an artist of feathers, sticks, insects, and leaves. "Go, walk up the path to the play park, you'll see what I mean."

We parked the truck at the Safeway, bought coffee, then walked past the vet clinic and the Subway and around behind the building. A thin asphalt trail pointed upstream, passing behind several double-wides and the Kingdom Hall of Jehovah

Witnesses. The dry, unremarkable Fountain sat constrained within a three-foot-deep channel rimmed with large boulders of pink Pike's Peak granite. Every twenty feet or so, a flood control structure made of the same granite spanned the creek. A man threw a Frisbee to his dog. A woman talked on her phone. I could hear sirens out on Highway 24. We walked among the ponderosas, working to stay in the sun. The breeze coming over the divide still held the winter's chill, but the scent of thawing soil filled the air.

Behind an auto repair shop, the Fountain disappeared into a gated culvert and, for about a quarter mile, travelled under the walking path. It reemerged briefly, just north of Sheridan Avenue. We came to the playground at Cavalier Park just as a child launched himself from the swing and into a muddy snowbank. His mother screamed. The kid threw himself into the mud and rolled. His mother howled again.

"Jeez. Let the kid be a kid," my father growled. "Can't have any fun if you don't get dirty."

A car alarm sounded. A semi-truck groaned past. "Is this it?" I said. And it was.

We scoured the area for signs that the Fountain continued further uphill, but the only things feeding the creek were the residential street gutters of Woodland Park. "I never realized the Fountain starts as street runoff." My father sat in one of the swings. "Makes sense though. They've always treated it like a sewer."

In the late morning, we sat in the sun on the boulders marking the rim of the upper Fountain, working over the future. Both his and mine. My father was worn, sad, and stressed. Within a month, Sylvia would be gone. At eighty years old, my dad faced a completely new life. Well, maybe not all new, I thought. We build on what has come before. My father would rise from his own flood. I wondered how to rise from mine.

"I guess we'll have to climb The Peak to find the source," I said.

"Not me." My father pointed at The Peak and then at the street gutters. "It makes more sense to start at the end," he said.

BONES

"The Earth is layer upon layer of all that has existed, remembered by the dirt."

–Adrienne McCree Brown

Just after dawn, a Chinook fell along the lee of the Southern Rockies. The sere wind drove a branch against the rain gutter running the length of the eave. The bang jarred me awake. The wind howled across the mouth of the chimney. I dressed in layers. It was March after all. I brewed a large mug of coffee, spilled half of it down my pants, and walked from my childhood home down to the creek.

The Fountain meets its terminus at the eastern edge of Pueblo. The Arkansas River, or "The Ark" as we call it in Pueblo, leaves its erosional takings miles upstream, behind the massive concrete dam that forms Lake Pueblo. As a result, where the two waters meet, a distinct line forms: a milky orange-red to the right, clear sea green to the left when looking upstream. The sediments from the Fountain trickle out near the confluence, forming bars and islands, points and riffles, in the watercourse. They also form a beach-like chevron of sand under the South LaCross Avenue bridge and along the left bank of the Arkansas for a hundred yards or more downstream. In the 1980s, when I was a teen, that stretch of sand was mostly bare. Later, it would grow in thick with grasses, reeds, and tamarisk.

Three cottonwood stumps, all cut long ago by beaver, pointed into the sky, the wood grayed and smooth. I saw two sparrows and a bobbing Eurasian collard dove. Then a coyote. I had seen this one before, a large female dressed in a luxurious gray and yellow coat the cast of late winter leaves. She watched me clamber down from the road to the water's edge, then she slipped into the cottonwoods and tamarisk. At the waterline there was a beaver print in the sand, a crushed beer can, and several plastic shopping bags from King Sooper's. A solitary Canadian goose waited on the sandbar. The late season Chinook, although somewhat warm, was not enough to clear the winter chill. I sipped what remained of my coffee, shoved my hands into my coat, and shivered, waiting for the fossil hunter.

The day before, I had met the red-haired collector along the creek north of the Pueblo Mall. His name was Luke, and he carried a stack of bones.

I had gone to talk to some of the unhoused people living along the banks of the Fountain. I parked at the Goodwill, grabbed my walking stick, and picked my way over stumbles of red granite boulders chained to the creek bank with steel wires and fencing. A feral footpath led into the tamarisk and willows. Broken plastic bags vomited their contents along the bank; shopping carts, sleeping bags, clothes, plastic bottles, batteries, toys, condoms, gloves, socks, a broken vibrator, beer cans, soda cans, diapers, and needles blanketed the ground. The stench curled my nose.

Under the Highway 50 bypass a man and a woman pushed bicycles up an embankment. The man lit a cigarette then leaned over and lit the smoke dangling from the woman's lips. They were filthy and tired and told me to watch for Tony's rottweilers. "You don't want to tangle with them." The woman sucked hard on her cigarette then trickled the smoke from her nose. She closed her eyes. "Plus, Tony got knives and a bat and he's a bit . . ." She formed a pistol with her thumb, index, and middle finger, put the imaginary gun to her head and fired. Her head wobbled, her eyes rolled, and she feigned a Hollywood death stumble. They mounted the bikes and pedaled south toward the Mall.

A series of well-managed camps of unhoused people lined the embankment. They were fenced with scraps of chain-link, wooden pallets, milk crates, construction waste, and old chunks of cut timber pulled from the water. Inside the fences stood tents, bicycles, charcoal BBQs, and the ubiquitous shopping carts. For privacy—and probably shelter from wind and dust storms—the owners had dressed the fencing in an array of blue, black, gray, and green tarps. I called out, asking if anyone was home. No response.

Ahead, a man leaned against a sour-looking elm. He carried a baseball bat and a long machete down his right hip. Tony, I thought. Butterflies filled my stomach. He called out, but not to me. Four dogs appeared from behind the embankment and raced my way, growling and barking. I swung my walking stick, keeping them at bay. The basset hound ignored the stick and fell at my feet. His eyes were rheumy and he drooled into the dirt. He rolled over and whined, his tail kicking up a tremendous amount of dust. The other three, a snarling Chihuahua and two indistinct, easily distracted mutts, stood a good ten feet off, barking, tails wagging. Rottweilers? I waved. Tony did not return the gesture. I thought better of the whole scene, rubbed my foot on the belly of the basset hound, then backed away from the dogs, keeping a close eye on the Chihuahua. As I approached the water, the dogs lost interest. I turned, and the collector popped out of the tamarisk carrying an armload of bones.

Luke was a big guy, broad and with a belly. He was young with a neatly trimmed, bright red beard and clipped red hair. "Deer!" He introduced himself and shuffled the pile of bones, gathering them in the crook of his right arm, and stuck out his left hand. I declined, blaming COVID, so we bumped elbows.

Luke had come to Colorado from North Carolina to attend a divinity program at a Christian church in Woodland Park, but COVID had cut the program short, so he and his wife set up in a small apartment in Colorado Springs to wait for the pandemic to end and for the divinity program to reopen. He took a job as a security guard at a local mall. She landed work as the manager of a women's clothing store in the same mall. Luke enjoyed the life of a security guard. He liked helping people. Life wasn't great, but they were able to get along until, out of nowhere, their landlord doubled the rent.

"We put most of our stuff in storage, packed the rest in the car, and came to Pueblo," he told me. "We slept in our car until we could find a place."

Luke landed another security job, this time at the Pueblo Mall, while his wife sold shoes at a nearby outlet. He had given up on divinity school. "Colorado has been brutal. Our new landlord says he'll keep the rent the same for one year. As soon as we got enough saved up, we're headed home to the Blue Ridge Mountains. Buddy, I never want to see Colorado again."

Luke was into anything and everything the outdoors had to offer, particularly bones, fossils, and rocks. He had a whole collection but was particularly interested in skulls: deer, elk, moose, antelope, skunk, beaver, and bear. "I got the bear skull right down here," he said.

"In the Fountain?"

"Yeah. Just over there. It was sticking out of the bank after a rain. I just plucked it out, rinsed the sand off, and . . . it's hanging on my wall."

"Does your wife mind?"

"She likes it."

The dogs did not bother Luke; he carried pepper spray. He was worried, however, that he might stumble across a dead body. The word about town was that several murdered women were buried in the soft sediments along the creek. "A couple of weeks back, I was a little further south of here on the opposite bank," Luke said. "I came across this homeless encampment. It smelled like death, man. There was a tent." He shook his head. "The flap was open and I looked inside. Dead guy in there."

"What did you do?"

"I went home and showered." He shuddered.

Luke claimed to have found several arrowheads and a bunch of strange teeth in the Fountain just north of Pueblo. One set of teeth, he was sure, came from an extinct camel. Two, possibly, from a giant ground sloth. Another set of shovel-shaped incisors might have come from a Pleistocene tapir. Luke had several jagged mastodon molars in his collection but most of the teeth were bison. "Some of them are for sure recent. Smaller. But I have a couple that are huge. *Bison antiquus* or something like that. You know, when Thomas Jefferson sent Lewis and Clark and Pike and those guys out here, he was sure mammoths were still alive and told them to bring one back to D.C."

From there, Luke dipped into a sort of crypto-zoology. Polar bear and grizzly mixes, moose and deer crossbreeds, Bigfoot, a ghost-white deer he'd seen in Appalachia, giants found in the Grand Canyon, and the chupacabra, which he was sure was real.

I told him how, in December of 1900, workers excavating gravel from a hill not far from the Fountain came across a mammoth skull. The men removed the six-foot-long tusks, setting them to the side while they worked on the rest of the skull and then the massive skeleton. However, the air and sunlight disintegrated the bones almost as fast as the men could remove them from the gravel. Within the hour, "only dust and a few heaps of pulverized bone" remained, reported one of the many Pueblo newspapers available in those days.

"They used to find them all the time," Luke said. "They were just laying around everywhere. Finding a mammoth would be a dream come true! But what I'd really like to find is the skull of a short-faced bear. Can you imagine being a caveman getting chased by a twelve-foot beast on two legs that runs as fast as a cheetah?"

"Can you show me some of what you've found?" I asked.

He said he would love to have me over to show off his collections but that his wife was sick. He worried it was COVID. We resolved instead to meet the following morning at the confluence to see what we might find.

But Luke never arrived. I wondered if his wife had grown sicker or if he had come down with COVID and was himself laid up.

Despite the wind, the day grew bright and warm. I pulled off my shoes and socks, rolled my pants to my knees, and zipped my coat to my chin. Then, I stepped into the Fountain. Intense shivers burst up my spine and the cold ached my shins. I did not make the decision to wade lightly. Hepatitis A and E. coli inhabit the Fountain. I had also heard stories, possibly apocryphal, of people disappearing into the quicksand of the Fountain. I had heard of a boy and a girl who had drowned in the 1970s. Some said it was the quicksand, others claimed the siblings were victims of La Llorona, a vengeful ghost whose own children were swept away by the creek. I had also heard of an entire freight train that disappeared into the sands of the Fountain, never to be found. That story may actually reference the Eden wreck in the way history clouds through time and stories overlap, blend, and become something entirely new, how each place develops its own particular lore, its own library of ghosts. I had heard these stories for as long as I could remember. I was unsure if they were true or not, but I told myself this was not a good day to find out. "Go slow," I said aloud and tilted into the Chinook, tracing step after cautious step to a sandbar in the middle of the flow.

To the north, a footbridge crossed the creek. Beyond that,

almost directly upstream, stood the snow-capped Peak. I could make out Cheyenne Mountain, Cooper, and Mt. Rosa.

To the east, cottonwoods and elms screened the growing workday morning traffic growling along South LaCross Avenue. To the west, a deep wall of buff-colored phragmites, a fan-like reed grass native to Africa and Asia, dipped and bowed with the wind. Past the reeds, in the haze, the Greenhorn Mountains marked the far western horizon.

South, beyond the confluence and across the furrowed surface of the Arkansas, a trash-strewn riverbank climbed twenty to thirty feet to the American Iron and Metal Company, and just beyond that the Evraz Steel Mill, formerly the Colorado Fuel and Iron Company (CF&I) and, for forty years, where my grandfather worked as train yard master. "The Mill" had, once upon a time, been the largest steel production plant west of the Mississippi and one of the largest in the world. Now, it was a Superfund Site, owned by one of Vladimir Putin's hydrocarbon oligarchs. I could also see portions of the neighborhoods of Salt Creek, Eilers, the Grove, and Bessemer, where my grandparents had lived, all now designated Superfund Residential Cleanup Areas by the Environmental Protection Agency.

A peacock screamed. Train wheels squealed across steel tracks. Two cop cars wailed down Santa Fe Drive. A putrid stench wafted from the poisoned creek trickling from The Mill. An empty Gatorade bottle bumped my shin and continued downstream followed by bits of plastic, a lonely shoe, and a bobbing Coke can. I retraced my steps from the sandbar to the shore where I cleared the sand from my toes, dried my feet in the wind, and put my boots and socks back on. It was warm and good.

Back in the forest, I met a man who lived in a tent. In fact, it was a series of tents knitted together with tarps, blankets, wire, and shoelaces. He had surrounded the structure in branches from the cottonwoods. His home resembled a poor version of a Tin-ne-ah "wickiup," the type you might see in Frank Randall or Edward Curtis photographs. I am thinking in particular of an 1880 Curtis capture from Arizona, minus the horse. The man stank of smoke, sweat, dirt, and shit, his eyes red and framed in purple bags of skin. He was originally from Indiana, he told me. He had been hurt on a job in Denver. The chronic pain from his injury wore him down. He fell into using opioids to manage the pain and his life collapsed. His girlfriend left him. He could not manage rent. "I went from the American Dream to the streets in eighteen months," he said. He had lived by the creek for several years. It was his home, but he was unhoused.

I left him and circled through the trees pushing through the brittle vegetation, tracing the bank of the creek. A robin rattled in the crisp grasses and litter of leaves. An early western kingbird stumbled north with the mercurial advancement of spring. An osprey perched in its aerie atop a power line pole near the railroad tracks. The wind buffeted the bird; it tucked its wings tight to its sides and leaned into the blow, eyes half closed.

I came across a man, a woman, and their dog. They were also unhoused, their shelter also a tent. They had seen the coyote. They knew her well and said that she denned down beyond the bridge, past the confluence, in a low cutbank next to the Ark. The woman said they got the dog for protection from "drunks" and "druggies," but the dog hid in the tent and whimpered whenever it caught scent of the coyote. "He's a good dog though," the man said and scratched the animal's ears.

There was another man. He squatted next to a shopping cart full of cans and buckets and canvas shopping bags, trying to light a fire in a tight ring of rocks sheltered by a blue tarp strung between the trees. Trash piled up just beyond his sleeping bags. The breeze turned in the brush, frustrating his lighter. He threw up his hands, sat back and asked for a cigarette.

"I don't smoke," I told him.

He struggled to get alcohol out of his life, he told me.

"Smoking helps with the cravings. The nicotine, I guess it's the nicotine, just keeps the desire under control." He shrugged. "I mean, smoking isn't good, but it's got to be better than alcohol."

I told him I knew the pull of alcohol and that he was probably right. He said he did not like going to the store for smokes because of all the alcohol. It was just too tempting. I promised that I would bring him some cigarettes.

"That would be really kind." He bowed.

Continuing past the steel and wood footbridge, I fell into a mass of phragmites so thick I bogged down. I could not move and I could not place the edge of the water. I retraced my steps and picked up the cement bike trail that seams the Fountain north for several miles. The water in the creek braided into dozens of tiny streams instead of one solid flow. The threaded, woven rivulets and the palette of reds, pinks, oranges, and browns that was the riverbed reminded me of my daughter's watercolor paintings. The creek bed was wide, perhaps fifty feet across. The roots of the stabilizing phragmites held the channel in place.

The osprey lifted and slid across the sky, heading downstream. He turned over the reeds on the opposite bank and disappeared behind a wall of tamarisk. Blues and reds among the reeds caught my eye. For several hundred yards along the opposite shore, dozens of unhoused Americans had created temporary shelters. There were tents and tarps, metal and wooden structures; there were clothes drying in the wind, waiting for the sun. There were carpets and blankets hung from lines between the trees lending shelter from the sun, winds, rain, and the winter that was not yet over.

Here stood an unsteady dystopian village of people without housing, on the floodplain of a once upon a time part-time creek, now a full-time river, in the middle of a post-industrial city at the edge of the prairies and mountains, in the richest country in the world, on a planet of worsening storms that grew warmer by the day.

—

The world is built on what came before.

"Landscapes . . . are palimpsests, laid down in layers over centuries," wrote Olivia Laing in *To The River*. "There are places where the past gathers as thickly and as insubstantially as pollen, places where it seems as oppressive as . . . a cancer eating up the present."

For thousands of years the original people of that land held the confluence as a place of importance. Oral histories point to the confluence as a place of ceremony for Indigenous nations of the region. At one time, I had been told, an ancient shrine of some sort stood at the confluence.

The confluence also marks some of the earliest Euro-American settlements in Colorado. In 1927, members of the Colorado Exploration Society unearthed the remains of an adobe fort near the mouth of the Fountain. Edwin B. Haver, a Pueblo real estate dealer, led society members to the spot. Haver had come to Pueblo in 1880 and he recalled how, at that time, the remains of an old fort were still visible. Less than a foot below the surface, the society encountered adobe brick walls and formalized fireplaces. Leaders of the expedition, Leroy P. Singer and J.W. Shy, claimed the ruins were those of the redoubt constructed by Jacob Fowler in 1803.

The 1803 date is probably incorrect. Fowler was born in New Jersey in 1764. A Revolutionary War veteran, Fowler left to what was then "The West," the upper Ohio River Valley, fighting in nearly every battle the American army waged against a powerful alliance of Ohio Indigenous nations. He joined George Rogers Clark to raid Shawnee towns across the Ohio River near Piqua on the Miami River, and was with the catastrophic Harmar and St. Clair expeditions of 1790 and 1791, military disasters that nearly ended American westward expansion before it began. Fowler, through sheer luck, escaped with his life when the Confederated Tribes descended on present-day Fort Recovery, Ohio. It was not, however, until 1821 that Fowler accepted an offer to serve with Hugh Glenn on an expedition to map the Arkansas River Basin. For thirteen months and thirteen days, the Glenn-Fowler expedition struggled across the plains and into the mountains. Pressed by the annoyed Numunuu, Fowler built a small redoubt and horse corral on a hill near the mouth of the Fountain and settled in to wait them out. It was barely a month before the men, starving, began to eat their horses and decided to leave. The Numunuu allowed the pathetic expedition to stumble its way east, the Americans arriving in Cincinnati by steamboat in July 1822.

Fowler's fortifications stood a couple of hundred yards northeast of the confluence. The ruins Haver saw at the confluence in 1880 may in fact have been part of the small fortification Lieutenant Zebulon Pike and his team constructed in late November of 1806. It also could have been something entirely different.

Pike built his stockade on a large tongue of land surrounded on three sides by the Arkansas where it once made a prominent bend before meeting the Fountain. The great bend in the river disappeared from maps in 1872 when the City of Pueblo straightened the Ark.

But in 1806, the Arkansas flowed as a wild river should, serpent-like, migrating across the landscape, creating bends, necks, promontories, oxbow lakes, and marshes teeming with wildlife. In his journal, Pike labeled the confluence the "grand forks." The Fountain was the "north fork" and The Peak "Blue Mountain." On Monday, November 24, the day after their arrival, the men cut fourteen trees and constructed a box-like breastwork five feet high on three sides with the fourth open to the water. Then, Pike, along with two others, set out to climb The Peak.

Unfortunately, Pike did not leave us with any decent description of the Fountain as it was in 1806. At most, what remains is a passage that may refer to the Fountain but could also be a description of the Arkansas River near the confluence: "The riverbank began to be entirely covered with woods on both sides, but no other species than cottonwood."

That's it.

Scouring the historical record for descriptions of the Fountain before widespread Euro-American settlement is an exercise in frustration. Members of Juan de Ulibarri's 1706 expedition labeled the Fountain "Rio de San Buenaventura," but apparently left no description. Juan Bautista de Anza came north from Taos in the summer of 1779, set on destroying bands of the Numunuu people lead by the legendary warrior Tavibo Naritgant, Dangerous Man. To the Spanish he was Cuerno Verde or Greenhorn, famous for the green-tipped bison horns that topped the headdress he wore into battle. De Anza aimed to secure the upper Rio Grande valley for Spain and the Crown's Tiwa and Tewa allies. Doing away with the Numunuu was key to achieving that goal. The Spaniards and their native auxiliaries prayed for success against Cuerno Verde at the confluence of the Fountain and Arkansas then returned after their victory to give thanks to God:

> I returned to the water place where the defeated enemy had been encamped. To this place the name of Rio del Sacramento was given [to the Fountain], this expedition having been dedicated to this most holy mystery.

The Spanish killed Cuerno Verde alongside his eldest son south of Pueblo near the St. Charles River. His headdress supposedly ended up in the Vatican where it disappeared into the Holy See's interminable collections.

Mentions of the Fountain trickled out through the first half of the nineteenth century.

There was Pike, then in 1820, John R. Bell of the Long Expedition recorded thousands upon thousands of bison at the banks of the Fountain, noting that after a particularly intense thunderstorm, the Fountain filled with bison dung "accompanied with a most intolerable stench, which impregnated the atmosphere for a considerable [stretch] from the creek." Thirst drove the hapless members of the expedition to try to filter then drink from the poop contaminated waters.

Captain Lemuel Ford, commander of Company G of the First Regiment of Dragoons, known as Dodge's Dragoons, marched sixteen hundred miles across Nebraska, Kansas, and Colorado in 1835, and left us with nothing more about the Fountain than a mention. "Thirty-six miles from the point where the fontaine qui bouille emerges from the mountains," he noted, "we left that stream to the right and pursued our march over a beautiful rolling prairie, to the Arkansas river . . ."

John Charles Fremont, on his way to California in 1843, passed a night next to the Fountain, noting that the creek was ". . . fifty feet wide, with a swift current."

Four years later, George F. Ruxton set camp somewhere in the middle reaches of the creek. He noted that Indigenous hunters had set fire to the prairie grasses in the winter, aiming to entice antelope, deer, and bison to the creek's edge with bright green grasses come spring. Evidently, it worked. "On this the animals fared sumptuously for several days . . ." he wrote. Meat on the hoof also brought predators. "While encamped on this stream, the wolves infested the camp to that degree that I could scarcely leave my saddles for a few minutes on the ground without finding the straps of rawhide gnawed to pieces."

This French name for the Fountain, *Le Fontaine qui Bouille* or *Le Fontaine qui Bouit*—The Fountain that Boils—derives from Indigenous names. The Tsistsistas called it the *esevoteohe*, or "seething river" while the Ka'igwu named it "boiling water." For the Hinono'eino it was the "medicine water." These names for the creek may hint at the Fountain's tendency toward violent floods. More likely, the names derive from the bubbling soda, iron, and thermal springs of Manitou where healing waters burst from the ground, gathering the people and adding to the flow of the Fountain.

What did the Nuuchiu call the Fountain? As far as I can tell, we don't know. Several Nuuchiu acquaintances told me that the name was lost to history. A friend, a Nuuchiu archaeologist, saw this as an example of just how thoroughly her people were genocided. It wasn't simply "just" ethnic cleansing—as if that isn't bad enough—it was a wholesale extermination of people, religion, philosophy, values, cuisine, language, and life ways. My friend Erin Elder, an artist of Monument Creek, explained how, growing up in Colorado Springs, she had been taught that there were no Indigenous people within the Fountain watershed. Her teachers insisted that the area had been more or less empty or rarely used, and that any people who had been here before colonization were completely gone and simply didn't exist anymore. Of course, this is entirely untrue. Thriving Indigenous nations made home in the Fountain watershed until they were pushed out by Euro-American settlers relatively recently. Native Americans are anything but gone.

In the cramped one-room collection center that is the Pueblo County Historical Society, I opened a rusty drawer crammed with maps. They were folded, rolled, and stacked, many crumbling and fragile. The drawer also held dozens and dozens of dried out, broken rubber bands that seemed like earthworms turned up at an excavation. I was curious how the Fountain was portrayed on historical maps and how its name changed over time. As I unrolled the maps, small, handwritten notes floated to the floor: "*proposed mountain water project for city of Pueblo circa 1936,*" and "*Side view of locomotive, circa 1910,*" or "*E.F. Gobatti,*" and one that simply said "*Foundry.*"

Growing up, we never called the Fountain by anything other than its Euro-American name. I am not sure I even knew the origin of the name until I was in my twenties. Yet on some maps as late as the early 1960s, the Fountain was labeled "Le Fontaine qui Bouille River."

The official 1890 map of Pueblo gives "Le Fontaine" a fair shake against the larger Arkansas, offering an aerial view looking south toward the confluence. An 1897 USGS map labels it as "Fountain Creek" and shows the channel hemmed on either side by the Atchison Topeka and Santa Fe Railway, the Denver and Rio Grande Railroad, and the Union Pacific, Denver, and Gulf Railway.

An undated map of downtown Pueblo shows the Arkansas and tiny Salt Creek, but not the Fountain. Based on the style and the layout of the town at the time, I am guessing this map was drawn sometime in the late 1890s. The only way someone would know that the creek runs through the city is by the odd placement of houses and buildings along either side of a tiny blank space snaking its way toward the Arkansas. The Fountain was not labeled, nor was it even distinguished as a waterway.

The 1907 "Complete Map of the City of Pueblo, Colorado, by William Peach, City Engineer" shows the "Fontaine qui Buille River" not as a wide, sinuous floodplain, but rather a set of straight, parallel, dotted lines marked "main channel." Noticeably, houses turn up right on the banks of the creek.

A map of postal routes in southeastern Colorado labels the waterway as "Fountain Creek." On a 1928 voting precinct map "Le Fontaine" is the boundary dividing voting precincts, the precinct lines running down the center of the creek. An undated Pueblo County zoning map I presume to be from the 1950s labels the creek as "Fountain River," while a 1942 Works Progress Administration map labels it "Fountain Creek."

Most often, the Fountain is but a single thin line on these maps while the Arkansas is usually drawn in fine detail with varying thicknesses, loops, meanders, and braided channels. Sometimes the Fountain is marked as a snaking set of parallel dotted lines, nothing more. Very few maps show the Fountain with any life at all. On a 1950 El Paso County, Colorado Department of Transportation (CDOT) map, the Fountain is but a single line without a label.

Quite frequently, the Fountain does not appear on maps at all. A "Water Resources Map" from 1936 does not bother to show the Fountain. In 1956, a CDOT map labeled simply "Pueblo, Colorado General Highway Map" rendered the Arkansas in beautiful, flowing hatchings. The Fountain does not exist. It is just not there.

It seemed to me that the way in which the Fountain was portrayed, or not, on maps reflected our society's ambivalence about such an odd little waterway. That so very many maps were produced without any acknowledgment of the creek made it that much easier to devalue, overuse, and exploit.

It was General James Wilkinson who sent Pike and his twenty men west. President Thomas Jefferson knew of the mission and approved, although he didn't appear to be as enthusiastic about Pike's expedition as he was for that of Lewis and Clark. Pike carried orders to explore the southwestern reaches of the fresh Louisiana Purchase. Pike was further tasked, secretly, with disrupting Spanish influence in the region, turning Native American nations into the arms of the fledgling United States of America, and mapping routes for future American conquest.

In many ways, Zebulon Pike typifies the early American republic. Pike was born in New Jersey in 1779 while his father was away fighting the British. In fact, Pike may have been born in George Washington's winter camp at Middlebrook. Pike joined the army at fifteen and served transporting supplies throughout the Ohio River basin. He proved himself capable, loyal, and devoted to the ideals of a young American nation. It did not take long before he caught the attention of the higher-ups. He was a dutiful, if uncreative, soldier—his loyalty fierce. In 1805, orders sent him north to find and map the headwaters of the Mississippi. He was also tasked to inform local Indigenous nations that there was a new boss in town. The "empire for liberty" as Jefferson called it, was on its way. The American juggernaut could not be stopped. Native people had best jump on board before they were run over. The Saux and Fox nations were skeptical. So too the Winnebago and Menominee. Pike struggled through the snows north to the headwaters and beyond. He was ordered west almost immediately upon his return from the frozen taiga.

Today, Pike's expedition to what became the American southwest is a sort of side note to the more famous Lewis and Clark expedition up the Missouri and over the mountains to Oregon. This is somewhat ironic as historian Jared Orsi points out in *Citizen Explorer: The Life of Zebulon Pike* because, in his time, Pike was a celebrity, a widely known and well-regarded pioneer and defender of the Republic, while Lewis and Clark were respected but less well-known. Yet Pike's apparent ineptitude, plus Wilkinson's later trial for treason for collaborating with the Spanish crown against the young United States, soured the public's view of the Pike mission.

Pike's expedition, as that of Lewis and Clark, was part of Jefferson's vision to expand the United States to the Pacific Ocean. Southern tobacco, corn, and cotton plantations, worked by enslaved people from Africa, had severely depleted southern soil. Erosion and declining productivity were major drivers in early western expansion notes Roger G. Kennedy in *Mr. Jefferson's Lost Cause*. The southern plantation economy consumed not only soil, but enslaved human beings and land belonging to Indigenous nations, enriching a few, impoverishing everyone else. "The practice of working soil to death and slaves to exhaustion was repeated over and over again, the desolating army of King Cotton moved on a broad front across the South drawing people away from home and leaving blighted hopes behind," penned Kennedy. The slave-powered plantation economy was not the only driver of westward expansion, but it played a dominating role.

Pike, a northerner, was only marginally aware of the factors driving America west. Yet, as a committed public servant, he rallied to the western visions of President Jefferson, himself the owner of hundreds of enslaved human beings and a plantation whose soils were washing to the sea. In the Louisiana Purchase, Orsi wrote, both Jefferson and Pike "saw an empire for the taking, a place so dimly known that it could be filled with any fantasy or scheme." It was just what the young Republic craved.

Fantasy, however, nearly proved Pike's undoing. At the time, respected publications imagined a West pleine with chimeric dreams and a menagerie of ancient beasts including the mammoths Jefferson believed the explorers would find. This was a West filled with savage humans, a lost tribe of Welsh warriors, giants, unknown animals, and fanciful landscapes of salt mountains, volcanoes, peaks higher than any other in the world, disappearing rivers, and, possibly, a vast intermountain lake that sourced the rivers flowing to the Pacific and the Gulf. Distances were likewise pure fantasy. Pike believed, for example, that Santa Fe was an easy two-week walk from St. Louis. Thus, Pike pushed west across the Great Plains, completely ignorant of what lay ahead.

And so, when Pike stood at the confluence of the Arkansas and Fountain on that frigid November morning in 1806, he peered north to The Peak, convinced he could reach the base of the mountain within a few hours, spend the night, summit, and return to the confluence stockade the following evening.

It is nearly impossible to fathom how Pike thought such a short, easy journey to The Peak possible. This is a mind-boggling footnote to history, offering lessons on how our brains become stuck and how that stuckness alters our perception of reality and may even warp reality itself.

From the confluence, as the crow flies, The Peak is about fifty miles distant. Obtaining even the base of the mountain requires traversing a difficult landscape of sand, rock falls, hills, gullies, and creeks. In late November, the land was probably covered in ice and snow. The actual travel distance was seventy, eighty, or even one hundred miles depending the route. From the confluence, The Peak just *looks* far away. Pike, somehow, saw it otherwise and that, for me, is difficult to comprehend.

A little after noon, Pike set out for The Peak. He started up the west bank of the Fountain accompanied by Dr. John Hamilton Robinson and Privates John Brown and Theodore Miller. When night fell, the four climbers found themselves far from The Peak, their only shelter, a lone cedar up from the water on the windblown prairie. "Without water and extremely cold," wrote Pike.

By dawn's early light, Pike made the bewildering decision to abandon the Fountain and lead the party straight north. This confuses me too because it is glaringly obvious that the Fountain could have only emanated from the snow-capped peak he aimed to conquer. Again, Pike completely misunderstood the landscape surrounding him. The men made a beeline for the mountain, setting out across the rugged foothills. Night brought them hardly closer. Another long day's march helped, but they remained far from where they had hoped.

Not only did Pike misjudge distance, he misjudged elevation. Pike assumed the climb up The Peak was only about three thousand feet, when in reality the ascent would be more than double that. At some point Pike must have realized the Grand Peak, as he came to call it, was over fourteen thousand feet tall. But when? Not soon enough.

On the morning of November 26, the team, leaving their food and blankets behind, set off up the mountain. They planned to summit and return by nightfall. The climb was brutal, however. "We commenced ascending," wrote Pike. "Found it very difficult, being obliged to climb up rocks sometimes almost perpendicular; and after marching all day, we encamped in a cave without blankets, victuals, and water."

At some point in the late 1990s, I too made a half-hearted solo winter ascent of The Peak. Mounting Ruxton Creek, I made my way several miles to a snowed-in meadow where, in the dark, I dug out a shelter, set my tent, and crawled into my sleeping bag. The climb left me drenched in sweat, which froze. I changed clothes, but by then my body temperature had dropped. My drinking water turned to solid ice. My camp stove refused to work. I could not find any firewood in the deep snow, and I fell into a shuddering sleep of ghoulish nightmares after gnawing my way through several stiff slices of jerky and a handful of trail mix. It was one of the most miserable nights of my life.

One foolish night in the snows of Ruxton Park nearly killed me. I had had the benefit of Gortex, Smartwool, waterproof snow pants, a tent, and a sleeping bag rated to zero Fahrenheit. Pike's men were dressed in cotton and thin wool. They had no blankets. No food. No water. They must have felt like absolute hell. But there was no complaining to be had. For Pike, avoiding physical discomfort or complaining about physical discomfort was a type of personal dishonor of the highest degree and something for which he had zero patience.

Before dawn, I woke with an incredible headache. My joints burned and my jaw hurt from chattering all night. I was not thinking clearly. I honestly thought I might die. And for what? To summit The Peak? Not worth it, I decided. As the sun rose east and below across the plains, I packed my things and set off, contouring down the creek, slipping on ice, and stumbling over masses of downed tree limbs and logs. Each footfall jarred my head. At the Pikes Peak Cog Railway Station, a porter clothed in a nineteenth century railway outfit took pity, filling me with hot black coffee and sticky donuts. He wrapped me in a wool blanket and set me next to a portable heater.

"Well then." The porter sat across from me with his own cup of coffee. "You're clearly not the smartest fella out there now, are you?"

From Pike's journal:

> *"27 November, Thursday—Arose hungry, dry, and extremely sore from the inequality of the rocks, on which we had lain all night, but were amply compensated for toil by the sublimity of the prospects below."*

I had crawled from my tent into a descending blizzard. Pike's men, sore, dehydrated, wracked by hunger and headaches, crawled from the cave to find a clear blue sky above and a sea of clouds blanketing the prairie below, stretching east as far as the eye could see.

> *". . . like the ocean in a storm; wave piled on wave and foaming, whilst the sky was perfectly clear where we were."*

Within an hour, the explorers had summited the peak. Except that, it was the wrong peak. Not knowing where they were, the team had climbed 11,500-foot Mt. Rosa, a mountain many miles southeast of their goal. They were crestfallen.

> *"The Grand Peak now appeared at the distance of 15 or 16 miles from us and us as high again as we ascended."*

Reality sunk in. Somewhat. They would never reach the top of the mountain. "I believe," Pike wrote, "no human being could have ascended its pinnacle." It took them three days to return to the relative comfort of their team and the confluence stockade.

Pike had vastly underestimated the distance to and the height of the mountain that would later bear his name. There has never been a moment when, standing at the confluence of the Arkansas and the Fountain, I have not wondered what it was Pike saw. Did he see what I saw? And what of his men? If the mountain appeared closer to Pike, did his men suffer the same mental distortion? Did Privates Brown and Miller, ordered north toward the mountain, look at each other and think, "Whoa. Bossman lost his marbles," or did they consider the whole adventure absolutely logical?

I try to imagine what the rest of Pike's crew, left behind at the confluence breastwork, thought about Pike's ability to lead. There's no evidence that they questioned him. The men either understood the world as Pike did, or they trusted him. Or, perhaps, they were simply obliged to follow orders. Probably all three. A little more skepticism of Pike's abilities was in order, however. Winter had only just begun and for Pike's team it would all get so much worse before it got any better.

On a clear day, you can see the Front Range of the Rocky Mountains from far out on the prairie east of Pueblo. Driving west, you first see the igneous masses of the Huajatollas, also known as the Spanish Peaks or Las Cumbres Españolas. The twin extinct volcanoes reach 12,688 feet and 13,631 feet into the sky southwest of the village of Walsenburg. As kids, we believed the name to be a Nuuchiu word for "Breasts of the World," but the truth is less titillating. "Huajatollas" is most likely a Numunuu name meaning "Double Mountain." First the Huajatollas, then you see The Peak appearing as a blue-gray cloud rising from the horizon just to the northeast.

Pike first saw the Front Range of the Rocky Mountains on

November 15th when the party was still some one hundred miles distant from The Peak and fifty-some miles from the confluence. From a small promontory somewhere near the present-day town of Rocky Ford, Pike scribbled that he was ecstatic at the sight of the mountains. Labeling the distant massif the "Mexican Mountains" or the "Blue Mountains," Pike wrote in his journal that he could see no difference between the Rockies and the Allegheny Mountains of Kentucky, Ohio, and Pennsylvania, and he believed he could reach the base of the Rockies by nightfall. In fact, it took them ten days just to reach the confluence. Today, Pike's understanding is laughable, but it demonstrates how he simply could not fathom what he was seeing.

Jared Orsi posits that Pike's brain was stuck on "Enlightenment Geography." That is, the fanciful vision of an American West full of bizarre phenomena and adhering to the strictures of "continental symmetry," a theory of geography President Jefferson found enchanting.

Rooted in the fifth century ideas of the Roman Macrobius and later Isidore of Seville, the idea of continental symmetry held that the world itself was divided into equal spheres, so too the continents: north-south, east-west, the world was orderly and balanced. Therefore, one great western river, they believed, drained the whole western half of the North America interior much as the Ohio River drained the interior of the eastern half of the continent. The source of all western rivers, Enlightenment geographers thought, was most likely a great lake or a common source somewhere in the Rocky Mountains.

In support of this theory, these geographers had collected the accounts of trappers, traders, and explorers—many of them relying on stories they heard from Native Americans. They accumulated maps and drawings and had, over time, developed a whole new theory of the West, one blending fact, fantasy, misinformation, and pure conjecture centered on the concept of "continental symmetry." Pike bought into these ideas wholeheartedly.

Orsi and others have noted that Pike had read Jonathan Carver's *Three Years Travels Through the Interior Parts of America* while journeying north to the source of the Mississippi. That probably didn't help his understanding of the West. In the 1760's, Carver and Briton Robert Rogers had searched for a water route across the continent. The book of their travels, chock full of exaggeration, claimed that in the center of North America a high-altitude plateau served as the single source of all the continent's great rivers. Pike took the Carver book quite seriously. Based on this information, logic dictated that a route up one western river, such as the Arkansas River, would naturally lead to all other rivers. Same with the symmetry of mountains. What was true on the east coast—the Appalachians and the Alleghenies—had to be true in the West. The Rockies, therefore, were believed to top out around 3,500-feet from their base.

I assume that when he set off west, Pike, being Pike, carried with him an 1802 map of the western interior drawn by British geographer Aaron Arrowsmith, another scholar Jefferson greatly admired. We do know that Meriwether Lewis carried a copy of Arrowsmith's map up the Missouri, but Pike's possession of the map is conjecture on my part. Regardless, it was a flawed and misleading map repeating many of the misconceptions held by Enlightenment geographers as a whole. Further, large swaths of the map remained blank, reflecting the general lack of information available about the region.

This is how Pike understood the American West, distorted, fanciful, and, for the most part, unknown to "civilized" peoples. From the confluence of the Arkansas and Fountain, The Peak surely appeared to him as the pinnacle of the continent Carver had mentioned, because that is what Pike expected to see. The Peak, he reasoned, was either the source from which all rivers issued or, at the very least, the place from which he could assess and map the headwaters of the Red, Platte, Arkansas, Columbia, Yellowstone, Colorado, Rio Grande, and even the Missouri Rivers. Several years later, still stuck on Enlightenment geography beliefs despite his on-the-ground experience in the Rockies, Pike testified to Congress that from The Peak, "I can visit the source of any of those rivers in one day."

For the young American nation intent on conquering and colonizing the entire continent, such a discovery would prove profound. From the source of all rivers, the whole of North America would fall under American control. From the source of all rivers, the American nation would drive out European powers and dominate Native populations. "Climbing the peak," wrote Orsi, "was no mere sport, rather, it was essential to the national objects."

It is possible that Pike knowingly lied to Congress. I have my doubts, however. Pike saw himself as a strictly honest and moral Enlightenment gentleman, dedicated to the national cause. Most likely, Pike fervently believed what he told Congress. Even after two years in the West and with on-the-ground experience, he still failed to understand what he had seen.

It is easy to ridicule Pike from the comfort of Google Maps, Google Earth, and ArcGIS, but Pike was operating at the time when Euro-Americans understood precious little about the western interior. Pike was no fool. Somewhat of an autodidact, Pike had taught himself French and Spanish, basic science, complex mathematics, and enlightened handwriting. He proved a voracious reader. Yet, at many moments in his life Pike was simply unable to see beyond preconceived notions and ideas. His mind could, at times, become incredibly and even dangerously stuck. The world was not what he expected nor wanted it to be, and Pike struggled to adjust.

The stuckness of Pike's brain when it came to geography put his expedition in extreme danger. Departing the confluence, the party pushed up the Arkansas River, gaining elevation as winter set in. Pike led his men, clothed in their summer cotton uniforms and wrapped in blankets, back and forth across the mountains needlessly—for fifty-one days. A number of times the men of the expedition nearly perished from either cold or starvation. Frostbite took fingers and toes. When one man refused to endure the cold any longer, Pike threatened him with execution. Later, floundering around the wilderness, Pike himself contemplated suicide.

It was not until the end of February 1807 that Spanish cavalry lead by Lieutenants Ignacio Saltelo and Bartholomew Fernandez, rescued Pike's expedition from a desperate makeshift fort in the San Luis Valley southeast of present-day Alamosa, Colorado. The Americans found themselves in a luxurious captivity. Treating the trespassing American soldiers as guests, the Spanish bathed, clothed, fed, and healed the expedition's members. Before long, the Americans arrived in Santa Fe and then the city of Chihuahua. If not for the Spanish dragoons, American history in the southwest would have taken on a completely different reality.

The world is built on what came before.

From the bank of the Fountain near the confluence, I watched as two women on the opposite shore washed clothes in the cold, muddy creek, then hung the shirts, pants, and socks in a Russian olive to dry. Just to the north of the women, a young man, bearded and tattooed, collected bricks from the sediments, stacking them in piles of six or eight, then carrying them back into the scrub.

Beginning in the late 1880s, the Standard Fire Brick Company operated at the edge of the Fountain, on the right bank just north of Pueblo's Mineral Palace Park. The company, run by a Chicagoan named Francis LeGrand Capers, grew to be one of the largest brick manufacturers in the country. Pueblo-made bricks can be found from Mexico to Canada and from California to New York. They also turn up by the dozens in the Fountain spread between the park and the confluence. The bricks are large, red, white, or pink, their edges rounded by one hundred years of being tumbled in the waters and sands of the Fountain.

The bones, arrowheads, manos, and metates that turn up along the Fountain's banks reminded me that Pike was a relative latecomer. The bricks assured me he was not the last. The Gatorade bottle, the plastic sacks in the water, and the ubiquitous Target shopping carts resting midstream or among the willow and tamarisk, tell that the Fountain continues to absorb and record the history of the watershed laid down in layers within its sediments. The Fountain is itself a palimpsest, a place where the past gathers thickly, at once insubstantially and oppressive.

In 2019, I walked the creek just south of the City of Fountain. I had hoped to photograph some of the blue herons I had seen in that stretch, but I was out of luck. For reasons known only to the birds, they had moved on. Instead, I pulled out my notebook and listed all the human debris I encountered: soda cans of all flavors, a car battery, various used water bottles, unidentifiable lumps of pink and blue plastic, a pillow case, coat hangers, a vibrator, assorted batteries, another car battery, syringes, one refrigerator, a large spring, an assortment of car and truck tires, lighters, an unopened pack of cigarettes, a blanket, men's underwear, women's underwear, pens, a phone book, a wide variety of small plastic liquor bottles, PVC pipe, a metal rod, plastic shopping bags, a shirt, a Marine Corps baseball cap, and of course the shopping carts . . . all the ingredients for a future plastiglomerate geologic layer, a type of rock made of sediments, human and natural debris, and all held together by plastic.

A geology of plastiglomerate will one day mark a moment in the Anthropocene. We use the term Anthropocene as shorthand for a moment in history when human beings dominate literally every aspect of life on Earth. It is not a term that is accepted by the scientific community as a whole. In fact, in early 2024, after an epic academic battle, the self-appointed guardians of the Earth's official geologic epochs rebuffed a proposal to declare an official Anthropocene period. And still, the term makes all too much sense.

The great English writer Robert MacFarlane says of the Anthropocene: "an epoch of immense and often frightening change at a planetary scale in which 'crisis' exists not as an ever-deferred future apocalypse but rather as an ongoing occurrence experienced most severally by the most vulnerable. Time is profoundly out of joint—and so is place." Or, to gently bend the words of William Gibson, 'the apocalypse is already here—it's just not evenly distributed.'

The Anthropocene is a geological age in which the atmosphere, the water, the biosphere, and most or all of the Earth's systems have been and will continue to be altered by humans. Humans have become the single most influential species on the planet creating an imbalance that threatens human survival itself.

If we as a species survive what we have created—and that is by no means assured—people thousands of years from now will know the Anthropocene as we know the Pleistocene, by traces of material culture collapsing from the stream bank. Or, perhaps working their way to the surface of the creek's sediments, appearing one day where they had not been the day before. Perhaps, if we survive, future geologists or archaeologists will excavate chunks of plastiglomerate. I imagine a teenage boy five hundred or one thousand years from now, searching the Fountain's sands as I once did. He comes across an ancient shopping cart embedded in a rock of cans, bottles, batteries, and used up vibrating sex toys. A river moves through time as well as space. The waters link us to our various pasts and futures. The creek binds us to where we have come from and to where we are going.

—

The Spanish released the Pike expedition in the spring of 1807. Instead of a mammoth, Pike delivered two New Mexico grizzly cubs to President Jefferson, who put them on display at the White House then sent them to a museum in Philadelphia. Pike and his men were never fully compensated for their struggles on behalf of the United States. Pike died a hero, his head pulverized by shrapnel while fighting the British at York in Canada in April 1813.

I continued north. By the afternoon, the air was fragrant with the liminal scents of ice, dried leaves, and thawing soils. The wind calmed, the sky cleared. A scattering of puffy, white clouds, grayed at the edges, floated overhead. Two teenage girls sat on a cottonwood stump swinging their legs, passing a joint back and forth. A Brewer's sparrow topped a sage, trilling reedy notes. An old man removed his coat, tied it around his waist, and pushed his bike up the asphalt path.

RIGHTS

"'But surely,' I said sweetly, 'we should all have access to swim in our rivers just as we should be free to walk in our own countryside. Don't they belong to all of us?'"

–*Roger Deakin,* Waterlog

On that map of the lung-shaped Fountain watershed that hung on my wall, blue marked the Fountain and its tributaries. Private lands were colored gray, sprawling military holdings, olive, public lands, a forest green. Two massive pink splotches marked the 2012 Waldo Canyon wildfire and the 2013 Black Forest fire. You could see by the dull yellow or beige color marking incorporated cities, towns, and municipalities that most of the Fountain watershed was urban or suburban.

I intended to walk the Fountain and many of its tributaries. My plan was to piece together a walking route of bike trails, streambed explorations, hiking trails, footpaths, paved roads, and overland routes in order to stay as close to the creek and its tributaries as possible.

I prefer to walk. For me, walking offers the opportunity to experience the world at its own pace. At the speed of walking, I can take note of the world around me: smells, sights, sounds, movement, the taste of the wind, the changes in the soil, the flutter of a leaf, the lift of a butterfly. A snowflake, a splash, a call. At the speed of walking, I have time to think and process what

I'm seeing. In my mind, the only way to truly know a place is on foot.

I am, admittedly, somewhat evangelical about walking. Probably annoyingly so. I learned the places I lived and visited by walking. In the winter of 1994-95, broken-hearted from a failed relationship with a Swiss woman, I walked from Bern to St. Gallen where I caught a train for Prague and a new chapter. The following year, I walked the length of the Var in France, from the source near the Col de la Coyolle to the rocky beaches near Nice where a bearded man with an enormous belly invited me to share a catch of fish while we sipped chilled wine from a cooler. In 2003, I spent five months walking 1,500 miles across Finland, interviewing Finns about their relationship to the natural world for my book, *Notes for the Aurora Society.*

Some types of walks require maps. The map I had concocted in my head was an imaginary realm spider-webbed with histories, memories, stories, wildlife migration routes, personal experiences, pure fancy, and prayers for the future.

The map on my wall, however, immediately indicated a serious problem in my reverie. Much of the Fountain, like much of the American West, is vaulted in private lands and infected by barbed wire. NO TRESSPASSING. DO NOT ENTER. TRESSPASSERS WILL BE SHOT ON SIGHT. Walking the length of the Fountain in a world dominated by private holdings would be difficult to say the least. Then there were the military bases. Should I bother navigating military bureaucracies for permission to explore the tributaries?

I didn't much like the idea of being shot on sight. How then, could I walk the watershed? One possible solution, the Fountain itself.

In Colorado, rivers are considered public. Waters of every natural stream, creek, or river theoretically belong to the people of Colorado and are therefore, theoretically, accessible.

Theoretically. There is a massive caveat. Private landowners are not required to provide access to public waters. The owner of any land a river flows through also owns the banks and even, perhaps, the streambed. You could float, raft, tube, canoe, or kayak down any Colorado river legally. However, if you touch the stream bank or even the streambed where private lands exist, you are trespassing and subject to arrest and prosecution. Many Colorado landowners interpret this confusion to mean that no one at all can utilize a water running through their property even if that person remains in a craft or never touches the streambed or bank.

In the 1990s, I worked as a raft guide in north-central Colorado. One gray afternoon on the Roaring Fork River, I bumped against a rock I should have missed and found myself sucked into a series of frothing holes that tipped the raft, pouring myself and my clients into the water. As shipwrecks go, this ranked among the least tragic. The only injury was to my pride. But my clients were stuck on a gravel bar in the middle of the flow while the raft slipped to river right and hung up in an eddy. Apologizing profusely, I made sure everyone was okay, then set off to retrieve the raft.

A landowner from the left bank appeared, rifle in hand. He screamed at my customers. He screamed at me. He accused us of trespassing and ordered my clients into the water. I shouted for them to stay put and assured the landowner that we would be gone in less than ten minutes. He refused to back down, alternately threatening to call the sheriff and/or shoot us. The landowner and I shouted back and forth at each other until a passing kayaker rescued my boat and brought it to the gravel bar. The landowner then screamed at the kayaker, this time pointing the gun. The kayaker looked at me, wide-eyed, dropped the raft, and high-tailed it downriver. I hustled the customers into the boat and pushed off, pulling hard at the oars.

There is no public "right-to-roam" or right to walk a riverbank in Colorado. In the Nordic and Baltic countries—Iceland,

Scotland, Finland, Sweden, Norway, Estonia, Lithuania, Latvia—the "Everyman's Right" protects the public's ability to access both public and privately owned land, lakes, and rivers for reasons of exercise and recreation. The only caveat is that one maintains a respectful distance from private houses and generally show respect for private property. Most Americans do not have this right and it constricts our ability to interact with lands and waters. Who owns a river? Should anyone? How do we access the waters that shape both our external and internal landscapes?

On a summer day in 2012, Roger Hill stood in the middle of the Arkansas River at the confluence with Turkey Creek, miles upstream from Pueblo. Fly rod in hand, the seventy-one-year-old angler enjoyed some of the best trout waters in the American West. Hill had fished that spot many times over the years and never encountered a problem.

Linda Joseph, however, was not pleased. From a bluff above Hill's fishing spot, Joseph chucked a baseball-sized rock at the angler's head. She missed, but only just. Joseph gathered up another rock, screaming at Hill that he was violating her private property rights, and again launched the projectile at the angler's head. Hill left. When he returned weeks later, Linda Joseph's husband, Mark Warsewa, left a threatening note on Hill's car. Roger Hill kept his distance for several years but in 2015, he returned to his favorite fishing spot with two friends. Warsewa pulled a gun and fired.

Thankfully, no one was injured. Warsewa spent a month in jail for his tantrum, but the fight was far from over. In 2018, Hill sued Joseph, Warsewa, and the State of Colorado for access to the Ark. The core of Hill's argument was this: federal law holds that "navigable" rivers belong to the states, not private individuals, and that state ownership of the riverbed is for the express purpose of protecting public rights to the river. The Supreme

Court of the United States long ago defined a "navigable" river as a waterway used as "highways for commerce" at or before the time of statehood. The Ark fit this definition. The river had, for years, been utilized as a highway for commerce. Traders used the Ark to ferry furs and other goods between the upper watershed and lucrative markets downstream such as Bent's Fort near La Junta, east of Pueblo. In the late nineteenth century, loggers sent tens of thousands of cut trees down the Ark to Pueblo for use as railroad ties. The Arkansas certainly had a history of commerce, Hill demonstrated, and was thus a navigable waterway held in trust for the public by the State of Colorado.

Colorado's river access laws are murky. Hill's lawsuit aimed to change that, or at least to clarify the rules. In December 2022, the Colorado Supreme Court agreed to hear Hill's case. Oddly, the Colorado State Attorney General, Phil Weiser, took the side of private property owners instead of exercising the State's public trust responsibility. Weiser reasoned that he was not opposing Roger Hill's assertion outright, but that changes to river access policy should be handled by the state legislature in a public process instead of in the court system. This reasoning is dubious however, given the legalized bribery and corruption at the core of America's legislative process—a corruption that directly benefits people such as Warsewa and Joseph at the expense of people like Hill and myself.

Colorado is somewhat of an odd bird when it comes to river access. States such as Idaho and Washington grant access to most waterways. Arkansas has a very liberal interpretation of "navigable," rendering most streams in the state accessible to anglers and boaters. Along Canada's navigable rivers, the government owns a strip of land three meters wide on either bank, which protects the public's right to utilize, enjoy, and experience the nation's waterways. Several other countries offer similar rights.

Hill based his argument on the "equal-footing" doctrine of the Commerce Clause of the United States Constitution. In the

Lessee v. Hagan (1845) decision, the Supreme Court held that under the equal footing doctrine, "a State, upon entering the Union, gains title to the beds of waters then navigable or tidally influenced, subject only to federal powers under the Constitution." Therefore, when Colorado became a state in 1876 the state gained ownership of all navigable waters.

As crazy as it sounds, Colorado's official policy holds that the state has no navigable waterways. None. Zero. Zilch. In 2012, the Colorado State Supreme Court ruled that the state's rivers were "nonnavigable within its territorial limits," meaning that, in practice, even the beds of good-sized rivers such as the Arkansas, South Platte, or Colorado, became private. Floating through private land was at least tolerable. Accidently bumping the streambed or touching the bank was trespassing, an illegal act that could result in fines or jail time. Or a shooting.

All this got me wondering. Was the Fountain ever navigable? If the creek was not historically navigable, it is now. While it certainly isn't "commerce," a kayak could nevertheless make its way from Colorado Springs to Pueblo almost year-round now, thanks to all the new water in the creek.

The Fountain was most likely navigable at times in the past, but surely not through the whole year. Juan Bautista de Anza mentions floating supplies on the Fountain for short distances during his expedition to hunt down Cuerno Verde. Historian Larry Obermesik, editor of *The Lost Gold Rush Journals of Daniel Jenks 1849-1865,* told me that settlers Dick Wootton and Loren Jenks maintained toll bridges over Fountain Creek at their ranches north of Pueblo. From the 1870s through World War I, dredging within the Fountain creek bed in Pueblo became a multi-million-dollar industry with Fountain Creek sand and gravel sold across the region for construction.

I am not sure any of this counts as "river commerce," but somewhere along the line, I ran across a historical account from the 1850s or 60s of a log raft, loaded with furs, gunpowder, supplies, and trade goods pulled up the Fountain from Pueblo to the trading post at Jimmy Camp. If the Fountain had indeed been used, even occasionally, to move commerce prior to or at statehood, did this mean that I had the right to walk the whole of the creek as long as I stayed in the streambed? Well, no.

Colorado is not the only odd bird when it comes to river access.

Through the early 2000s, private landowners increasingly sought to bar public access to waterways in New Mexico by draping barbed wire across the flow. As anyone who has ever paddled a river knows, barbed wire strung across a waterway is incredibly dangerous. A paddler, propelled by the current, may not have enough time to stop or change course before becoming tangled in the brutal, bloody noose. Signs screeching PRIVATE PROPERTY and NO TRESSPASSING proliferated. Such extremism reached fever pitch in shootings like the one Hill endured. In the mountain town of Taos, a private landowner viciously attacked a farmer with a shovel resulting in severe injury. The farmer's transgression? Cleaning a spring-fed irrigation ditch along a recognized public right-of-way that crossed private land. Since the late 1990s, angry landowners have frequently pulled guns on anglers, kayakers, and bird-watchers.

In 2015, the New Mexico state legislature quietly shuffled a bill to the desk of then-Governor Susana Martinez, a Republican. The new law barred public access to waterways long considered public. America's legalized system of political grift worked its magic. The Governor and State Legislature sided with private landowners against the people of New Mexico. It also put them at odds with then-Attorney General Gary King, who insisted the state constitution provided New Mexicans with the right to wade or float in streams running through private property, provided they remain in the stream. In one late night, hush-hush session, New Mexico state lawmakers removed what had been a centuries-old right.

The same thing happened in other western states. In 2010, the Utah state legislature cut off access on streams running through private property, rendering 40 percent of Utah's fishable streams out of reach.

Throughout the American West, wealthy Americans are working to keep the rest of us riffraff off public lands and away from shared waterways.

In May 2023, the United States Supreme Court, in a case known as *Sackett v. EPA*, stripped federal protections for all ephemeral streams and wetlands in the United States. The ruling limited Clean Water Act protections to permanent standing waters for rivers that flow year-round. It also limited wetland protection to those wetlands that are immediately adjacent to standing bodies of water such as a lake.

This ruling was purely political. It ignores ecological and hydrological reality. A creek is made up of far more than the water we see flowing through the actual channel. Once again, the whims of private landowners trumped the greater good.

In the ruling, Justice Antonin Scalia referred to the American West as "immense arid wastelands," a truly astounding statement for anyone who has ever been west of the Mississippi and a direct thumb in the eye to those of us who call this land home. Not only was the statement enraging but also somewhat ironic, reflecting poorly on Scalia's education and intellectual curiosity. The very reason people like Scalia view the American West as "arid wastelands" is due directly to choices we made as a nation, particularly wetland and stream destruction by overgrazing, the massacre of our native wildlife, the decimation of beaver populations, the draining and paving over wetlands and springs, and the genocide of the Indigenous nations that respected the way in which water works. America turned what once was a lush western landscape into a desert.

New Mexico's Rio Grande, indisputably a major waterway that occasionally goes dry in stretches, may have lost all protections with the *Sackett* decision. In fact, almost 100 percent of waterways in New Mexico, Arizona, and Nevada—not to mention a significant number of Colorado's waterways—ended up without protections, much less rights. For waters of the American West, the *Sackett* ruling is potentially disastrous. What *Sackett* means for the Fountain is unclear.

The war over access to rivers is all part of a larger battle over who controls access to nature. Who has rights and who does not. In Wyoming, pharmaceutical tycoon Fred Eshelman purchased a fifty-acre tract adjacent to designated wilderness for the express purpose of blocking public access to publicly owned Elk Mountain. In northern New Mexico, private landowners blocked a public road to White Peak, a treasured hunting area owned by the people of New Mexico. In southern Arizona, a rancher blocked access to public lands aiming to turn the area into his own private hunting reserve, hoping to sell exclusive access to those able to pay upwards of $10,000 a day to hunt. In Colorado, nearly one million acres of public lands are blocked. As of 2023, throughout the American West, sixteen million acres of public lands are off limits to the public thanks to private landowners.

On June 5, 2023, the Colorado Supreme Court ruled on Roger Hill's case. The ruling was nothing short of bizarre. The court held that Hill lacked legal standing, claiming the angler could not sue for being kicked off a public waterway if the waterway had never been deemed public in the first place. In other words, Hill did not have the legal standing to *prove* the riverbed was public because the riverbed had never been proven public in the first place. A mind-numbing ruling to say the least and a major step backwards for public access. Even more confounding, the ruling appears to incentivize anglers to purposefully trespass and get arrested in order to prove standing.

In New Mexico, the news was better. The state Supreme Court eventually ruled that New Mexicans have the constitutional right to waterways flowing through private lands provided they don't step ashore. The new state attorney general, Raúl Torrez, proved aggressive in enforcing this right, suing a number of private landowners who continued to block access. New Mexico Game and Fish officers, on the other hand, have been remiss in their duties to enforce open access. Probably because three wealthy landowners who had installed unlawful barriers of metal and concertina wire across streams donated thousands of dollars to the New Mexico Conservation Officers Association, of which New Mexico Game and Fish officers are members. Yet another example of America's system of legalized bribery.

The idea that ownership rights are absolute strikes me as absurd. It is also a demonstration of a growing anti-social behavior that harms us all. Some private landowners are irrationally stuck on the idea of maximalist ownership in its most extreme, ignoring the reality that property exists within social, economic, and ecological contexts. Property does not exist in a vacuum. This thinking has property owners clinging to the idea they have the right to put others in danger, be it via strands of barbed wire or weapons. What many Americans forget far too often is that with rights come responsibilities.

This maximalist thinking also results in other forms of public endangerments such as pollution, which kills hundreds of thousands of Americans each year. According to a 2022 study in *The Lancet*, an estimated nine million people die worldwide each year from polluted air and water.

Take for example the spraying of pesticides or herbicides such as Roundup. Private property owners have the "right" to use these known cancer-causing agents on their own land. Of course, those chemicals do not stay on the land of the people who used them. They get into the air, water, insects, and wildlife, resulting in human cancers, fish kills, and the deaths of birds, bees, and butterflies.

Those who use these chemicals put their family and neighbors at risk, which results in even greater social harms.

Several states—Pennsylvania, Montana, Illinois, Massachusetts, Hawai'i, and New York—have provisions within their constitutions guaranteeing a citizen's right to a "clean and healthful environment." A similar Colorado proposal failed to pass the state legislature in 2014. Several other states—New Mexico, New Jersey, Maine, Nevada, Oregon, and Vermont among them—are looking to amend their Constitutions to protect the people's right to clean air and water. They face an uphill battle. There is no such provision in the US Constitution and, in fact, on the world stage, the United States, under both Republican and Democratic leadership, has consistently stood beside Russia and China to oppose the fundamental right to a clean environment.

The 2024 New Mexico proposal reads that residents "shall be entitled to clean and healthy air, water, soil, and environment; a stable climate; and self-sustaining ecosystems, for the benefit of public health, safety and general welfare."

For most of us, such a protected right is a no-brainer. The right to a clean environment is fundamental for a healthy and fruitful life. Yet this idea is somehow controversial. These proposals meet with considerable opposition from powerful polluters such as the mining and oil and gas industries, chemical companies, some ranchers, timber operations, and energy producers. Most lawmakers do not like these laws, and courts rebel against them. New Mexico's proposal appears stuck in the state legislature for the time being. The Interwest Energy Alliance, a partnership of renewable energy producers and environmental groups including the national Sierra Club, also opposes such amendments, claiming they could curtail green energy projects. It seems odd: if your green energy project does not protect people and ecosystems, is it actually green?

The efficacy of such Constitutional amendments is also questionable. In the United States, laws do not always apply to the rich and powerful and constitutional amendments are frequently ignored. Advocates push on, however, pointing to situations where the amendments have worked. While all bad development has not been stopped, such amendments can curtail the worst of the worst when it comes to pollution and environmental destruction.

A blade of grass bent into the Fountain. The flow pulled it in an arc, a half circle, tracing a line across the water that rippled then faded to foam. The blade of grass, pulled to its limit, snapped back, stood straight, then dipped into the water again, arching a fresh line across the surface.

I had parked my truck outside a half-abandoned shopping center in Colorado Springs and followed a feral footpath through a copse of elm, olive, and willow. The elms were black. They tilted over the water, stretching for sun. A butterfly, its colors dull, flickered past. The scent of the Fountain filled the air: a unique, meaty, humid mélange of ash, urine, moss, coal, and concrete. The Fountain's odor is disturbingly human.

David Burnham sat on the creek bank, rummaging through a box of flies. "Water's pretty damn clear today. I'm going to try this little bugger," he held up a black, hand-tied fly.

"Alright," I said. "I'll run with something a little more flashy."

"See what happens."

"See what happens."

I joined Burnham on the bank. We attached our flies, adjusted our wading gear, and carried our rods past an old tire to the middle of the Fountain. With a small thermometer, Burnham took the creek's temperature. "Bit of a fever today—sixty-seven degrees. That's crazy warm for a mid-October morning in Colorado." He shook his head. "I'd bet the water hits seventy or seventy-five by noon. We should knock off before that. Fish will be stressed."

In the middle of the creek, the water splashed my waders. Where the river carved the bank into pools and eddies, the water could be knee-deep, but in some places, it was almost hip-deep. It was these deeper holes we aimed to fish. The best hole I knew of was to the right bank, just below a low, concrete wall draped across the Fountain's flow. Half a dozen or so of these two to three-foot-high walls cut the creek along its path through Colorado Springs. I have never been able to figure out why these little walls exist. Perhaps they are sediment or flood control structures. Whatever their purpose, they appear old, the concrete crumbling.

Trash collected just below the cement wall. The tumbling water curled as it topped the structure, gouging deep troughs in the sediments below the surface, trapping foam and flotsam above. Plastic Kum-and-Go soda cups, Coke and Pepsi bottles, bits of plastic, and grocery bags swirled in the muck. A pink and yellow soccer ball, partially deflated, rolled in the flow but was held firmly in place by the roiling water. Two months previously, we had fished the same spot. The soccer ball had not moved since.

Burnham, the local chair for the conservation group Trout Unlimited, had retired after decades in the National Guard. A passionate advocate for fish and waters, Burnham drove for Uber and Lyft in the afternoons so his mornings were free for fishing. Work, he had told me at one point, was the price you pay to go fishing. Burnham knew every creek and, it seemed, every individual fish in central Colorado. "I caught that rainbow in a little hole on Bear Creek two years ago. I got him again, same fish, last week. He'd grown but it was the same fish."

"How do you know it was the same fish?" I asked. "Don't they all look alike?"

"Every individual is unique, man. You just got to pay attention. Hell. They probably think we all look the same too."

I cast my flashy fly above a right bank hole, beside a bobbing plastic Starbucks cup and a Gatorade bottle. The fly turned in the flow without breaking the surface.

Along the bike path, a runner passed. He stopped, turned, and came to the creek's edge. "There's no fish in there! What are you doing?"

"Watch!" Burnham smiled.

The man folded his arms and leaned against an elm.

Burnham picked a hole in the Fountain's center, just below the cement. His first cast was off, his second perfect. A trout hit the fly and dove. Burnham whooped. I reeled in, grabbed the net, and waded over as backup. Burnham tightened the line. The rod bent nearly to the water. "Big one," he said. The trout surfaced just outside the foam, thrashed about, and dove again for the hole, bending the rod.

"Well I'll be . . ." the runner pushed himself off the tree and stepped to the water's edge.

Burnham moved toward a sandbar, working the fish to the shallows. It rested near the surface and I scooped it into the net. The hook popped from its mouth and Burnham looked up. "Eighteen inches at least," he said. "What a beauty!"

"I never thought . . ." said the runner on the bank. "There were never fish in here before!"

Burnham shrugged. "There's always been fish in here, just not trout."

The brown trout measured in at just over twenty inches. He, or she, was thick with red and coffee-colored spots. A European salmonid, the hardy, adaptable brown has been introduced to rivers throughout the world.

There was something else. Burnham turned the fish over

and pointed. A painful looking lesion throbbed from the side of the fish. It was round and yellow, like mucous. "That's no good."

"Pollution?" I asked.

Burnham nodded and slid the trout back into the water.

"You're not going to eat that?" The runner asked.

"I wouldn't eat anything out of the Fountain," Burnham said. "Gorgeous fish, but . . ." he made a face as if he were about to puke. "It's still a sewer."

We fished the two holes until the water temperature hit seventy-one degrees. I pulled in a foot long rainbow trout, another non-native species, and then a nine-inch brown. Burnham landed two more browns, both smaller than the first. One of his browns also had a lesion. The fish was worn and did not fight. We unhooked it and placed it into a calm pool. When I let it go, the fish went sideways, pushed against the flow, surrendered, and floated downstream, unable to fight the current. Burnham shook his head. "That's it. Water is too hot to fish and I got to Uber. Let's try up near the park next time."

Alone then, I folded my rod and waded downstream. Two unhoused men sat in camp chairs near a small, smoky fire. They waved hello. I waved back. "Don't eat anything out of there!" One of the men called out.

I gave him the thumbs up and kept wading.

Sweaty and hungry, I sat for a lunch of carrots and chips. The grass caught my attention. The blade arched across the surface of the creek. It stood, bent, then traced the half-circle in the water. Then again. And again. I lost track of time.

I walked south for an hour until I came to a pile of bones jutting from a dried over pelt, tan and fringed in white. The deer's hooves poked from a ramble of beaver-chewed willows a few feet away, the meat gnawed from the leg bones. The Fountain licked at the carcass and sighed.

—

Across the world, rivers are being afforded basic rights themselves. The general idea—details vary by location—is that in order to protect human communities, rivers should be given rights similar to those afforded human beings.

In February 2021, Canadian authorities granted the Mutuhekau-shipu (Magpie River) legal personhood. The move, taken as part of the fight against a series of hydroelectric dams, granted the river nine distinct rights, including the right to flow, the right to be free of pollution, and the right to have legal guardians who could sue on behalf of the river.

The rights of nature concept builds on the work of legal philosopher Christopher Stone. In 1972, Stone, a professor of law at the University of Southern California, proposed that forests and rivers should be afforded rights under the law.

"Until the rightless thing receives its rights," Stone wrote, "we cannot see it as anything but a thing for the use of 'us'—those who are holding rights at the time. Throughout legal history, each successive extension of rights to some new entity has been therefore, a bit unthinkable."

For Stone, the extension of rights to nature was a logical step, building on the right of women to vote, citizenship belatedly granted to Native Americans, and the Civil Rights legislations of the 1960s. "What is needed is a radical new theory or myth," he wrote, "felt as well as intellectualized—of man's relationships to the rest of nature."

A river's rights might include the right to flow, the right of the river to evolve, the right to remain unpolluted, the right to maintain its ecological functions and the biodiversity those functions generate. Stone expanded on these ideas in his 1974 book *Should Trees Have Standing: Law, Morality and the Environment.*

For many years, Stone's radical proposal hung in the ether, marinating. Eventually, several native nations—the Yurok and Ponca among them—began to explore how Stone's concept might be applied to issues facing their communities. For Indigenous peoples, the concept makes sense. Stone's argument was not plucked from thin air. He had built a legal framework based on age-old concepts of nature's animacy held by Indigenous nations throughout the world. That is, that nature—birds, rocks, rivers, forests, mountains, winds, fire—are beings just as we are beings. For Indigenous people, nature is animate. Being and animacy extend beyond the human, and therefore so too should rights. Author and ecologist Robin Wall Kimmerer calls this "the grammar of animacy," the idea that nature is a "relative." Kin. Family. Not a "thing" for exploitation.

If this sounds silly, consider that in the United States of America we have long accepted the legal theory that corporations are no different from humans. A corporation only exists on paper, yet corporations have been awarded "personhood" by the Supreme Court, meaning that paper entity retains the same rights as you and I . . . living, walking, breathing beings. We barely even question this legal absurdity despite its profound and distorting impacts on our politics and economy. If corporations have the rights of personhood, so should rivers.

In 2016, the government of New Zealand conferred rights on the Whanganui River. Ecuador gave rights to the Alpayaco River. The Indian state of Uttarakhand extended rights and personhood to the Ganga and Yamuna rivers—then came the Mutuhekau-shipu. Australia, Mexico, and Bangladesh are all considering the rights of rivers. Rights are even being considered for the abused Colorado River. Residents of Toledo, Ohio, drew up a bill of rights for Lake Erie stating that "Lake Erie, and the Lake Erie watershed, possess the right to exist, flourish, and naturally evolve." In February 2020, a federal judge struck down the law as "unconstitutionally vague."

Dr. Erin O'Donnell (no known relation) of the University of Melbourne has her doubts about the efficacy of these rights. The problem, she says, is few of these new laws grant the river a right to *flow*. Those that do, fail to offer a legal mechanism to ensure that right. Rights for a river, O'Donnell explained in legal articles and a book on the subject, means nothing if the river does not have the right to the water flowing between its banks.

Along New Zealand's Whanganui, for example, 80 percent of the river's water is diverted for hydropower. In India, the Ganga and Yamuna continue to be polluted and diverted.

The rights of nature movement may be slow, but the idea is gaining ground.

Colorado does have an in stream flow program. Since 1973, this program has guaranteed some minimal rights for about 9,700 miles of stream and 480 natural lakes. While flawed in some important ways, the program at least gives Colorado something to build on.

At the dawn of 2024, the Board of Trustees of Nederland, a community forty-five miles northwest of Denver, appointed two "guardians" to serve as formal representatives for Boulder Creek. This follows a 2021 decision by the town to recognize that Boulder Creek and its watershed were living entities possessing "fundamental and inalienable rights." Boulder Creek was afforded the right to exist. That may seem a bit silly, but when it comes to public acceptance of the rights of nature, it is a big step forward.

Nederland isn't the only Colorado town to recognize the rights of a local waterway. Other towns have passed resolutions recognizing Grand Lake, the St. Vrain, and the Uncompahgre Rivers as living entities with rights.

To be clear, O'Donnell and others who critique the concept of legal rights for nature are not calling for the idea to be flushed. Quite the opposite. By pointing to weaknesses in the application, they aim to see those holes plugged and for the rights of rivers and the rights of other natural beings to have real teeth. This will have "the most transformative potential in terms of the way that people relate to the river," O'Donnell said in a 2021 *Guardian* article. Affording rights to nature overturns the paradigm of human domination over nature. "When we see the river as a living being, that is when we start to say, hang on, what do we want for the river?"

All these moves are a net positive. It is the right direction for us to take. Still, the rights of nature movement is largely human-centered, as the other O'Donnell points out. Rights for nature typically come about because of a human need. We continue to use nature for our benefit. That is okay. It is understandable. This is an evolution. But we can go deeper.

Upon Deakin's passing, Robert MacFarlane got a hold of the wild swimmer's notebooks. One line in particular seemed to strike MacFarlane. "All water," Deakin had written, ". . . river, sea, pond, lake, holds memory and the space to think."

The rights of nature movement is a Western legal concept rooted in a worldview born of Indigenousness. Water is not a what; it is a who. Nature is alive. A river is a being. Water is alive and water is family. A tree animate. A mountain has a soul. These too are family and should be treated as such. Water, tree, mountain . . . they have a right to exist. After all, without nature there are no rights at all.

The idea that "things" such as rivers, rocks, trees, and birds are actually more than inanimate objects and are imbued instead with their own sentient beingness is at the root of human spirituality. It is our species' fundamental worldview, born in a distant time, when the boundaries between human beings and the rest of the world was barely a thin veil. For early humans, life was precarious, the world deeply real. Daily experience and the continuation of that existence was subject to the vagaries of wildlife and weather. Survival depended on one's ability and willingness to pay attention, close attention, to the world around.

When you pay attention that closely, the world becomes something more that it appears when seen at a passing glance.

Our ancestors paid attention to survive, and in doing so, they saw the truth about the world around them, that it is full of sentient beings with their own intentions and forms of communication. Ravens bear messages, leaves bring seasonal tidings, the mountain forecasts the year to come while retaining memories of years past. A fire cleans and heals. A falling rock, the bison on the steppe, the stars mapped across the sky, and a gurgling creek with something to say—and it says, we're mostly water.

In Lapland, an old hunter once explained to me that in the Finnish language, the word for human being is ihminen. The root for this word is (arguably) ihme, connoting miracle or wonder. Human as miracle. A river, wrote Edward Abbey, is also a miracle, though crazy old Abbey was not focused so much on the water itself. His understanding of a river stretched beyond the stream banks. "Miracle to miracle," he wrote referring to the entire process of a river, a watershed, the water in context.

When I think of a river as miracle, a river as a being, I am reminded of Borges. "A miracle," penned the blind Argentinean poet, "has the right to impose conditions." In other words, a miracle has the right to demand rights. A miracle has authority above human law.

OSPREY

October 26: Fifteen miles north of Pueblo

A kestrel hung above the channel separating the Fountain from the hay fields and the low wooded hills. She dove for something in the scrub, a mouse, a prairie dog, or a chipmunk. But she thought better of it and perched on a snag. East of the creek, a tangle of dry tamarisk and willow disappeared to the cutbank where stubby prairie grasses and cholla spread to the horizon. I sat to watch, but the kestrel dropped and disappeared west so I walked on.

The blue sky reached from the equally blue mountains to the yellowing rim of the plains. But for a scattering of wispy cirrus, the sky was empty. A luminous gold dripped from the elms. The leaves of the cottonwoods rattled orange and crisp. That year, summer stretched to October. Autumn would not end until nearly Christmas. The Fountain's forest blazed yellow—in every direction nothing but yellow, yellow, and the blue above.

The osprey arrived from the south and hovered above riffles in the flow. He pushed upstream into the breeze, hovering again above a pool, then circled back to the riffles for another look.

Held aloft by long, narrow wings, the osprey's head angled slightly downwards, yellow eyes scanning the water. A wood duck called, and a scatter of song sparrows settled on dried teasel heads that bobbed with the weight of the feathery friends. Crows flocked to a snag in the brush.

Where the creek wound through the cottonwoods, the osprey rose on the breeze and approached. He circled, maybe fifty feet above, taking stock of this solitary human making his way along the bank gravels. Satisfied, he spiraled up and east over the cholla and an abandoned farmhouse. He returned to the creek, pushing into the northerly breeze, wings bowed, then outstretched, flapping steady, easy. He hovered again, folding his wings, leaning just back, pushing the air in front so that he hung in that blue sky, barely moving. Then, his wings unfurled, he fell to his side and straightened to a dive, his white legs stiff, dark talons wide. He hit the water and lifted above a sandbar, talons empty. He made for one of the cottonwoods on the right bank, squatting into a perch. The brown and white feathers on the back of his head stood straight, crown-like. Even from across the creek I could see those beaming yellow eyes.

About fifteen minutes later, a raft of ducks moved up from the south, settling into the creek bed along a rounded bank where the flow had dug a trough. Either they failed to notice the osprey or the ducks did not care. The osprey noticed, however. He lifted his feet one by one, flexing talons in anticipation.

Two mallards turned into a side channel and made their way to the main stem. The flow caught them up, and they turned circles in the current before drifting downstream. The osprey leapt from his perch, wings folded and dove at the ducks. He adjusted, extending his talons in front, wings angled just back, white underside fully exposed.

The ducks squawked and burst into the sky straight at the raptor. Confused, the osprey tried to adjust but missed, diving just past the ducks. They turned again and angled north. The other ducks exploded from the water in a panicked chaos of squawking, quacking, and flapping wings. By the time the osprey broke from his dive and returned to the sky, the ducks were gone.

I walked up from the bank to a barbed wire fence covered in dried tumbleweeds. I lifted a downed branch and lay it over the wire, pushing until it bent, then collapsed. I struggled through the tumbleweeds and into the cottonwoods beyond.

The day had grown long, and I'd lost track of time. I could see the shadows bend across the yellow. The strips of light pulled oranges and reds from the leaves and the breeze of the day fell away. I walked for ten or maybe twenty minutes more then decided to make for the road.

As I approached a gate, the osprey appeared from the south, wings weighted and slow. Gripped in his talons, a fish twisted as its life force faded. It was a trout, although it seemed too far south and warm for trout. Still, there it was, a trout in the grip of a great raptor. The osprey turned west into the deepening blue.

ALL TAPPED OUT

"I tell you, gentlemen, you are piling up a heritage of conflict and litigation over water rights, for there is not sufficient water to supply these lands."

–John Wesley Powell

A man raised his hand. "We don't have enough water for *thousands* of new homes." He removed his baseball cap and scratched the back of his head.

The developer, a representative of La Plata Communities, pushed back. "There's plenty of water, we just have to get it here." He smiled.

The reporter, a small woman from Denver, leaned into me and whispered, "The City of Colorado Springs shouldn't exist. Makes no sense." She had torn up her lawn and planted native flowers. She'd looked into a rain catchment system for her house, but she couldn't afford one. Not yet anyway.

A woman stood and pointed at the man with the baseball cap. "Look. This isn't hard. You get the water from where it is, and you move it to where you want it to be. That's the Western way."

I thought wait . . . I've heard that before and I could not decide if it was sarcasm or a genuinely held belief. I turned to the reporter. She shrugged. I shrugged.

"Can we drink money?" asked another woman. "Can we use some magic and turn money into water? Yeah. I don't think so."

I sat next to the reporter, in the back of a town hall meeting on the Amara annexation, a proposal to bring 3,200 acres of unincorporated El Paso County into the City of Colorado Springs. La Plata Communities aimed to build thousands of high-end homes in a master-planned community on the old TeeCross and Kane Ranch properties near the City of Fountain. There was a problem, however. Water. Or, the lack thereof.

Colorado is a "headwaters state." Generally considered high desert, many of the iconic rivers of the American West are born in Colorado. The Arkansas River, the Platte River, the Rio Grande, and, of course, the once-mighty Colorado River. Colorado is home to eight major river basins, large aquifers, and thousands of lakes and reservoirs.

Yet within Colorado, water supplies cannot meet current demand, much less the demands of the future. The Colorado Water Plan states that "competition for scarce water supplies is driving up water costs and posing challenges to meeting future municipal, industrial, and agricultural needs while protecting and enhancing the environmental and recreational opportunities."

Translation? "Holy Shit!"

The Colorado Water Plan sees a supply-demand gap for cities upwards of 750,000 acre-feet by 2050. The plan projects municipal water demand to increase from 35 to 75 percent in coming years, depending on the development scenario. Farmers and ranchers face a two to four million acre-feet gap. Climate change will not make things better. Climatologists point out that Colorado is becoming permanently drier, a process known as "aridification."

Holy shit indeed.

Earlier that day, after several chilly nights in the upper reaches of Monument Creek, I checked into a motel in downtown Colorado Springs, closed the door, stripped, and beelined for a hot shower, only to find the water already running.

Several gallons per hour gushed from the faucet. I fiddled with the valves and the diverter, but the water continued to pour into the tub. Here was water, piped at great expense from the Colorado River basin, through and over the Rocky Mountains, cleaned for domestic use, pumped to that motel, only to leak away into the Fountain while developers and residents argued over how much water was available for new homes.

I showered, notified management about the leak, and made my way to the town hall meeting. When I returned late that evening, the water continued to run. Three days later when I left for Pueblo, the leak had not ceased.

Of course, "wasted" is a term burdened with human values and judgment. That "wasted" water runs into the sewer, to the water treatment plant on a bluff overlooking the Fountain. From there it is piped back into the Fountain where it makes its way to Pueblo and the Arkansas. For the Fountain, the leak is a gain. For the people of Colorado Springs, that leaking water is a loss. For Pueblo the extra water in the Fountain is an erosion, flooding, and sedimentation problem. Fountain Creek, like Colorado Springs, is an enigma. Neither should exist. Not as they do today, anyway.

In the 1970s, our family often drove from Pueblo to my grandmother's house in Fort Collins, north of Denver, for the weekend. Of course, youth and memory distort time, distance, and nearly everything else, but what I remember of those Friday night drives was a vast, lonely stretch of dark highway from north Colorado Springs to Castle Rock, with a solitary rest stop at Monument Hill. Only the lights of ranch houses punctuated the night. Now, thousands of homes, businesses, shopping centers, and streetlamps light the entire way.

Roads of all types are so common within the Fountain watershed that an overlay of maps extinguishes the creek, its tributaries, and the landscape in general beneath a cobweb of asphalt and gravel. The urban and suburban sprawl follows the roadways spilling across the map pell-mell from one outlet mall to the next.

As of 2023, more than nine hundred thousand people lived within the 927 square miles of the Fountain watershed. More are coming. It is challenging to describe just how much construction and development is underway within the watershed.

Two million people total lived in the "Centennial State" when I was born at St. Mary-Corwin Hospital in Pueblo in 1970. By 2023, almost six million people lived in Colorado. Between 2010 and 2020, Colorado added nearly a million new residents. Colorado Springs, the largest city in the Fountain watershed, grew by about 2 percent annually from 2010-2020, to 490,000 residents. Pueblo grew more slowly to a population of 115,000. All up and down the Front Range, once remote areas where our family rode horses, camped, jeeped, and hiked, are now covered in pavement, track homes, or oil and natural gas sacrifice zones. From Pueblo to Cheyenne, Wyoming, Colorado's Front Range has become one mega city, and will only become more so. Urban planners and geographers label this "megaregion" the Front Range Urban Corridor. More than five million people lived there as of 2020. More arrive daily. Eight to nine million people are expected to live in the corridor by 2050.

That's a lot of people needing water and while 80 percent of Colorado's population lives on the Front Range, 80 percent of its water is on the West Slope.

I found the Amara controversy difficult to wrap my head around.

"That's probably 'cause the whole thing really doesn't make much sense," the reporter said.

Colorado Springs should not exist because it lacks water. In reality, Colorado Springs is the high desert. Only about sixteen inches of precipitation fall in the region each year and that amount is declining. The Springs (as Pueblo people call it) is also the only city of its size in the country without its own river.

As far as I could make out, the City of Fountain annexed the Amara properties on La Plata's behalf, promising water and other utilities for the proposed subdivision. Then, a new water study indicated that the City of Fountain would not have enough water to supply the fresh sprawl. La Plata sought to de-annex the properties out of Fountain and instead court annexation by Colorado Springs, which promised to deliver the water. The City of Fountain, however, would not let go. Fountain denied the de-annexation request, reasoning the city was working to find more water and that fresh funding meant a new reservoir would eventually come online. Sometime. Maybe. In the future. Perhaps. La Plata sued Fountain. Meanwhile, Colorado Springs' move to annex TeeCross and Kane Properties moved ahead. Until it didn't.

In late 2022, Colorado Springs Utilities (CSU) stepped on the breaks. CSU sought an ordinance requiring the city to have enough water on hand to meet at least 130 percent of current and projected demand. Existing water was to be reserved for developable land already within the city boundary. Annexations were, for all practical purposes, halted for a decade, if not more.

In January 2023, the Colorado Springs City Council approved the measure. The Norwood Development Group, the most powerful developer in the area, cheered. Norwood, after all, already owned the majority of developable land within the city. They already had their water. La Plata Communities, on the other hand, cried foul, claiming they had been misled by Colorado Springs and that the new rules meant that Norwood held a near monopoly on development within the city and would for years, cutting La Plata out and driving up costs for consumers. El Paso County was not terribly happy either. Responsibility for any new development such as Amara would fall on the county and water for growth would have to come from the already stressed Denver basin aquifer and local non-renewable groundwater wells—wells already showing troubling signs of depletion plus contamination by so-called "forever chemicals" from Peterson Air Force Base.

"The risks [uncertainty in the Colorado River basin] have been greater than what we planned for originally and are coming sooner," the CSU General Manager for Planning told the *Colorado Springs Gazette*. He argued for at least some caution when it came to new development. The then-mayor of Colorado Springs seemed to agree, stating that the city government had an obligation to protect residents from a future serious drought that might see a cut in Colorado River water to Colorado Springs.

It may come as a surprise, even to many Colorado Springs residents, that more than half of the city's water supply comes from the Colorado River basin, across the mountains on the west slope of the state. The Springs pulls upwards of 80 percent of its water from the Colorado, a system famously hammered by overuse, abuse, decades-long drought, and climate change. Only about 13 percent of Colorado Springs water comes from within the Fountain watershed. "It's like smoke and mirrors," a Colorado Springs city councilor said referring to how the city manages its water.

Open-ended growth in Colorado is simply not sustainable according to the Statewide Water Supply Initiative. And yet it continues nonstop.

"It's not unrealistic to imagine a day when the Colorado River water dries up," a CSU employee told me over coffee. "It's crazy to think about it," he said, "but it would be irresponsible to *not* think about it. If the Colorado dries up, then what?" I leaned forward, expecting him to answer his own question. He shook his head. "Well, I guess it's not terribly hard to imagine a future Colorado Springs half abandoned for lack of water."

Colorado Springs and El Paso County have painted themselves into a corner. The whole region has chained its economic well-being to endless population growth, and yet the water resources to sustain that growth never existed in the first place.

Colorado Springs' contentious new water rule seemed like a clear, if weak, step in the right direction. Seemed. While the rule was expected to halt Amara, some creative water accounting and recalculating resulted in a CSU decision that Amara does indeed meet the requirements of the new rule, and the annexation and development are expected to proceed—and still more sprawl remains on the table. The 1,834-acre Karman Line development and the eighteen-thousand-acre Banning Lewis Ranch are all expected to move forward as well—water conservation rule or not.

Endless growth, after all, is at the core of Colorado Springs self-identity.

John Harner is a professor of geography at the University of Colorado at Colorado Springs and the author of *Profiting from the Peak: Landscape and Liberty in Colorado Springs.*

"In reality," he told me, "Colorado Springs has more than enough water. In theory."

Water has never been an impediment to growth in Colorado Springs. City managers have been extraordinarily proactive in buying up water rights and planning for future development. "We probably have thirty to fifty years of water rights in reserve," Harner said. "Of course if the Colorado River goes dry we'll have a major problem on our hands."

CSU water managers, developers, and several elected officials I talked to, all assured me that Colorado Springs would be just fine going forward, that there were hurdles to overcome but that Colorado Springs' water future was secure. They could be right but I am not so sure. While the Colorado River will never fully dry up, chronic overuse and a historic climate change-driven mega drought have reduced the river's flow by more than 20 percent according to the United States Geological Survey. Despite a wet winter here and there that momentarily boosts flow, the overall trend does not bode well. Staking Colorado Springs' future on Colorado River water is like tiptoeing across a lake covered in preciously thin ice.

"We already own those water rights!" A pro-development speaker shouted at a 2021 public meeting I attended about development. "They can't take those rights away from us!"

"Water rights are just paper," a woman responded. "Paper is meaningless if there is no water."

The relationship between Colorado Springs' obsession with growth and its need to secure more water may indeed be "smoke and mirrors." It is also a house of cards. Almost all climate models point to an increasingly dry American West with less precipitation in general. The precipitation that does arrive is shifting from predominately snowpack to patterns dominated by brief, intense rain events. Colorado Springs' water infrastructure is a system reliant on the snowpack, not rain, and it is a system constructed with very little conservation in mind.

It is not development *per se* that is the problem. It is the type of development. Colorado Springs has long encouraged expensive, resource-intensive, car-dependent sprawl, the worst kind of development when it comes to managing natural resources and creating vibrant human-centered communities.

"Colorado Springs has always had this libertarian mindset of no taxes, no regulations, let the private sector sort it out and so on," Harner told me. "The idea is that if you mess up, you will be held accountable by the market. The problem is, the accounting never happens. Nobody in Colorado Springs ever pays a price for what they are doing. They just get the feds, the state or the taxpayers to cover their screw ups. The people of Colorado Springs want nice things; they just want someone else to pay for it."

It is a simple system really. Large companies like Norwood

and La Plata build thousands of car-dependent, single-family track homes in developments with no community center. This sprawl is often adjacent to generic big-box retail developments dominated by gargantuan, half-empty parking lots. The developers make millions of dollars while leaving taxpayers to pick up the tab for roads, sewers, water, fire protection, public safety, and stormwater drainage. Capitalize the profits, socialize the costs. Colorado Springs not only allows this to continue through lack of decent regulation, the city actually subsidizes the sprawl at the root of so many of its own problems.

As Colorado Springs sprawls further and further with increasingly lower housing densities, paved surfaces such as parking lots, driveways, sidewalks, and roads show up everywhere. These surfaces are "impervious", that is, they cannot soak up water, and that water runs off into the Fountain, gathering pollutants along the way, eroding creek banks, eating roads and houses, and washing away productive farmland in Pueblo County.

A tubby plastic ghost wobbled in the breeze, "Happy Halloween! Boo!" scrawled across its chest. A window box of geraniums drooped in the heat.

I parked my truck in the American Legion Post 38 lot, put on my COVID mask to keep the dust out of my lungs, and joined a group of elected officials from the City of Fountain, Colorado Springs, and El Paso County. On hand were several engineers, stream restoration specialists, and members of the Fountain Creek Watershed Flood Control and Greenway District. They milled about next to a cement barrier. A Colorado Springs mayoral candidate handed me his card and insisted the Fountain would be a top priority were he to be elected. (He wasn't.) A Fountain town councilor pointed at him saying, "I hope so," and she walked away.

The whole group, two dozen at least, crawled over the cement barrier blocking Southmoor Drive and crossed the road to the edge of a precipice. Increased flow in the Fountain from development in Colorado Springs had eaten away the left bank, creating a 150- to 200-foot-high cliff. The flow had undercut the road, and it was collapsing into the creek. Several people had lost access to their homes.

The Colorado state legislature created the Fountain Creek Watershed Flood Control and Greenway District in 2009 to deal with the growing array of water quality and erosion issues along the lower reaches of the Fountain. The District was just one result of a complex series of lawsuits, rulings, negotiations, and decrees dating to the late 1990s, when the Sierra Club, Pueblo County, the Environmental Protection Agency, the Colorado Department of Health and Environment, and the Lower Arkansas Valley Water Conservancy District all launched various lawsuits at Colorado Springs for the damages it caused to the Fountain, downstream users, and the riparian ecosystem. Colorado Springs lost and lost again and was forced to pay millions in civil penalties. The courts forced the city to create an $11 million fund for water and pollution mitigation projects within Colorado Springs itself. A massive sewage spill into the Fountain in 2005 resulted in yet another lawsuit against Colorado Springs. The Clean Water Act violations forced a settlement of $50 million from CSU to Pueblo for impacts. It was this money that was used to create the District, tasked with downstream restoration projects in Pueblo County. As of January 2024, the fund had spent more than $40 million on work.

The situation mirrored another conundrum where the Fountain, bursting with water from The Springs, nearly toppled the Riverside Mobile Home Park into the flow. El Paso County spent several million dollars to buy the trailer park, move the residents, and turn the area into county open space. Several bridges have likewise fallen victim to the Fountain's increased flow—repairs coming at a staggering cost.

After looking over the eroding banks and collapsing roadway at Southmoor, the engineers and restoration specialists resolved to spend millions to reroute the creek, stabilize the cliff, and eventually repair and reopen the road.

I won't lie. I laughed out loud. The situation was absurd.

Developers dozens of miles upstream and miles from Fountain Creek had contributed in no small way to the collapsing road in the City of Fountain. One would think that developers such as Norwood should either cough up the money for the stabilization work or, at the very least, be required to install proper storm water drainage system in any fresh sprawl they build. Instead, the federal government, the City of Fountain, the State of Colorado, and Colorado Springs taxpayers will pick up the multi-million-dollar tab.

This is a peculiar facet of free-market capitalism called "externalized costs." That is when the true cost of doing business is not included in the market price of the goods and services being produced. Those unaccounted for costs are "externalized" onto someone else. This trick comes in many forms, from under-paying workers who then rely on food stamps and other public funds to make ends meet or when an oil and gas company leaves abandoned oil wells behind to be cleaned up using state and federal funds. Or when developers refuse to install proper storm water drainage infrastructure and downstream users have to deal with the problem. *All* pollution for that matter is an externalized cost, allowing a small number of people to make a tremendous amount of money while the rest of us pick up the true cost of their enterprise.

And it's not just the water. Colorado Springs simply could not exist without the largesse of the federal government, an ironic situation for a conservative city full of libertarian attitudes.

All this sprawling growth has earned Colorado Springs the nickname "Sprawlorado Springs." In urban planning classes, Colorado Springs is often held as an example of what *not* to do and of car-dominated culture gone nuts.

Norwood and La Plata both claim they are simply responding to market demands. An independent contractor at one of the Amara meetings made the point for them. "We're simply providing a product the consumer already wants," he said. "This type of development benefits the whole community. Housing, jobs . . . that's the beauty of capitalism."

But it isn't that simple.

From the days of legendary founder General Palmer, Colorado Springs aggressively marketed itself as a destination for gold seekers, land speculators, those made physically ill by the horrors of nineteenth century industrialization, and, most recently, the military and outdoors enthusiasts. Colorado Springs actively drives its own growth, encouraging people to come. Entrepreneurs, business organizations, real estate agents, developers, and community boosters have worked diligently to meddle with market functions in ways that drive urban development and suburban sprawl. The result is a mostly complacent population that has internalized the idea that such growth is natural, inevitable and a net positive, and a city government hamstrung by influential developers and its own trajectory.

Even that "benefit to the whole community" trope is questionable. Yes, there are jobs. Yes, there is economic activity. Yes, there are some taxes paid to the public coffers, but in a community obsessed with low taxes, that tax money is woefully inadequate to cover the costs of the sprawl, much less really benefit the city. Thus, many of the costs associated with the apparent success of Colorado Springs are foisted on the feds, the state, and future generations. *And*, those costs are quite literally washed downstream in the Fountain.

The idea that developers are simply giving people what they

want is specious at best. Polls and surveys conducted through the years show that lifeless suburban sprawl is emphatically *not* what Americans want. A 2023 survey from the National Association of Realtors found that 77 percent of Americans want to live in a neighborhood where they could easily walk to amenities like parks, stores, and restaurants. Developers and the housing industry are not giving consumers what consumers want; they are giving consumers what *the industry* wants.

Social critic James Howard Kunstler labels Colorado Springs-type suburbia the "national automobile slum" and "the greatest misallocation of resources in human history."

It is not as if Colorado Springs is unique. Denver is a mess of sprawl. Even Pueblo is spilling north. Smaller Colorado cities such as Grand Junction, Glenwood Springs, and Durango, clogged with traffic jams, suffer this great misallocation of resources. In fact, the entire nation has become a giant automobile slum.

Suburbia has still other costs. One afternoon, I took my notebook, climbed on my bike, and peddled north from downtown along Nevada Avenue to a colossal shopping center of Costco, Petco, Kohl's, and Lowe's. A brewpub, cookie store, ice cream shop, sushi place, and Starbucks defined the periphery. The big box circus stood just above Monument Creek on the left bank of the Fountain's main tributary. The parking lot stretched so far you could nearly see the curvature of the Earth. I jest, but it was indeed enormous, studded with but a few sad trees. I locked my bike to a lamppost. There were no bike racks. I wandered the place wondering how I might describe this moment in the American experience to someone living two hundred years from now. How could I possibly relate this? The first thing I noted was the heat. The parking lot was twenty to thirty degrees hotter than the nearby Greenway Trail. That heat was like a punch in the face and shoppers avoided it, rushing from air-conditioned vehicles to air-conditioned stores and back to air-conditioned cars. It reeked of oil, acrid and unhealthy. Then the noise. The endless snarl of the interstate. The bumper-to-bumper traffic of Nevada and Austin Bluff's Parkways, which are really highways misleadingly labeled as roads. A guy walked by carrying a pistol. Airplanes and helicopters passed overhead.

Another thing that stood out was how each business blocked access from its parking lot to the one immediately adjacent. If you were ridiculous enough to drive from the bundt cake place to the burrito place not twenty feet away, you had to drive out of the lot, onto the road, circle around, and access the Chipotle on the other side. Why might you do all that instead of just taking two minutes to walk? Because being outside your car in these retail centers is simply dangerous. These are incredibly unfriendly environments. Worse, these giant parking lots are rarely, if ever, full.

After many minutes dodging cars, I crossed the wide roads surrounding the retail center into the adjacent neighborhoods. Here were hundreds of cookie-cutter tract homes arrayed along a confusion of nearly treeless streets (ironically named for trees) that, from above on Google Earth, look like a confusion of spaghetti fallen from a plate. The nearby school felt like a prison, featureless gray walls surrounded in fencing with a police car parked out front. A groundskeeper with a brush hog made sure not a single chunk of vegetation should mar the field of dust, gravel, and broken glass.

In my notebook I wrote, "Dear person two hundred years from now, I know it is hard to believe but as a society, we actually *choose* to live like this."

These suburbs create their own set of expensive social ills: isolation, despair, substance use disorder, suicide, and violence. Children cannot, or will not, walk or bike or meet with their friends. People struggle to interact. Public life and community disappear. People sit inside watching TV. Lonely children resort to screens. These suburbs are places not worth caring about and places that impart a message that nobody cares about you and nor should you give a damn about anyone else. "There is not enough Prozac in the world to make people feel good about these spaces," Kunstler proclaimed in a 2004 TED Talk.

Colorado Springs' growth machine enriches a few while creating knock-on social and environmental costs, costs everyone else is forced to reckon with.

At the water's edge a menagerie of birds jammed a drooping, sunlit tamarisk. House sparrows, white-crowned sparrows, robins, a hermit thrush, and even a lesser goldfinch. An American dipper picked at something in the water near the bank. I counted at least two dozen birds from eight different species soaking up the sun. All the bird life at that spot surprised me. I had seen very few birds of any kind that entire week.

It was just before midwinter. The noontime sun hung far to the southwest. The creek seemed sluggish, viscous, and thick. I pulled a third coat from my pack, jerked my wool beanie over my ears, and stamped my feet to keep the blood flowing.

I had walked north from State Highway 47 in Pueblo, pushing across mudflats, outcroppings of delicate gray shale, and through tangles of willow, tamarisk, phragmites, and olive. I-25 growled to the west. Cars and trucks swarmed the Wal-Mart, Ross, Pet Smart, and Big Five. Unhoused people huddled in silence around small fires. A solitary blue heron stood on a sandbar. There was no snow.

A trail appeared and I followed, sliding down past a fox's hole then over a partially eroded peninsula of beige and rose-colored sediments, into a burned-out homeless encampment. Melted tents, sleeping bags, and clothes hung from black, ghostly stumps and the grasping branches of faded elms. A dead dog lay in the ash. The stench was mind numbing. Just past the burn, a man sat in a plastic lawn chair wrapped in blankets. He puffed at a stubby cigarette. Behind him, a woman dug into the embankment with a snow shovel, the handle broken off part way up. She had excavated a semi-cave in the dirt, inserted her tent, and partially walled it off against the winter with green and brown plastic tarps. The trail disappeared.

For several hours, I stumbled through the vegetation, up and down eroded banks and across icy sandbars in the middle of the creek. The frozen sand provided a decent series of steps to move upstream leap-by-leap. I could not have done this in summer; the sand only held because it was frozen. I tracked under a power line and over an exposed natural gas pipe jutting from the bank. It was rough going. I sweated but my feet were icy from the creek. Eventually I came to a cottonwood gallery. The 70- to 80-foot-tall trees wrapped me like a grandmother's embrace, cutting the breeze, brightening the world in yellows, and smoothing the way for tired feet. A deer watched. A wild turkey crossed in front. An inquisitive blue jay paralleled my path. "This," I stopped to write in my journal, "is sweet-walking."

The creek had migrated west at some point, and I dropped into the old gravel channel for half a mile then turned west to regain the water. Near the bank, the cottonwoods gave way to willows, tamarisk, and olives so thick I dropped to my hands and knees to move forward. I heard my coat tear. I stood and an olive stabbed my cheek, blood squirted on the inside of my glasses. I tripped down the bank, leapt over a braid of water onto an icy sandbar, then, still not in full control, over another braid of creek to a still larger sandbar rimmed in windows of ice and covered in tubes of frozen goose poop. The blood again squirted onto my glasses, and I could not see out of my left side. Once I regained my footing, I cleaned my glasses and got the blood under control.

Traversing the creek in this disjointed way, instead of all at once in a bottom to top or top to bottom trek, had become a lesson or a practice in patient jigsaw-puzzle exploration, linking sections on the map with sections on the ground, connecting journeys of one season with journeys of another, then navigating access to the next.

The sun dropped behind a skiff of thin, gray clouds. A deep chill took hold. The birds huddled into their feathers, turning to featureless puffballs. Their chatter stopped and an icy loneliness overtook me, morphing my spirits into something dark and suspicious, tinged with anxiety. I burrowed into my coats, ate a snack of jerky, and decided I had had enough for the moment. My feet, iced over, ached in the bones. I made my way east toward Overton Road.

Just as I exited the cottonwoods, a man waved me down. "Oh shit," I hissed. I was trespassing.

"Well? How you doing there?" Dr. Bill Barr was a Gandalf-like figure. Tall and narrow, wizened with a gray beard and an easy smile, he stood at the top of a small rise like some Middle Earth forest denizen making the daily rounds about the Mirkwood. He stuck out a huge hand and invited me for cookies and coffee.

I followed Barr up from the creek while he explained that he was two weeks out from hip replacement surgery. I was astounded. He moved slowly but he was solid as a rock. "Hell, a gust of wind could blow me over right now." I didn't believe him. He opened the door, and the warmth of the house beckoned. "Excuse the mess," Barr said. "We're doing some remodeling and well . . . you know how it goes."

"I do."

Bill and Barbara Barr took to farming in 1984. She grew up in Pueblo. He had migrated down from a ranch in Wyoming. Dr. Barr was already a successful veterinarian, Barbara a schoolteacher. Their real passion, however, was farming. Particularly raising lambs.

Sometime in the 1970s, the Aetna Life Insurance Company

acquired what became the Barr Farm from Sharkey Mass, a Pueblo entrepreneur who had put the land up as collateral to help fund another endeavor. Mass went bust and lost the land to Aetna in bankruptcy. Aetna then leased the land to the Barrs in 1984. They purchased the farm in 1993.

Sharkey Mass was actually Frank Masciantonio. Between 1885 and 1925, Pueblo welcomed a large number of Italian immigrants. Some went to work at Rockefeller's giant steel mill. Others started small, mostly food-oriented businesses. Most became farmers. Dozens of Italian families settled along the Fountain to grow food. Cabbage was a major crop, Barr told me. He pronounced "Italian" with the Pueblo accent, morphing the word to "eye-talian" with a hard accent on the first syllable. During World War II, many Pueblo Italians changed their last names to something more "American," both to show their solidarity in the fight against fascism and to avoid being labeled as potential enemies. They had seen their Japanese-American neighbors suffer that fate and wanted none of it. That's how Masciantonio became just Mass. Most of these families reverted to their traditional names in the 1980s, 1990s, and early 2000s.

"It was a junkhole when we got it," Barr said. "But we turned it around."

"He would work all day, come home, and farm until midnight," Barbara said. "One of the worst inventions ever was when they decided to put lights on tractors. The man would work all night if I'd let him."

The Barrs grew mostly alfalfa and corn to feed lambs and cows. They sold permits to close friends and family to hunt on the property. There were ducks, deer, and turkey to be had along with the occasional elk.

"There are three major headaches trying to farm along the Fountain," Barr told me. "The homeless, the trains, and the creek."

An unhoused couple had set up a semi-permanent camp

back among the cottonwoods just north of where I had turned toward the road. They built a structure of pallets and plywood covered in a yellow tarp and surrounded by a fence cobbled together with chain link and barbed wire. "I can't imagine how they got all that stuff down there," Barr raised his eyebrows. "Floated it down or up, I guess. Like the old days." He explained how a fight between two unhoused men resulted in one man losing an arm. Then the police showed up and raided the camp, driving everyone out. They were back within weeks.

Justin, Dr. Barr's adult son and heir apparent to the ranch, worried about fire. They'd already had a near miss when flames from a homeless encampment blew north, nearly engulfing their property. That was 2019. It happened again in 2023. The fire department arrived in good time, Barr said, but then several of the homeless men attacked the firefighters and the police had to secure the situation before the firefighters could do their job.

Justin feared that just one spark from the couple's camp could ignite accumulated years of dried leaves and grass, the fire feeding from downed branches and old trees. "We'd have a disaster on our hands," Barr said. He was reluctant to force them out, however. "You know, you hate to get ornery about this stuff, but it causes a lot of stress. And then, where else are they going to go? It's not fair they're on our land but it's not fair to be stuck outside so . . . we do . . . what?" He threw up his hands and sat back. I asked for more coffee.

Another problem plaguing the Barr farm was theft. Someone had taken off with tools, a pump, and some hay. Someone stole $8,000 worth of solar panels from the array that powered the irrigation pumps. A few weeks later, Justin confronted a man trying to steal a pickup truck; the man bolted for the cornfield and disappeared. Barr wondered if the two problems were linked but he had his doubts. It probably wasn't the people experiencing homelessness that were doing the stealing, he thought.

Yet another challenge? "The goddamn train," Barr moaned.

Fountain Creek splits the Barr farm in two sections. The Burlington Northern Santa Fe Railway (BNSF) regularly blocked access to their land on the west side of the Fountain. There were four tracks on the west (right bank) side. Two for hauling freight and two for "building" trains. As the BNSF puts their increasingly long trains together, they frequently blocked a county road that the Barrs used to access their fields. This is against the law, but no one seemed willing to enforce the rules and take BNSF to task so the violations continued. Several times, the Barrs had been blocked from their fields during harvest time. At least once, the trains blocked the way out *during* harvest and the Barr's could not get their goods to market. The contracted workers doing the cutting were furious. They could not get their equipment and semitrailers out, keeping them from the next job. Everyone lost except BNSF. At the time I visited, the Barrs were having problems finding someone to do the harvest as everyone was nervous about the trains.

"We've tried to talk to them. We've schmoozed them multiple times. They just don't care," Barr said. "So, we'll probably have to file a lawsuit." He frowned, clearly unhappy about the idea of going to court.

By far the biggest problem facing the Barrs was the Fountain. Specifically, all the excess water in the Fountain coming as a result of Colorado Springs' rapid urbanization.

"It used to be a reliable little waterway," Barr said. "Yes, it flooded at times, but the base flow was gentle and consistent. Then, in . . . well . . . I want to say the mid-80s sometime, the base flow started going up. It went from a creek to a river and when it flooded, the floods were just worse than we'd seen before. They've created a water highway."

The 1999 flood pushed the Fountain into a new channel and the bank erosion grew serious. Several acres of productive farmland washed downstream. The left bank of the Fountain went from a gently sloping rise to fifty- to sixty-foot cliffs in spots, the cliffs shear, erodible, collapsing into the creek. On the Barr's property, the flow had also dug out several natural gas pipelines creating a further hazard.

It was not just the Barrs.

"There's only one way to win when it comes to water." Jay Frost pointed at an eighty-foot-high cliff known up and down the Fountain as "The Great Wall." The cutbank, eroded out by years of excess water in the creek, ate away at upland pasture. "Don't fight."

Jay, the smiling patriarch of the Frost Ranch, was born in 1960 and raised along the banks of the Fountain a few miles north of the Barr Farm. The Frost had once been part of the sprawling Hanna Ranch, a multi-generational cow operation that bucked the conventional ranching wisdom and stirred a storm of debate by fighting Colorado Springs and focusing on conservation.

The day I visited, Jay's wife Bonney was in the hospital, suffering a severe bout of West Nile Virus. All up and down the southern reaches of the Fountain, ranching families were falling victim to the mosquito-borne disease migrating north. Jay himself had suffered a minor stroke ten years before and occasionally he stuttered, stumbling to find the right words. Still, his sense of humor shone through.

Jay's father was born in Detroit. The family moved west during the Great Depression, seeking opportunity in California. After serving as a Seabee in the Philippines during World War II, Jay's father bought a ranch on the Rio Puerco south of Albuquerque. Once a lush grassland, the Puerco today is an arroyo—a scarred, desert landscape ruined by sheep grazing. Drought ruined Jay's father. His wife died and he borrowed just enough money to buy three small ranches along the Fountain north of Pueblo in 1959 and was able to obtain 314 acre-feet of water rights dating to 1863. He joined the parcels into one property and took to raising cows.

"He'd learned something," Jay told me. "He'd seen how the Puerco had been just . . . just ravaged. You know, it wasn't always like that. The Indians did just fine running things. When we Anglos showed up, everything went to shit."

The elder Frost wanted to do things differently. He aimed to leave the land better off than he found it. He met and married Jay's mother, a widowed single mother who owned the neighboring Hanna Ranch. Before long, the ranches were joined and nine kids, including Jay and his half-brother Kirk, were running up and down the Fountain.

"We had the run of the place. The creek was our playground. You know, what I remember about those days was the stability. And the optimism. We don't have those today but for us back then? Life was good."

Jay didn't plan to run the ranch. That he left to his older half-brother Steve. Jay was interested in the larger world, he told me, and he left for college in New Mexico right out of high school. Family, the Fountain, and a tragedy would bring him home.

Kirk, too, left the ranch. He prospered as a commodities broker in Denver through the 1980s. When Steve left the ranch in 1989, Kirk came home filled with new ideas about ranching, conservation, and the urban sprawl he saw as a threat to Colorado's agricultural communities. Kirk adopted HRM or Holistic Resource Management as the guiding principle for the ranch. HRM is a controversial grazing regime that originated in South Africa. It calls for rotational grazing, care for the soil, goats for weed management, and the restoration of streams and wetlands.

Kirk was labeled the "Eco-Cowboy." He reached out to work with The Nature Conservancy and Colorado Open Lands. He fought Colorado Springs and he made a hell of a lot of enemies, a story central to the 2014 film documentary *Hanna Ranch*, produced by Eric Schlosser, author of *Fast Food Nation*.

"He pissed off a lot of people," Jay told me. "But how else do you make change?"

Kirk did piss off a lot of people, but not everyone. He ended up head of the Colorado Cattleman's Association, and there was talk that he might one day be governor of Colorado.

But Kirk struggled. Depression is all too common in rural communities that see their life ways and culture as under threat. On a snowy night in the winter of 1998, Kirk took his own life on the banks of Fountain Creek.

The Hanna and Frost ranches split and Jay took over the Frost, selling several parcels to pay debts and buy out siblings who had no interest in ranching. With his three children, Jay started over carrying on his father and brother's land care values.

"Between the trash, the erosion, and the sediment, we're having a hard time. You know, in the '65 flood, all our fences got wiped out. Dad replaced them. Since, we've taken down a lot of that fencing but we left the fence posts out there and they became a sort of . . . what do you call it . . . gauge to measure the sediment. You go out there and look around now and you'll see that only a foot or two of the fence posts are above ground. There's been that much sediment build up. Hell, I have to take the bulldozer out there a couple times a year to keep our irrigation intake free of all the sediment."

The Great Wall alone dumps over one hundred thousand tons of sediment into the Fountain each year. A multimillion-dollar restoration plan from the Flood Control District was in the works but Jay was not happy. "You know, the more I learn, the less I like it."

"What?"

"All of it. Everything. We're caught in a free-market capitalism fuck. The Springs sucks in everything it can and rich people are gobbling up huge amounts of land all over the West. That's not democracy. It will all be upside down before too long."

—

A series of torrential downpours hit the Fountain watershed in late spring 2023. Landowners in Pueblo County lost dozens of acres of land. Cathy Todd lived along Overton Road south of the Barr Farm. She had watched for years as the Fountain crept ever closer to her property. That June, a flood washed her land downstream, leaving her barn teetering on a ledge above the creek. She called around for help but found none. As if the barn weren't bad enough, Todd worried about her ninety-two-year-old mother, whose home sat just across the creek. The water was closing in on her place too.

To be sure, Colorado Springs is a major source of this problem. That so many people built homes, barns, and other structures within the Fountain's ancient floodplain only makes matters worse. Building in a floodplain is asking for problems.

I wondered if it might be in everyone's best interest if, over time, the State of Colorado, the feds, and the Greenway District bought people out, removed houses and structures, and freed up the Fountain's floodplain to work as it should.

At the Barr Farm, Dr. Barr poured me another cup of coffee and sat back down across the table.

"Colorado Springs has changed things quite a bit," Justin said. "The Big Straw allows them to suck up all the water they can get their hands on, then force us to deal with the return flows."

"This wouldn't be allowed in other states," Dr. Barr added. "Dumping return flows into the Fountain is lazy and cheap. All that excess water should be piped down to Pueblo Reservoir, not dumped into the creek."

I sat back, wondering how that would even work. Much of the excess Colorado Springs water comes from the street runoff. CSU could theoretically pipe water from the wastewater plant to the Pueblo Reservoir, but I could not quite wrap my head around all the contingencies of such a project.

"We get all their trash, all their sewage, all their erosion problems. Colorado Springs would call us up and say: 'Ooops. We had a sewage spill yesterday. It's toxic. Stay out of the creek.' But we had cattle in the creek!"

One year the Barr's saw more than 20 percent of their heifers miscarry. They had never had that before. Only later did they learn that it had happened after a sewage spill, but by then it was too late to ask for compensation.

"One of these days," another rancher told me months earlier, "we're going to all get together and sue the pants off of Colorado Springs. They've screwed us over and don't give a rat's ass. Let's just say . . . we're talking to lawyers."

I asked Jay Frost about a potential lawsuit against Colorado Springs. "Awww. It's a good idea but I don't got time for that shit." I asked Dr. Barr the same question. He raised an eyebrow and smiled. "Oh . . . I don't know about that."

Justin stood and put on his baseball cap. He reached out and shook my hand. "You see, I worry about our kids, man. Not just mine, yours too. All of them. All the kids. I worry about what we are leaving them. I just don't get why we always got to be jacking with Mother Nature. We had a pretty good little creek here and now we got one mess on top of another."

THE BIG STRAW

"In the West, it is said, water flows uphill toward money. And it literally does . . ."

–*Marc Reisner,* Cadillac Desert

At first, Colorado Springs' founders—not to mention land speculators and early development boosters—aimed to enrich themselves by privatizing every possible service a city needs to function. It did not take long for them to realize, however, that privatization of water might wreck their investments. As early as 1875, putrid drinking water jeopardized the health spa tourism industry. Typhoid ran loose. *My Family Visited Colorado Springs and All I Got Was This Lousy Case of Dysentery* was not the slogan early boosters sought. Then, a series of costly fires in 1876 destroyed sections of the business district. Strategically placed barrels of mosquito-infested water, noted then-Mayor Matthew France, were not an adequate fire suppression strategy. A harsh drought the following year proved the last straw. Mayor France put the issue to the people. In April 1878, voters approved an $80,000 public funding bond measure by an overwhelming majority. It was an easy sell. Without question, clean water and fire suppression are a public good. Developers agreed. They also saw the benefits of spreading the price of development onto city residents. "Cost sharing" with taxpayers meant more money in developer's bank accounts. Within months of the referendum, construction of the "south slope water system" was underway. First up, Ruxton Creek.

It was barely fifteen degrees Fahrenheit when I set off to find the Ruxton diversion. I carried a copy of a woodcut print of the intake dam and pond. The dark woodcut had appeared in the *Colorado Springs Gazette* in 1888, the same year Colorado Springs city engineer H.I. Reid authored an annual accounting of the Colorado Springs' water resources. There was enough water coming from Ruxton Creek, he concluded, to "supply the city's want for many years to come." Ruxton, Reid believed, held enough reliable water for more than triple the population.

In the *Gazette* illustration, a man stood just below the dam. He wore a top hat and carried a cane. Behind the dam spread a pond, divided in two by a wooden pipe. Beyond that, a two-story structure of some kind faded into the trees.

Ruxton meets the Fountain in a little park just off the main drag in Manitou Springs. It flows through a neighborhood of Victorian and Edwardian homes decorated in gay pride flags, Denver Broncos flags, and Christmas wreathes. A six-foot-tall plastic velociraptor peered from a porch. The creek flows in a deep cement channel crossed by bridges of hewn red stone. Some of the houses were wonderfully gaudy, painted in turquoise, blues, purples, and yellows. Several were on the market, asking prices ranging from $2.5 million to well over $5 million.

Sluggish in the cold, Ruxton's waters pushed under thin sheets of raggedy ice fractals and tube-shaped icicles dangling from willow branches bent close enough to the water to catch the splash of the creek. Splash. Freeze. Splash. Freeze. Splash. Freeze. The icicles grew day by day, bending the willow to the water.

Above Manitou and for most of its run, Ruxton is a small, raucous, snow-fed waterway, pouring through Englemann

Canyon on the east slopes of The Peak. It is unclear to me what the Nuuchiu, Ka'igwu, and Hinono'eino people named the creek—more evidence of the intentional erasure of Indigenous history—but the English language name for the creek came from George Fredrick Augustus Ruxton, a British itinerate and author who, at age seventeen, served as a lancer under Diego de León. Later he visited the San peoples of South Africa, trapped beaver with the Numunuu, and authored several books, the best known of which, *Ruxton of the Rockies*, portrays his life among the mountain men of the American West. Ruxton squeezed an impressive amount into a short time. Dysentery took him on a visit to St. Louis in 1848. He was barely twenty-seven years old.

The year before his death, while hunting along the Fountain, Ruxton got it in his head to do what Pike could not, mount The Peak. His plan was to follow the creek that now bears his name all the way to the summit. Probably the route Pike should have taken had he been more in tune with the landscape. In any case, young Ruxton did not make it far. A Nuuchiu family, upset to find a white man trudging through their sacred waters, sent him packing. Yet, somehow, he left his name behind.

Snow had fallen the night before my climb. It was not much, perhaps an inch, and it crunched and squeaked under my boots. When I stopped, the hollow gurgle of water channeling through ice filled the air. I followed the creek to the Iron Springs Chateau and then behind the main building of the Pike's Peak Cog Railway. Unsurprisingly, I ran up against a NO TRESSPASSING sign and a private road. I diverted from the creek and into the empty railway station. There, a sign warned tourists about altitude sickness. A cat curled next to a heater. I tried to mount the tracks since they paralleled the creek for several miles, but a man appeared explaining that I was, again, trespassing. I returned to the station then walked out to the parking lot. A cluster of underdressed Texans shivered, teeth knocking and babies crying.

"I'm going to die up there!" A woman hissed. Her husband

rolled his eyes. I walked to the edge of the parking lot. Men in bright yellow jackets appeared.

"You can't go there," one said.

I changed directions.

"Can you go around please?"

"Look out buddy!" another shouted.

"Watch the traffic!" yet another man told me. "Are you doing the Incline? Are you lost?"

"I'm trying to walk Ruxton Creek. I did it when I was in my twenties and . . ."

"Oh, you can't do that. It's illegal."

I ignored him and walked on. There was another sign:

DO NOT ENTER
PRIVATE DRIVE
WRONG WAY
TURNAROUND

More tourists arrived for the cog railway trip to the summit. I passed through several parking lots and mounted a steep road, slippery with the fresh snow, hoping to find a way back to the creek. Another NO TRESSPASSING sign greeted me. This one, metal, dangled from a large gate. I hesitated, then saw three sets of fresh footprints in the snow, one made by cowboy boots, the other two by hiking boots. Dog prints danced along the human trail. I ducked under the gate and followed the tracks down to the water and up Englemann Canyon.

In 1891, barely eighty-five years after Pike assured the world The Peak could never be conquered, *The Illustrated American* published an account of the Englemann Canyon. It was "a narrow valley," the author observed, "with a steep mountain rising on either side, and the clear, sparkling Ruxton Creek rushing parallel to the track, sometimes dashing over rocks hundreds of feet below the trail, and sometimes pausing for a moment to form a deep, smooth pool, such as the speckled trout loves to haunt . . . waterfalls innumerable are passed, some of them showing the most romantic beauty." By 1891, Colorado Springs to The Peak and back was a trip of less than five hours on the train.

The Ruxton I climbed was not so different from the Ruxton in the 1891 description. The creek tumbled over and through large boulders bearing faces of giants, elves, and dwarves, spilling into deep, smooth pools. The speed of the flow varied. Here it raced full force, throwing a mist into the winter forest. There it slowed, spreading into lips, eddies, and pockets sheltered in coral or flower-like fans of frozen liquid. Linked smooth balls of ice resembling lava or thunderstorms on a hot July day grew in stacks and piles on creek bed boulders. There was clear ice, cloudy ice, rabbit ice, needle ice, and sheets of layered ice that reminded me of the inside of a geode. I never did see a trout.

Another sign: DANGER. DROWNING HAZARD.

A natural pool about twelve feet across and four to five feet deep spread just beyond the sign. A grated steel bridge crossed the pool leading to a set of steel stairs and another bridge that cut through rocks and past what might have been a wooden sluice.

Someone had recently cut down a bunch of trees. The trunks and the slash were dumped into the creek. It made for a slow, difficult climb. I scrambled through thick brush, the logs and slash, and over slippery rocks. For several hundred yards, I followed the fresh tracks of a bobcat, not more than an hour old. The water in my Camelbak froze, and I regretted leaving my thermos in the truck.

For several hours, I struggled my way up, just feet below the cog line. Frequent stops slowed my progress. The ice kept my attention. I took dozens of photographs and sat at times seeking words and phrases to describe the singing voice of the creek.

I also fought to stay dry. A fall into the water at fifteen degrees Fahrenheit might prove deadly. I suffered through severe hypothermia once in my life; it is not an experience I wish to repeat. The memory of my 1998 winter trek up Ruxton sat in my mind and I wasn't keen to repeat that either. The cog passed and I could see the Texans, peering at the winter from behind fogged windows.

The way forward was elusive. I descended about twenty feet, crossed the creek, and mounted a steep slope only to come across a well-worn trail. I felt stupid. Cowboy boots had been there. The two pairs of hiking boots had not come this far, but the dogs had continued with the human. I followed cowboy boots up the feral trail to the Ruxton intake.

To me, the cement structure did not appear much different from the 1888 illustration. No doubt it had been upgraded and repaired multiple times since, but it was basically the same structure: an eight- to ten-foot-high dam, a pool, and even a wooden sluice or pipe exactly like the one in the woodcut. Water tumbled from the lip of the dam through a thick tube of ice. The only thing missing was the man with the hat and the two-story building.

From the Ruxton intake, Colorado Springs engineers laid collection pipes to channel Ruxton's flow to the city's new reservoir: Mesa Number One. The reservoir spread across a flat promontory west of downtown Colorado Springs above Monument Creek. With a two-hundred-foot elevation difference between the reservoir and the city, those getting Ruxton water also received the luxury of pressurized water. According to historian James Earl Sherow, a certain Reverend Cross of the Colorado Springs Congregational Church praised the new water system . . . and made the most appalling of claims. Pure water, he pronounced, made beer and whiskey irrelevant. Citizens could no longer blame contaminated water for their vices. Beer and whiskey irrelevant? I could never . . .

The race for water was on. In 1886, Colorado Springs constructed yet another mesa top reservoir and extended the

Ruxton intake further upstream. H.I. Reid was sure it was enough. City Fathers—and they were most certainly all men—disagreed. They wanted still more water. Reid obliged, boring the Strickler Tunnel in 1900 and the St. John's Tunnel in 1904 to tap Beaver and Boehmer Creeks and transfer those waters to Ruxton and then to the mesa top reservoirs. Reid also took Mystic Lake, Ruxton's natural source, and enlarged the glacial moraine holding the lake so that it could store more water. By 1908, Colorado Springs, under Reid's leadership, had constructed eighteen high-elevation reservoirs, many miles of flumes and ditches, two massive tunnels, and two storage reservoirs.

The path was set. For the next one-hundred-plus years, Colorado Springs would aggressively pursue any and all water it could get its hands on.

William Ellison Smythe called for Americans to do anything and everything to make green the wastelands of the West. Writing in *The Conquest of Arid America*, Smythe painted America's western destiny as one to "grapple with the desert, translate its gray barrenness into green fields of gardens, banish its silence with the laugher of children."

The founders of Colorado Springs aimed to do just that. Reid's Ruxton development was not Colorado Springs' first attempt at securing water. Early Euro-American settlers dug dozens of irrigation ditches from the Fountain and the Monument to water orchards and gardens. The Colorado Springs Company sunk a number of wells to supply their new colony. The El Paso Canal began diverting water from the Fountain in 1871. That six-and-a-half-mile ditch snaked its way through the settlement, supplying laterals that fed municipal trees and urban lots. This water turned the dry prairie into a moist, shaded city. This water enabled the Colorado Springs Company to attract settlers and then tourists.

Still, the Ruxton and Beaver water transfers marked a turning point. Beaver Creek ran outside the Fountain watershed, flowing instead to the Arkansas. Taking water from one basin and moving it to another watershed was not unprecedented. Colorado's first inter-basin diversion was on the Ewing Ditch in 1880, which moved 2,400 acre-feet from the Colorado River basin to the Arkansas River basin over Tennessee Pass. Yet the scale of the south slope water system opened eyes. No longer was a community limited by the water available within its immediate watershed. Suddenly, all the water resources a community might ever want and need were available for the taking. With enough money and engineering, massive amounts of water could indeed be made to run uphill and from one basin to the next.

"The American West," wrote Donald Worster in *Rivers of Empire* "can best be described as a modern hydraulic society . . . a social order based on the intensive, large-scale manipulation of water and its products in an arid setting."

Colorado Springs is nothing if not a hydraulic society.

The City of Pueblo also wanted in on the water act.

The Tanks. The Old Res. In high school, kids from Centennial, my high school's crosstown rival, threw "kegger" parties out at the old Northside Reservoirs on the north end of Pueblo. Kids like me, from the south side, trekked across town for the beer-soaked festivities. My friends and I packed into my little white Toyota Corona and plowed up a rutted two-track across cactus-studded clay hills tracking the light of distant bonfires. We parked at the edge of an earthen rampart and skidded down concrete slab walls to the bottom of The Old Res to join the party. As far as I can tell, The Tanks are no longer a party spot. They've been filled, leveled, and covered in tract homes.

These Northside Reservoirs were part of an ambitious project known as the "Fountain Underflow." The idea was simple, as complex unworkable projects often appear. The Pueblo Water Supply and Power Company aimed to bury approximately ten and a half miles of thirty- to thirty-six-inch perforated pipes deep into the sands and gravel underneath Fountain Creek near the village of Piñon north of Pueblo. The pipes would gather naturally filtered water, utilizing gravity to carry the water a mile downstream to a proposed hydroelectric power plant and then to The Tanks. The two sixteen-foot-deep Northside Reservoirs could hold up to eighteen million gallons, a significant addition to Pueblo's water bank. Construction began in the fall of 1905.

It was the Arkansas Valley farmers that worried the City of Pueblo. They too had joined the Western Water Rush, grabbing up every teaspoon of water they could get their hands on. City officials, including then-Mayor John T. West, understood that water constrained Pueblo's future and they scrambled to secure their clean, domestic supplies before farmers soaked it all up.

At the village of Piñon/Pinyon, a tent city grew, replete with cavernous cook tent, offices, evening entertainment, and a wood-framed building so that workers, assembling pipe from two-foot sections, could labor through the winter. Mayor West, on a visit to the camp on October 28, 1905, expressed "surprise" at the extent of the operation.

There were problems however. One big problem actually. The water was unusable. In the summer of 1905, the Santa Fe railroad erected a new water tank for its engines not far from the future Fountain Underflow intake. The company had known for years that the Fountain water was far too alkaline for human consumption and ordered train crews to utilize Fountain waters in case of emergency only. The fear was that the alkali in the water would damage the locomotive's boilers. Determined to protect its investments, the Santa Fe chemically treated the water pulled from the Fountain to neutralize the alkali. Company engineers explained that even after chemical treatment the water would be "utterly unfit to drink" and was probably only good enough for washing clothes or minimal irrigation.

Judge C.C. Robinson took note. He told The Pueblo Star-Journal that: "It looks very funny to me that these Fountain Underflow people should be attempting to make the citizens of this city believe that they can supply it with an abundant supply of pure and wholesome water, when a railroad company which is getting ready to use the same water from the same point only a short distance from the place at which the [water] company proposes to take its supply, does not dare to use the water until it has been chemically treated."

It was a precarious project plying troubled waters. Still, the Ball brothers of Muncie, Indiana bought in. The Balls manufactured glass fruit jars, the famous canning jars still in use today. The Balls imagined a relatively easy return from the Fountain Underflow. Instead, they lost their shirts.

In a classic example of the "sunk cost fallacy," the Ball's water company plowed on despite the warnings, hiring a Professor Schuyler—then considered the nation's premiere water quality chemist—to analyze the Fountain's water. Schuyler gave the thumbs up. The company then hired a Chicago-based chemist and then a Denver-based chemist, and ultimately a chemist from the Colorado School of Mines. All returned favorable reports to the Pueblo Water Supply and Power Company.

Something did not add up.

It is impossible to say if the Balls paid their chemists to return positive results or if the chemists sought only to please their employers. It could also be that the samples sent to the chemists were not Fountain Creek water. Either way, no one trusted the results of these analyses. Independent chemists and those hired by local ranchers reported that the Fountain waters were simply not suitable for human use.

And so, when Fountain Underflow water poured into the Northside Reservoirs in early 1908, citizens reported the water as an odd color of blue, reeking of carbonic gas, the taste "hard" and "acidic." The Pueblo Water Board threw up its hands and walked away, labeling Fountain Creek water "not drinkable, potable, or wholesome."

The Balls sued. The city and the water board counter sued. Others joined the fray and lawsuits flew like panicked ducks. The legal sparring dragged on for years. The power plant was never built and in July 1911, the Tabor-Skinner Irrigation Company purchased the Fountain Underflow project, hoping to bring tracts of land north of Pueblo under cultivation. This apparently never happened either. Farmers pointed out that the alkali water would kill the soil in less than a decade and most refused to use it.

It is unclear what happened next. The court case was never resolved and according to Eleanor Fry, writing in 2001, the case simply disappeared from the docket. The Fountain Underflow never delivered a single drop of water to Pueblo's municipal supply.

Meanwhile, Colorado Springs had run into its own problems. The mining center of Victor, located just over the mountain, was not terribly happy with Colorado Springs and its interbasin water high jinks. Colorado Springs was getting an unpleasant lesson in water law. The city, it turned out, did not have rights to Bear Creek. Four claims dating to 1861 were already on the books. The diversion was illegal.

Victor sued. Other lawsuits piled on. El Paso County sued the city, other municipalities took Colorado Springs to court, and downstream agricultural producers joined the Lawsuit-a-Palooza. Bear Creek was not the only issue. Colorado Springs' high-handed and aggressive pursuit of water upset seemingly everyone. Again and again, the city lost in court, learning along the way that it's best to obtain water rights *before* investing in infrastructure.

Of course no one bothered to ask the Nuuchiu, Ka'igwu, and

Hinono'eino people for permission to take control over, reroute, or utilize their traditional waters. Indigenous Coloradoans were simply ignored and pushed aside, their relationship to the waters erased.

The back and forth in court over Colorado Springs' pursuit of water was key in creating the legal framework that became today's Colorado Water Doctrine: all surface and groundwater in Colorado is a public resource, a water right is a right to utilize a portion of the public's water resources, and water rights holders can build facilities on the private land of others in order to exercise their water right. Yes, you read that correctly. The Colorado Doctrine grants more private property rights to a water right holder than to a landowner without water rights. In 1891, the courts ruled in *Strickler v. City of Colorado Springs,* that cities could buy and transfer water rights as long as other water rights holders are not injured.

All these lawsuits did nothing to stop Colorado Springs' pursuit of water. Instead of giving up, city leaders learned and adapted, finding ever more ingenious ways to turn the dusty bowl of a city into a thriving garden. Colorado Springs eventually got a hold of the Bear Creek water. Throwing around its economic weight, the city bought out downstream farmers and older water rights.

Having secured south slope waters, Colorado Springs next looked to the north slope of The Peak. In 1933, utilizing Congressional funds allocated for Depression-era public works, Colorado Springs diverted French Creek, dammed the Crystal and South Catamount Creeks, and then piped that water into the Ruxton system. In 1960, the North Catamount reservoir opened. In 1970, Colorado Springs enlarged the 1924 Rampart Reservoir. Pipelines and straws spiderwebbed across the mountains west of Colorado Springs.

—

What is a river?

The Fountain muddied my understanding of rivers. That human choices alter landscapes is nothing new, we've been doing it for a half a million years, at least. But there is a difference between nudging the system slightly and reengineering it wholesale. That we take a scrappy, high desert creek and morph it into a lush riparian zone blessed with a continuous flow struck me as something unique and, if not unique, surely unusual. When a scrappy, mostly dry creek becomes a full-time river through human manipulation and with the sole intention of benefitting humans it might no longer be a creek or a river, but something else entirely.

Nearly every definition of the term "river" contains the word "natural." *The National Geographic Society* tells that "a river is a large, natural stream of flowing water." Wikipedia and the USGS agree. "A river is a natural flowing water course."

So too with definitions of "watershed." Again, *The National Geographic Society*: "A land area that channels naturally occurring rainfall, snowmelt into a common body of water."

Leaving aside the problematic definition of "natural," it would be a stretch to say that Fountain Creek—filled with street runoff, Colorado River and Arkansas River flows, as well as fossil water mined from distant aquifers—doesn't come close to meeting the definition of "natural."

In a world where almost every waterway, every lake, pond, wetland, creek, brook, stream, river, and run has been altered and manipulated by and for people, perhaps there is no such thing as a "river" anymore. Perhaps there are only canals and pipes. I wondered, does a creek like the Fountain render terms like "river" or "watershed" obsolete?

One speaker at the 2023 Arkansas Basin Water Forum referred to the Fountain as a "canal." A canal is an entirely human-created piece of infrastructure constructed with the sole intent of serving human needs and desires. Ouch. I cringed. That was certainly not how I wanted to think of the Fountain.

If the Fountain is not a river, nor a canal, might it be something independent of each? But what?

Water law in the American West is complicated to say the least. But there are a few basic concepts that might help to make sense of it all.

First, we measure amounts of water in acre-feet. One acre-foot is the volume of one acre filled with water to a depth of one foot. That is approximately 326,000 gallons. Imagine an American football field covered in water one foot deep. One acre-foot is imagined to be the annual water consumption of a single-family suburban household, although actual use varies greatly from region to region. Cities in the American Southwest have cut consumption to half an acre-foot a year per household, and some have even dropped consumption to a quarter acre-foot a year.

We also measure water in cubic feet per second or CFS. One CFS is the equivalent of one basketball moving past every second. Thus, five hundred CFS equals five hundred basketballs passing every second.

Next up: beneficial use. Western water law holds that all water must be put to "beneficial use." That means the water must go for agriculture, industry, municipal use, recreation, mining, or a handful of other uses defined by the federal government and individual states. Leaving water in the flow of the creek or river is not traditionally considered a beneficial use. That has begun to change. In 1973, Colorado recognized that fish, wildlife, and wetland preservation just might be a beneficial use after all. A number of other states have since joined, noting that some forms of recreation and wildlife constitute "beneficial use."

Then there is the Doctrine of Prior Appropriation, probably

the most vital concept of all western water law. This idea holds that when water is in short supply, the right to use water is determined by the date that water was first put to "beneficial use." In other words, the older "senior" water rights get water first while the "junior" right holders must settle for less water or none at all. A farm with an 1861 water right is senior and thus has priority over a neighbor with an 1885 appropriation. In a dry year, the 1861 right will probably get water while the neighbor may not. This concept is also known as "first in time, first in right." Colorado's oldest Euro-American water rights date to the 1850s.

The Doctrine of Prior Appropriation is a relatively new invention. Donald Worster points out that, traditionally and throughout the world, no one could own a river nor own water as property. People who lived along riverbanks had rights to use the water but not to own, transfer, nor diminish the flow. A river, Worster wrote, belonged to no individual person but rather to everyone including God and the river itself. "No individual was free to enrich himself by seizing it for his personal use to the exclusion of others."

American colonizers rejected this ancient concept in favor of the ability to exploit nature and in particular, water. More personal freedom, less collective responsibility.

Many historians make the case that western water law and, specifically, the Doctrine of Prior Appropriation, came about due to the aridity of the West, that a traditional way of valuing waters would have made settlement impossible. Worster rejects this idea, as do I. We see these traditional values functioning in arid regions the world over. Western water law in fact developed because colonists believed that waterways and nature itself existed solely to benefit the bank accounts of certain individuals. A more ancient and traditional form of water management could have worked just fine in the American West and probably would have worked better than what we ended up with.

Colorado is unique in the West in that it sets water right

seniority in Water Court—or courts, there are seven of them, one for each major basin. These courts do not create water rights but rather clarify rights. No other state in the West really does this. New Mexico's water rights adjudication process, for example, is a mess where no one wants to take any responsibility and the can is forever kicked down the road.

The fourth key water law concept is that of "use it or lose it." If you do not put your water right to "beneficial use" for a certain period, you might lose that right. If you utilize less than your right allows, you may also lose the unused portion. For example, if your right is enough to water one thousand acres of land but you only use enough to soak five hundred acres, you might lose the other five hundred. If you choose to leave your water in the river, you risk losing it all. When a water right is not exercised for ten or more years, it is presumed "abandoned." Such a system incentivizes the waste of water, the destruction of soils, and devaluation of pretty much everything a river is supposed to be. This too has recently begun to change through water leasing programs, but the changes are far from ideal—the pace of change is glacial.

Finally, there is "paper water" versus "wet water." Acquiring a water right does not mean you have actual water. It means you have been granted paper water, a legal claim to a specific amount of water for beneficial use. Wet water is the real, tangible amount of water that might come your way in a given year based on your paper right. Again, during dry years, that paper water does not guarantee you wet water.

The Doctrine of Prior Appropriation pushes cities like Colorado Springs or the Denver suburb of Aurora to chase down older water rights for purchase. An 1880 right is far more valuable and reliable than a right with a priority date of 1910. Going after older rights gives Colorado Springs more water security and that means drying up agriculture.

Some Western states are experimenting with ways water

right holders might leave water in the river and not lose their rights. Yet the system overall has little flexibility. Water in the West is over appropriated, meaning that every drop of available water has been claimed. In fact, water right claims exceeded available water as early as 1890. This inflexibility combined with nonnegotiable interstate water sharing compacts makes true water conservation nearly impossible.

Despite all the re-piping of water within the Fountain's watershed, the creek itself saw only minimal impacts. At first, Colorado Springs had stuck with regional water for the most part. That all changed in the 1930s and 1940s.

Thirsty Front Range cities looked west for water as early as 1914, when Denver envisioned a massive tunnel through the mountains to fill its reservoirs with water from the Colorado River basin. At that time, West Slope water was abundant, seemingly inexhaustible, and ostensibly underutilized. Colorado Springs was not to be out done by Denver. In 1949, the city embarked on the Hoosier Tunnel, a one-and-a-half-mile-long straw (pipe) dug straight through the mountains. Known as the Blue River Project, it put The Springs at odds with many of its neighbors, and soon Colorado Springs again found itself in court. Still, the project moved forward, and the first West Slope water trickled from Colorado Springs faucets in 1961.

Between 1950 and 2010, the population of Colorado Springs exploded by more than eightfold, from 45,000 people in 1950 to 416,000 people in 2010. City elected officials called for still more water.

As Blue River water greened up fresh suburban lawns, Colorado Springs signed an agreement with the City of Aurora to build the Homestake system, 130 miles of straws, tunnels, reservoirs, diversions, and pumping stations that increased the city's supply by more than 50 percent. That was just Phase I.

Colorado Springs and Aurora aimed to expand Homestake in Phase II by grabbing new rights, boring fresh tunnels and flooding still more valleys with storage reservoirs.

Around 1980, sustained flows in the Fountain at Pueblo began to rise. By the time I graduated high school in 1989, hydrologists could see that something fundamental about the Fountain had changed. USGS hydrographic data showed that sustained high flows were not only sticking around but were increasing. Flood stage flows were also consistently higher on the average. Colorado Springs, through its development, had altered the Fountain.

But times, they were a-changin'. By the 1970s, the era of ginormous, federally funded water projects was on the wane and the age of conservation had, sort of, begun. Through the 1980s, Colorado Springs ran headlong into a wall of lawsuits from landowners, other cities, other counties, as well as conservation organizations like the Sierra Club.

As of 2024, Homestake II has not happened . . . yet. Throughout the early 2020s, I listened to numerous Colorado Springs leaders and developers fantasize about a rejuvenated Phase II. They want it. The rest of the state? Not so much. Colorado Springs' somewhat arrogant and pugnacious pursuit of water was, and continues to be, an irritant to the rest of the state. At the Arkansas Basin Water Forum in April 2023, one of Colorado's lead water managers told me "You won't hear it in public, but pretty much the entire state is pissed at Colorado Springs. From the Governor on down, Democrat and Republican alike. We've got a water crisis on our hands and this city's unwillingness to play ball has everyone . . . frustrated, let's say."

With Homestake II at least temporarily off the table, Colorado Springs pivoted to simply buying water. In 1972 and 1976, the city purchased water rights at Twin Lakes at the top of the Arkansas River near the old mining city of Leadville.

As early as the 1890s, irrigators east of Pueblo, 150 miles

downstream, joined to enlarge the cerulean blue natural lakes to hold more water. Thirty years later Colorado bore a tunnel through the mountains to bring Roaring Fork River water from the West Slope to Twin Lakes. Managers released that water into the Arkansas then diverted it for irrigation via the Colorado Canal east of Pueblo. When The Springs bought those old agricultural water rights, they did not intend to extract that water in particular from the lakes and pipe it northeast to the city. That would have meant billions more in infrastructure and, probably, decades in the courts. Instead, Colorado Springs released water from the upstream reservoirs to benefit downstream irrigators along the Ark. In exchange, they extracted more water upstream from Twin Lakes and Turquoise Lake on the Homestake project. By 2015, 90 percent of the water stored in Twin Lakes was owned by cities and various industries.

And still, it was not enough.

The prairies of southeastern Colorado are strikingly flat, the landscape punctuated by farming communities with names like Swink, Rocky Ford, Manzanola, Sugar City, and La Junta. For about one hundred years beginning in the 1860s, settlers turned the biologically rich short grass prairie into an agricultural bonanza. Towns across the plains thrived.

Then, in the 1970s, Colorado Springs began purchasing enormous amounts of senior water rights in Crowley and Otero Counties east of Pueblo, drying up tens of thousands of acres of productive farmland. The result was the near economic destruction of southeast Colorado. In 1975, Crowley County had some fifty thousand acres in irrigation. By 2020, it was less than five thousand, and in some dry years, no more than two thousand acres received water. John Harner labeled this move by Colorado Springs as "devious," pointing out that the Arkansas valley farmers accused both Colorado Springs and the city of Aurora of "political blackmail and excessive use of economic and legal power" in their pursuit of water.

In the late 1970s and early 1980s, our family made frequent trips to the town of Rocky Ford for farm festivals and markets, a large statewide swim meet every Fourth of July weekend, and to pick cantaloupes, corn, beets, and pumpkins from a friend's farm. Rocky Ford in Otero County was a thriving community. Today, irrigation ditches are dry, noxious weeds fill fallowed fields, and winds whip dust into choking clouds. Rocky Ford is nearly a ghost town. Without water, Crowley has turned to America's prison industrial complex for economic development. As of 2023, nearly 50 percent of Crowley's population was in the slammer. Crowley County is the poster child for just how bad things can get when cities buy up farm water. Under Colorado water law, once the water is gone, it is gone for good. Understandably, this reality does not sit well with much of rural Colorado.

And yet, there is a case to be made that farming in the high desert is not the best use of water anyway. It is also true that many of the Otero and Crowley County farmers who sold their water were elderly and did not have any children willing to carry on the family tradition. Farming is hard. So too, those who defend the urban water rights grab point out that cities are far more efficient when it comes to water use. This is true, and perhaps we should not have been farming the lower Arkansas River valley in the first place. Still, the death of once-thriving communities is painful for individuals, families, and whole regions.

The thirst for water dumps us into a legal, ethical, cultural, and financial quagmire.

I've singled out Colorado Springs for its obsessive pursuit of water because Colorado Springs is central to the Fountain watershed. Yet, the city is hardly alone in its thirst. The Denver suburb of Aurora has been as aggressive as Colorado Springs if not more so. The Front Range cities of Firestone, Castle Rock, Windsor,

Erie, and Lone Tree are all in need of a drink, growing at a rapid pace, competing to slake that thirst.

For eastern Colorado agricultural communities the stakes were high. Tens if not hundreds of millions of dollars lay on the table. One family of multi-generational dairy farmers sold their 175 acre-feet in water rights for nearly $5 million. Debt-burdened farmers lined up to sell. Not everyone wants to trade water for cash, however. Urban water purchases pitted community members against one another, some fighting to save their rural economy while others aim to exercise their private property rights. Wild and bitter accusations of "traitor" and "communist" fly at public meetings. In 2012, Jay Winner, then head of the Lower Arkansas Conservation District called the water wars "a nasty, nasty business."

To my father, a very conservative Libertarian type, interbasin transfers are "one of the dumbest things this country has ever done." I agree. Nevertheless, water transfers are not going away. We are, apparently, stuck with them. For now. Laws prohibiting interbasin transfers have been introduced to the Colorado State Legislature dozens of times. Each one of these so-called "basin of origin" protection bills has failed. Yet the movement grows. That nasty, nasty business creates some odd alliances. Environmentalists and conservative types generally find common ground when it comes to drying up farms and using public monies to shuffle water from one basin to the next.

Rural Colorado has decided to push back on future water transfers. In 2023, six counties in south central Colorado's San Luis Valley, horrified by what happened in Crowley and Otero Counties, banded together to turn off the spigot. After months of public hearings and legal wrangling, residents created a regional oversight board designed to put the kibosh on Front Range cities working to grab the valley's aquifer.

It's an uphill battle. The cities of Aurora and Colorado Springs maintain permanent offices in the lower Arkansas

Valley, with staff dedicated to identifying landowners who wish to either sell or lease their water rights. In 2022, Colorado Springs purchased 3,000 acre-feet of water from Bent County farmers, water expected to supply some nine thousand new homes. That 3,000 acre-feet is part of an estimate 15,000 acre-feet Colorado Springs plans to obtain from Arkansas Valley farmers over the coming years, and they plan to go after another 10,000 from other Colorado farmers by 2050.

Front Range cities perfectly demonstrate Worster's 1985 assertion that "The hydraulic society of the west . . . is . . . a coercive, monolithic, and hierarchical system, ruled by a power elite based on the ownership of capital and expertise."

Modern water policy makes mockery of the cherished free market. Freedom plays no role when it comes to water.

And still, it wasn't enough.

Watching the construction of Pueblo Reservoir is one of my earliest memories. My mother drove me to Liberty Point, a sedimentary bluff high above the Arkansas River where we watched with binoculars. I remember the giant digging machines, the cement trucks, the ever-growing concrete dam and the swarm of workers, ant-like from that vantage.

The Pueblo Reservoir was part of the Fryingpan-Arkansas Project or Fry-Ark. Six new storage reservoirs, seventeen diversion dams, two power plants, twenty-seven miles of new tunnels, and hundreds of miles of canals and straws to move water throughout eastern Colorado and Kansas. Colorado Springs and the suburbs of Widefield, Security, and Fountain joined in constructing a forty-five-mile pipeline known as the Fountain Valley Conduit from the reservoir, giving Colorado Springs still more access to west slope water. Naturally, this too was a federally funded project.

And still, it was not enough.

In 2000, Colorado Springs and its partners announced the Southern Delivery System (SDS), another fat straw to move Arkansas water from Pueblo Reservoir. This time to fuel the city's sprawl to the east. When complete, eleven pumps will send tens of thousands of gallons of water each day fifty miles and 1,500 feet uphill to two yet-to-be-built reservoirs at Banning-Lewis where another two hundred thousand homes are in the plans.

The number of transmountain diversions is astounding. On the Colorado map I'd hung on my office wall, I marked in red every diversion I knew of. I counted forty-four, most somewhere along the continental divide.

The SDS pushed the long-simmering tensions between Pueblo and Colorado Springs to the boiling point. Pueblo elected officials joined Bob Rawlins, a vocal free-marketeer and long-standing editor of the *Pueblo Chieftain*, in opposing the SDS. All that water after all has to go somewhere. It doesn't just disappear. At issue was not the Pueblo Reservoir, but the Fountain.

Not only has all the paved over development in The Springs added water to our intermittent creek-cum-river, but decades of water diversions and the newer cross-mountain transfers of Colorado River basin water swelled the Fountain as effluent. By the late 1990s, the Fountain held four to five times more water than it had historically. As we've seen, all that extra water changed the very nature of the Fountain and it continues to cause large-scale erosion and increased flooding from the south end of Colorado Springs to the confluence with the Arkansas.

As in 1965, June 2023 saw an unusual, persistent weather pattern set up along the mountain chain above Colorado Springs, resulting in day after day of bucketing rain and hail from Cheyenne to Pueblo. Some areas received over half their annual precipitation in just a couple of hours. City streets turned to rivers.

The confluence in Pueblo flooded, CDOT closed several bridges, fearing collapse. Justin Barr texted several videos of the swollen Fountain eating away at his fields. "Well, there it is," he said in one of the videos as chunks of land sloughed into the roiling waters. There was despair in his voice.

The SDS gave Pueblo some leverage to deal with the erosion and flooding. If Colorado Springs wanted its Pueblo Reservoir water, changes were in order. Pueblo wanted its northern neighbor to deal with its runoff and effluent issues once and for all. Without a land use permit from the Pueblo County Commission, construction on the straw could not proceed. Desperate for the water, Colorado Springs promised Pueblo they would make changes and the city created a "Stormwater Enterprise," hoping to tax landowners based on the amount of property covered with impervious surfaces. Pueblo, believing their northern neighbor would finally fulfill its promises, issued the land use permit and construction on the SDS straw took off. But Colorado Springs' anti-tax fundamentalists cried foul, sued, and won, halting the stormwater tax plan. Next, Colorado Springs put the idea before the voters. Again, it was rejected. Voters again said no in 2014. Pueblo felt cheated, Harner wrote. Colorado Springs got its water, but it didn't live up to its promises.

In 2016, Pueblo again threatened to shut the SDS down unless Colorado Springs stepped up. Stuck between a rock and a hard place, The Springs settled and the two cities agreed on a twenty-year, $460 million plan for Colorado Springs to fix its storm water issues. Finally, in 2017, Colorado Springs voters approved a new stormwater fee. The SDS moved forward. It was not simply past mistakes that would be socialized, but the future. Colorado Springs continues to sprawl east and north and current residents are expected to cover the costs of that sprawl through stormwater taxes, "unjustly subsidizing both future residents and the housing development industry," wrote Harner.

—

In 2023, 80 percent of Colorado Springs' water arrived via pipelines from the Western Slope, two hundred miles away. Like many Front Range communities, Colorado Springs owns paper water from the Colorado River basin. Paper water, not wet water. As long as the water flows, Colorado Springs can continue as it has. But as the Colorado River basin dries from overuse and climate change-driven drought, will Colorado Springs face a moment when most, if not *all,* of their Colorado River water is nothing but worthless paper?

CSU seems aware of just how precarious the city's water situation is. In the fifty-year water plan, CSU hopes to add 41,000 acre-feet of water to its annual supply, a cost estimated at something like $40 million. No doubt an underestimate. That 41,000 acre-feet would include additional water rights purchases and additional storage at the Montgomery Reservoir near Hoosier Pass and at Clear Creek reservoir near the mountain town of Leadville, as well as a deeply controversial possible new reservoir near Holy Cross Wilderness area.

The winter of 2022-2023 offered the Colorado River basin a breather. Lake Powell, after falling for years, rose a foot a day well into the summer. Even in a multi-decadal drought there will be wet years, sometimes even several wet years in a row. Yet climate and water models point to a long-term or even permanent drying across the West, wet winters like 2022-2023 are but a momentary reprieve. Colorado River-dependent communities and industries breathed a substantial sigh of relief, but the stay is temporary.

Colorado River basin users appear determined to avoid reality. In May of 2023, three of the Colorado River states—California, Arizona, and Nevada—announced a deal to cut their take of water. Initially, hailed as "groundbreaking" and "innovative," the plan was a hoped-for, massive step forward in solving the Colorado River crisis. Except it was none of that. Water experts across the West took one look at the so-called plan and realized it was nothing more than the states kicking the can down the road.

The plan conserved barely one million acre-feet of water, and only for three years, falling far short of the four million acre-feet that had to be conserved *permanently* just to begin tackling the problem. The agreement also sidestepped water development plans in the Upper Basin states—Colorado, Utah, Wyoming, and New Mexico. Twenty new dams, diversions, and pipelines were planned for places like Aurora, Denver, and Colorado Springs; infrastructure that would pull an additional 500,000 acre-feet per year from the Colorado River system. The plan required Washington, D.C. to subsidize the scheme to the tune of $1.2 billion, essentially paying people not to do what they should not have done in the first place.

Apparently, the Colorado River states are not going to bite the bullet. Kicking the can down the road will only create more misery in the long run and, at least for the moment, that is where we are headed.

In northern El Paso County sits a pump station, part of the Cherokee Metropolitan District, an agency supplying water to nearly twenty thousand customers on the northeast edge of Colorado Springs and some areas of rural El Paso County. Instead of the Fountain or Colorado River basin, the Cherokee pulls its water from the wells of the Denver Basin, a Cretaceous clay and sandstone formation underlying northeast El Paso County, the city of Denver, reaching north nearly to Fort Collins, and east to the plains. The Denver Basin wells are in steep decline so the district bought surface water rights on the Fountain to stave off the inevitable.

Yet, those water rights are for water south of Colorado Springs, some thirty miles distant. So, the Cherokee aims to pump that Fountain water north through a $140 million system of ditches, reservoirs, pumps, and pipelines. This proposed "Loop" system would serve customers in the Cherokee and nearby water districts. Once used, the Fountain water would be mixed with Denver Basin groundwater, treated at a wastewater facility, and discharged into Monument Creek, the Fountain's largest tributary. Some of the water will make its way to Pueblo and the Arkansas, some will get picked back up south of Colorado Springs and sent north again for reuse.

Another term of art among water managers is the concept of extinction. Certain waters, like those from the Denver Basin wells and the Colorado River basin transfers, can be "used to extinction," meaning it can be used and used again until every molecule is gone, none of it has to go downstream. The Loop would be a "use-to-extinction" system.

If constructed, this Loop will prove an extraordinarily complicated and expensive system. Just the water transmission lines will run over a million dollars a mile, the Loop's backers admit. By the time construction begins—*if* it begins—$140 million will prove a vast underestimate.

The idea of recycling and reusing drinking water is nothing new. Since the earliest days of human settlement, upstream communities the world over have dumped wastewater into rivers, only to see that water reused downstream. The Loop is a wastewater recycling system with the Cherokee District utilizing the Monument and the Fountain as an "environmental buffer" diluting the cleaned effluent in the creek instead of returning treated wastewater directly to consumers.

Reuse is not a bad idea, yet the concept rankles many who do not realize they are already consuming treated, diluted effluent. The environmental buffer is mostly an aesthetic choice. The idea of water going directly from the sewage treatment plant to the kitchen sink grosses most people out. Yet the waters pulled from the Fountain are no different. The Monument and

Fountain are mostly treated effluent and stormwater runoff at this point anyway, so while it may somehow seem better to put the water in the creek before reuse, it really doesn't matter and the concept of environmental buffers may be on its way out anyway.

In November 2022, Colorado's water quality agency approved the concept of "direct potable reuse," that is the process of treating sewage and returning it directly to your kitchen tap without first diluting it in a lake, aquifer, or river. Colorado was the first in the nation to adopt such rules for direct potable reuse. Florida, California, and Arizona are not far behind.

Detractors label this "toilet to tap," but toilet to tap it is not. Wastewater is extensively treated utilizing an array of membrane filters, ozone gas, ultraviolet light, and reverse osmosis that remove solids, contaminants, bacteria, and viruses. The water dribbling from the other end, so to speak, is cleaner than most of Colorado's famously crystalline high-altitude streams.

With water resources dwindling and population growing, no western state will escape the need to recycle wastewater and to keep their water supplies flowing through an endless loop system.

Still, conservation is perhaps the most consistently undervalued and overlooked source of water. In 2021, *Fresh Water News* looked at fifteen cities across Colorado to assess how permanent water restrictions impact water use. They found an average savings of up to 40 percent. The city of Castle Rock—located along I-25 between Denver and Colorado Springs—saw a 20 percent reduction per person per day since enacting restrictions. Aurora's water use dropped 30 percent. Permanent water restrictions work and work extremely well.

Colorado Springs residents, traditionally opposed to any sort of regulations, did not look kindly on the idea of permanent landscape water restrictions as a way to save water. But in January 2020, after years of controversy, the city adopted outdoor watering rules which resulted in a 5 percent drop in water use. Not a wild success, but the savings amounted to about 12,000 acre-feet per year.

One challenge with water conservation is that the pro-development community tends to look at such savings as a completely new source of water, as if a new well was tapped or a previously unknown creek was discovered. "See?" they say. "Now we can build another 12,000 homes with that saved 12,000 acre-feet!"

Some imagine an even bigger straw as the answer to the West's water issues. These visionaries seek a gargantuan straw sucking billions of gallons of water per day from somewhere else, forcing it uphill to satiate the arid West.

Such pipe dreams have taken a variety of forms over the past hundred years. One plan aimed to pull water from Canada's Hudson Bay. Another imagined a straw from the Yukon River to California. One dreamed of water shipped from Canada to California in oil tankers. Yet another imagined a five hundred-mile-long reservoir, extending the length of British Columbia, diverting Arctic water through a series of pipes and canals into the Colorado River. These proposals got Canadians thinking—and worrying. A 2004 Canadian TV drama, *H2O*, fretted that the United States, after assassinating the Prime Minister, would force Canada to sell water to its desiccated neighbor.

More often than not, however, the Mississippi River is the target of the pipe dreamers. In 2022, the Arizona state legislature passed a resolution demanding an updated Federal feasibility study to move Mississippi water west. The old study, they said, was outdated. And anyway, they didn't like what it said.

In the 2013 study, the Federal Bureau of Reclamation (BOR) looked at the idea of piping Mississippi River water west. They estimated it would take thirty years and $14 billion to make that dream come true. Thirty years and $14 billion *at least*. In reality, such a pipe would take fifty to sixty years and more than $30 billion to build. At least.

The BOR study raised more questions than it answered. How do you obtain the land to build a pipe 70 to 100 feet in diameter and 1,400 miles long? What are the environmental impacts to the Mississippi, the Colorado, and everywhere in between? How many lawsuits might be filed against such a project, how long would they take to resolve, and how would the whole project be secured from sabotage? Then there is the power needed to push that water 1,400 miles uphill. Where does that come from and who pays for it? How will that impact climate emissions? The whole idea also ignores the fact that the Mississippi is itself an unreliable source, frequently drying as it did in 1937, 1940, 1988, 2023, and years in between.

The desperation is palpable.

HERON

July 27: Clear Springs Ranch

Where the Fountain turned then flattened, a solitary heron waded beneath an overhang of grasses. He was blue-gray from the distance, white about his face, with a black line of feathers above his eye that trailed behind his head. His snake-like neck flowed with each step.

I had come across the fields and through a stand of cottonwood elders filled with jays. They dropped into the grasses and shrubs, gathering insects and the fruit of the red and yellow current lining the trail. The jays squawked and called, mimicking crows, ravens, and the red-tailed hawk perched in a snag near the bridge.

Rain was coming. I pulled on my jacket and jumped from the bank to a gravel bar dividing the creek. I trailed the heron, keeping distance. The western horizon, framed by the mountains, disappeared behind a curtain of falling water.

The heron continued upstream, plodding, scanning. A pair of snowy egrets perched near a pool formed by a triangle of stone slabs. The water, spilling over the rocks, frothed silver bubbles. The egrets fished minnows and chubs, swallowing them in gulps. The heron arrived and poked at the egrets. It was not a violent stab, but a sign to move on, as if to say: This is my spot. My pool. The egrets crossed the Fountain to another hole upstream, this one formed from a beaver-cut cottonwood that had collapsed into the flow. The heron hunched, a spring poised on long stilts of legs.

I left the gravel bar and sat on the bank, watching. For an hour or more, the heron stood, unflinching. He waited for fish to come and be eaten. The creek moved on, glassen.

Water has the magical power to create beauty, or at the very least, to conceal what is broken. Water buries the shopping cart, whisks plastic bags away, and washes drug needles to the Gulf of Mexico . . . or at least into the Arkansas. Over time it smoothes over the shotgun casings and rounds the edges of broken glass into colorful stones a child can safely stuff into her coat pocket. Sitting by the creek, watching the still pools reflect the sky and the current ripple the sediments, it was hard to imagine the Fountain full of sewage, forever chemicals, microplastics, and viruses.

Along the treetops, the hawk circled, the pale of his under feathers crisp against the blackening sky. He may have been out hunting before the rain. If he was, he wasn't serious about it. He turned, circled, and only once called out a hoarse *keeeeee*. Then he glided down, swept up, and flew off. Something else caught my attention: a pair of porcupines scurrying across the cottonwood branches, gnawing bark.

Just after two, a man walked along the forest path. He carried a bulky camera topped with a massive lens. He fumbled with a tripod and said he was looking for western tanagers. I told him I had seen none. Instead, I pointed to the porcupines, the egrets, and the heron. He claimed to be on a mission for the tanagers and had not expected rain. He hustled downstream. Ten minutes later, I could see him where the Fountain curled east. A rush of mallards, goldeneyes, and teals poured over his head, making north into the storm. He seemed not to see the birds. Then he was gone.

The heron had not moved.

The clouds dropped to the treetops. The creek—wide and still—mirrored the near black of the storm. Rain arrived and the drops scattered the mirror in thousands of concentric circles. I opened my umbrella and zipped my jacket. The heron bent, sodden, then struck. The speed at which a heron snatches a fish, or in this case a frog, boggles the mind. I've seen it now, dozens of times, and struggle to comprehend—probably because my feeble human body could never spring like a heron.

The bird swallowed the frog. The rain came in sheets. The Fountain rose, turning a dank orange-ish, filled with sediment. I thought I could wait out the storm, but the wind folded my umbrella and my boots filled with rainwater. I raced for the cottonwood grove. Lightening arrived. Thunder raced the heels of the flashes. The Fountain pushed its banks. The heron had not moved. The photographer was gone, and I made for the sheltering bridge.

DARK WATERS

"You're glumping the pond where the Humming-Fish hummed!
No more can they hum, for their gills are all gummed.
So I'm sending them off. Oh their future is dreary.
They'll walk on their fins and get woefully weary in search of some water that isn't so smeary."

–*Dr. Seuss,* The Lorax

About a mile north of the Target and Goodwill stores in Pueblo, I came to a screen of tamarisk so thick I could not find a path through and back to the waters. Instead, I scrambled up a steep, crumbling bank of dry clay and shale angling away from the creek and walked toward the railroad tracks. I passed a pile of discarded tires, several masses of construction debris and household trash, and a shopping cart filled with plastic bottles. I peered into the next arroyo, finding my way.

Two men sat in the arroyo amidst broken bags of trash, still more construction materials overcome with weeds and several rotten mattresses. One of the men had a bicycle. He had locked it, with a massive chain, to a Volkswagen-sized rock. I could not tell how old the men were. They looked rough, dirty and worn out. The lines on their faces spoke to an extremely difficult life of living unhoused next to the Fountain.

The men collected water from a pipe poking from under the railroad tracks. The pipe drained from the Interstate running just a couple of hundred yards to the west. They filtered the water from the pipe through a stack of t-shirts and into a five-gallon bucket. They made me nervous those men, so I went down to talk to them.

"Hey," I said.

Both nodded but remained focused on the t-shirts, keeping them aligned with the water tumbling from the pipe and into the bucket below. One of the men was missing his front teeth. I dropped into the dirt and crossed my legs. Several crows passed overhead and a flock of sparrows crowded into a dry chamisa. Minutes passed me, mesmerized by the water and their silent focus. I expected them to offer some sort of explanation. I also expected them to ask me for some sort of explanation. They did neither. More minutes passed.

"What's the water for?" I asked.

"Camp."

"Why don't you get the water from the river?" I asked.

"The creek?"

"Yeah, the creek."

The man missing his teeth turned to me and scowled. "That shit's dirty, man," he said.

Dr. Velma Campbell was a semiretired occupational physician and community activist in Pueblo. She had worked in public health in New Orleans before that, toiling alongside her husband on eco-justice issues up and down Cancer Alley. When we met in Pueblo at Mauro's for tacos, she brought along Jamie Valdez, a longtime water protector and self-described "justice warrior." Valdez had spent most of his life fighting air and water pollution, first in his Pueblo East Side community next to the Fountain, and later across the entire lower Arkansas River basin.

Jamie and Velma were close friends. For years they had fought for the people of Pueblo, teaming up to force the eventual (2031) shutdown of the Comanche coal-fired power plant just east of Pueblo, to fight off a proposed nuclear reactor, and to restore rights to Pueblo's beleaguered and poisoned Salt Creek. I'd known them both for a while, and it was good to catch up on family, community, and local political gossip. To me, people like Jamie and Velma are heroes. I was humbled to share a pile of tacos with people like that.

The State of Colorado lists the Fountain as "impaired." When it comes to water quality, the state also suggests you think twice before wading into Fountain Creek. At least not without some protections. There are "sharp objects" the state says, referring to broken glass, nails, and used needles. The "impaired" designation comes from the presence of high amounts of E. Coli and naturally occurring selenium that regularly turn up in water samples. But that's not all. Hepatitis A is also present in the creek. Mercury turns up in the fish that live in the Fountain. Lead is also present, as are artificial hormones, pesticides, pharmaceuticals, antibiotics, and an as of yet unknown amount of microplastics and other toxins.

The men filtering water from the I-25 culvert instead of lifting it from the Fountain were correct. That shit *is* dirty, man!

For Velma, PFAS remain the biggest challenge facing the Fountain. Jamie agreed, telling me that there are days when he actually has anxiety thinking about it.

PFAS (per- and polyfluoroalkyl substances) are a toxic, cancer-causing family of chemicals typically used in firefighting foam and fire-resistant materials. PFAS are used in everyday household products such as non-stick cookware, stain resistant furniture, mattresses, waterproof clothing, carpets, car seats, cosmetics, lubricants, paints, and even items that hold our food such as grocery story packaging, pizza boxes, and popcorn bags. The PFAS family of chemicals is everywhere. Literally. They are called "forever chemicals" because they take millennia to break down. Some researchers say these chemicals are indestructible and that there is no safe level of exposure.

The crazy thing is that those who manufacture products containing PFAS are not required to disclose to consumers that the chemicals are present in their products and the Environmental Protection Agency (EPA) did not regulate or even test for PFAS until about 2016. And PFAS move, easily making their way throughout our ecosystem via water—getting into aquifers and creeks—making them extremely challenging to contain.

Even at very low levels of exposure, in the parts per quadrillion, they are a serious public health issue. Kidney and testicular cancers top the list, but they are also known to disrupt hormone production, cause liver and thyroid disease, and abnormal fetal development. PFAS are particularly dangerous for children and have even been found in breast milk.

"People wonder why there is a cancer epidemic in this country," Jamie rolled his eyes.

In early 2016, PFAS turned up in the City of Fountain's drinking water. Mike Fink, then head of the city's water utility was at a loss. Where did it come from? How long has it been in the system? What were they going to do about it? Some seventy thousand residents depended on that water. Then PFAS turned up in the drinking water of the nearby communities of Security and Widefield. The numbers were shocking.

"We're used to having a playbook, a set of rules that tells us what to do when a known contaminate is discovered and has to be removed," Fink told Water Education Colorado soon after the discovery. The problem was that PFCs [PFAS] were unregulated; there were no clear state or Federal guidelines to follow. "We had no playbook."

The city turned off the wells. Fink and his colleagues in

Security and Widefield scrambled to secure surface water to make up for the loss of groundwater. Poor water quality means less water quantity.

Numerous military bases and facilities sit within the Fountain's watershed. Fort Carson is by far the largest, but the United States Air Force Academy, the Cheyenne Mountain Space Force Station, and the Schriever and Peterson Space Force Bases all lie in or near the watershed. All of these bases utilize firefighting foams loaded with PFAS or PFAS-related chemicals. That foam washes into the creeks and streams that feed the Fountain, seeping into the aquifer. Peterson has admitted to pouring thousands of gallons of PFAS into the Fountain. The other bases, likewise, have admitted to various levels of culpability.

"The military is for sure at fault," Campell said. "But there is something else. PFAS get used in a variety of industries. Oil and gas production is a big one and we got oil and gas all over the state. So there are other sources. We also think PFAS are seeping out of the shale along the creek somewhere. Maybe near the racetrack kinda by Clear Springs Ranch."

I wondered out loud if that too was from Fort Carson. Valdez didn't think so, but he wasn't sure. "There is a concentration of this junk somewhere, but we're not sure where exactly and we're not totally sure of the impact," Campbell said. "Problem is, nobody wants to pay to get it all figured out."

"Ignoring it won't make it go away," Valdez frowned.

"But that seems to be the plan for now," Campbell threw up her hands.

Later in 2016, the EPA finally set health advisory guideline for PFAS. Seventy parts per trillion (ppt). Instantly, dozens of Colorado water districts were out of compliance, some registering PFAS levels two hundred to three hundred times the EPA limit. Then in 2021, the EPA lowered the limit from 70ppt to 4ppt, indicating a fresh realization that PFAS were a major public health crisis. Dozens more Colorado water supplies were then deemed unsafe. It seemed that almost no one in the state had clean drinking water.

PFAS researchers say that even the 4ppt level is too high. It should be 2.5ppt said one expert. Not more than 1ppt said another. "Zero is the only acceptable level," a Colorado Springs Utilities employee told me at the Arkansas Basin Water Forum.

In the 2019 movie *Dark Waters*, a West Virginia farmer by the name of Wilbur Tennant approaches corporate lawyer Rob Bilott. Tennant's land was contaminated with PFAS-related chemicals produced by behemoth DuPont—the "Better Living Through Chemistry" people.

Bilott was an odd choice for an ally. For years, he had defended companies like DuPont from citizen lawsuits. But the injustice of Tennant's situation—and the complicity of local authorities—put Bilott on the road to Damascus, and the corporate lawyer became an eco-justice crusader. Before long, Bilott found himself representing more than 70,000 individuals in a colossal class action lawsuit against DuPont.

Dark Waters is based on a true and incredibly frustrating story: how DuPont knowingly dumped the PFAS-related chemicals into local streams and aquifers, contaminating people's drinking water and the surrounding landscapes.

Even after a multi-million dollar fine from the EPA, DuPont refused to put money towards a good faith clean up effort, instead spending twenty years and significant financial resources on a losing legal battle. Meanwhile, more people fell sick and died from PFAS-related cancers and diseases. Eventually, Bilott prevailed, but the winnings were a paltry $671 million—benefiting only the 3,500 plaintiffs who could prove their cancers were caused by the chemicals. Tens of thousands of other individuals were never compensated at all.

The family of PFAS chemicals was not banned (and won't

be). Contaminated water and soil remain. And for multi-billion dollar companies like DuPont, huge legal bills and settlement payments are more like tax write-offs than a crushing defeat.

Chemical companies like DuPont made billions and billions of dollars putting "those chemicals out there, knowing that they would get into the environment and into our blood," Bilott said in a 2019 interview. For them, it is just another example of externalized costs.

"And in fact," Velma Campbell told me, "they've known PFAS were dangerous since the 1940s, but nobody ever said anything. Now, 99 percent of Americans have one or more of the PFAS chemicals in their blood. I have it. You have it. Jamie has it."

I looked at Jamie. He raised an eyebrow and frowned. "It gives me anxiety."

The EPA has identified 120,000 sites across the country where Americans are exposed to unsafe levels of PFAS. Colorado tops the list with a jaw-dropping twenty-one thousand or more contaminated locations, the highest in the nation.

Chris Higgins, a PFAS expert at the Colorado School of Mines labeled PFAS "one of the greatest environmental drinking water containment challenges of our time."

In 2018, Bilott filed a fresh lawsuit to force companies like DuPont to pay for an independent science-based advisory body to clearly establish the heath impacts of the PFAS family of chemicals and to prevent them from entering the environment and our bodies. To this date, the chemical companies continue to fight Bilott and other activists, dragging it out, avoiding, and delaying what is obviously their responsibility.

While *Dark Waters* is a fictionalized account of a true story, *The Devil We Know* is a documentary of the same series of events, featuring the personal stories and battles of people who worked at the DuPont facility in Parkersburg, West Virginia, and the people in the region whose lives were upended or destroyed by the PFAS. The film's title refers to an internal DuPont memorandum of sticking with "the devil we know," meaning the continued use of PFAS instead of developing a safer alternative. Instead of keeping people safe, DuPont chose to make more money. The documentary is as maddening and wholly depressing as the fictionalized account. Perhaps more so.

Colorado launched an emergency program to fund infrastructure to remove PFAS from drinking water in 2021. Further, the program aimed to remove PFAS from all firefighting foam in the state. Other states have made similar moves.

The City of Fountain called the Air Force. Whatever the conversation, the result was a $9 million payment from the Air Force to the city to develop a new water treatment facility that could remove most if not all PFAS from the water supply. The military also offered to help Security and Widefield.

To remove the PFAS, the City of Fountain initially used a fine carbon filter, but the filters had to be replaced every few months. It was inefficient and expensive. Instead, the city changed out to large tanks, filled with tens of millions of ion-exchanging resin beads the size of a pencil tip. The beads were positively charged to break the chemical bond between the water and the PFAS. The PFAS bind with the beads and the water moves on, clean. Fountain's water quality now exceeds EPA PFAS guidelines—in a good way.

The problem isn't going away, however. PFAS infect a significant chunk of the Fountain watershed. Who will pay for the long-term upkeep of the City of Fountain's facility? That remains to be seen.

Many Puebloans see the Fountain as Colorado Springs' dumping ground. Colorado Springs using the Fountain as a "sewage pipe" is something you hear frequently in public meetings held in Pueblo. True or not, the sentiment is strong.

"Pueblo is a sacrifice zone," Valdez said. "We're a low-income, mostly Hispanic community. The rest of the state looks to Pueblo as a place to dump things they don't want."

The amount of E. coli in the Fountain, particularly the upper Fountain, is another violation of the Federal Clean Water Act. The Feds required Colorado to put the Fountain on what is called the Section 303d list—an inventory of all the sickly waters—which demanded the state figure out what was causing the problem and to develop a plan to fix it.

The source and impact of E. coli in the Fountain is somewhat of a mystery at this point. For years, researchers believed the high E. coli load in the creek was caused by bad septic storage tanks and livestock in the upper watershed. However, an extensive study by the USGS in 2008 and 2009 showed the worst contamination was downstream of Manitou Springs, indicating that something else was going on.

The main problem in dealing with E. coli in the Fountain is that there is not one particular point source of the pollution. It is not as if Manitou or Colorado Springs sewage treatment plants are dumping sewage directly into the Fountain—although that has happened in the recent past. Rather, there are hundreds of sources for the E. coli scattered throughout the watershed. To be sure, the number of unhoused people living along the creek contributes to the problem. Wildlife crowding into the narrow riparian corridor as pavement increasingly dominates the watershed is also an issue. One DNA test indicated an incredible amount of E. coli came from birds. That study has been knocked about quite a bit and called out of date. But, to be sure, wild and domestic animals, street runoff, and bad septic tanks all contribute. There are also other possible sources.

From about 1980 to 2010, my father owned a two-man plumbing business in Pueblo. It was just him and his buddy Danny

Carrillo, a Mexican immigrant who had served as an underage tank gunner in the Korean War.

Sometime in the early 1990s, dad got a call from a nursing home located near the Fountain on the south side of Colorado Springs. Something had gone wrong in the laundry room and the basement had flooded. My father and Danny drove north to the nursing home and starting looking around—detective plumbers on the job, trying to find a busted pipe.

As I heard the story, Danny went out behind the nursing home seeking a crawl space entrance or basement. Instead, he found a large, half-buried cast iron pipe poking from the nursing home. It was all grown over with grass and weeds and was hard to see, but it was big enough and long enough that it caught his attention. He called my father over and the plumbing detectives followed the pipe to a hovel of rocks, sheltered in elms, at the edge of Fountain Creek. Sewage poured from the pipe, sliding down the creek bank and into the water—a putrid, muddy slurry of feces, urine, bleach, laundry detergents, and medications.

"It was a nursing home," my dad told me one evening over beers as we watched lightning flash across The Peak. "Do you know how much medication old people cram into their bodies each day? Hell, I'm relatively healthy and I've got a lineup of pills on the counter. Can you imagine?" He laughed then listed all the drugs that might end up in nursing home sewage.

My stomach turned.

"It's not as odd as you think." He told me about other nursing homes in Pueblo, Fountain, and Colorado Springs, all doing the same thing. Over the years, he discovered several hotels, campgrounds, and individual homes—none connected to the local sewer system, dumping their waste into either the Fountain or the Arkansas. "Dozens of them," he said.

When Danny and my father approached the manager of the nursing home, he seemed genuinely surprised. The dumping had been going on for years. My father told him he had two choices: One, they could report the violation, and the nursing home would be on the hook for a serious fine. Two, the nursing home could pay the two plumbers to get the building hooked to city sewer and remove the pipe to the Fountain. If they agreed, my dad promised he would keep his mouth shut. The nursing home manager chose city sewer and the two plumbers completed the work within a week.

TRIBUTARIES

"There is a river whose waters give immortality; somewhere there must be another river whose waters take it away. The number of rivers is not infinite; an immortal traveler wandering the world will someday have drunk from them all."

–Jorge Luis Borges, The Aleph and Other Stories

Somewhere along the way I got it in my mind that there were two Turkey Creeks. One emptied into the Arkansas River where Roger Hill had been on the receiving end of a stone-throwing private landowner. That one I knew well, having fished several sections. The other Turkey Creek—the one that didn't actually exist—emptied into the Fountain somewhere just north of Pueblo. At least in my mind. This second Turkey Creek was sort of like the Rio Buenaventura, an imaginary river that led early Euro-Americans astray for nearly one hundred years. Like Pike, I'd gotten this alternative reality so stuck in my mind that I frustrated myself for months trying to find it. I was sure the maps were wrong. But alas, it was me.

In the late 1880s, someone murdered my maternal great-great-grandfather on the grassy steppe bordering Turkey Creek. Well, maybe murdered. That was the family lore. A newspaper article from the time speculated that he died of a stroke. Julian Coudayre was a French immigrant born in disputed

Alsace. A discharged veteran of Napoleon III's Grande Armée, he'd married my great-great-grandmother Bridget McNamara, an Irish woman he'd met in Lyon, and they migrated to the United States sometime soon after 1865. They married in Idaho Springs, Colorado, created two children, and moved to Pueblo.

At some point, Grandpa Julian purchased a plot of land northwest of Pueblo along Turkey Creek, hoping to find something valuable. Maybe gold. Maybe silver. Maybe he just wanted to run cattle. We don't know. We have no idea if he ever found anything of value, but if he was indeed murdered, either someone wanted that land or what he found on that land. Perhaps he had a run in with the Indigenous people who didn't want their land taken away by some random European. On the other hand, maybe Julian had simply pissed off the wrong person. There was one story of a poker game gone awry. Or maybe he simply had a stroke. Either way, someone found his body in the sage and grass, belly down, hat on head. His children were teenagers.

Perhaps that's why I was so focused on Turkey Creek. I had hoped to make yet another connection between family history and the Fountain. However, it was not to be. Another Rio Buenaventura evaporated.

A tributary, in the context of geography and hydrology, refers to a stream or river that flows into a larger body of water, such as a lake or main river. The Fountain is not only the main channel running from Woodland Park to Pueblo. The Fountain is a whole system that shapes the course of the larger narrative. Tributaries bind the entire system. If the Fountain watershed is a lung, Fountain Creek is like an artery and the tributaries the veins. So too, each tributary is its own unique system fed by even smaller waterways, the capillaries if you will. Each has its own feel and character, its own ecosystem, its unique human communities. Some Fountain tributaries are born in the mountains, others emanate from the prairies. Some are northern and cold, some southern and warm. Some tributaries are purely wild, others nothing but urban.

If I was going to get a full understanding of the watershed, I had to understand all the pieces that make up the whole, and so I set out to explore as many of the Fountain's tributaries as possible.

MESA CREEK

September

Mesa Creek trickled into the Monument from under I-25, just north of the Colorado College campus. I had thought it might pour from a culvert I could traverse under the Interstate, but the pipe was far too small. I walked down the right bank of the Monument, past a pile of used drug needles and their discarded orange caps, to Unitah Street, where I passed along a sidewalk under I-25, then trekked back north until I reconnected with Mesa Creek. Sweat pooled in my shirt and trickled down my legs.

When it came to exploring the tributaries of the Fountain, this would be my pattern. Start at the point where the tributary met the Fountain or Monument and head upstream from there.

Mesa Creek snaked its way through several blocks of residential housing. There, it was a dark, wet tunnel overgrown with elm, ash, willow, and Virginia creeper. I could not push my way through the green and instead made my way through the neighborhood while not straying into anyone's backyard. Eventually, I arrived at Sunderman Park, eighty acres owned by the City of Colorado Springs. The houses and pavement fell behind. At last, I could follow the creek.

Mesa Creek widened from the narrow conduit snaking between houses to a four-foot-wide stream running across a slightly incised channel. Trails spiderwebbed the park and city open space beyond. Soon, the riparian zone grew to about fifty or seventy-five yards across.

The forest was dark and cool, a relief from the heat. Virginia creeper snaked along branches of bursting feathery flowers amongst crimson leaves. The black of the waters caught up the tableau of the red creeper, the lemony leaves of alder, the faded yellow grasses, and the still green of the elms, cottonwoods, and willows; a shimmering glasswork of reflections, like a confluence of Monet and Klimt.

I came to an area where a beaver had dammed the creek at some point. But no more. The dam had been either breached or had burst in a flood. A maze of logs, mud flats, and flow spread through a French braid of streams, piles of sticks, spongy sediments, and large willows wrapped, long before, in wire to protect them from the beaver. For a walker, it was a difficult section to navigate, but it was rich and lovely and worth the effort.

So much of the Fountain watershed is a study in harsh contrast. As I moved upstream, I held the riparian wonderland to my left. To the right, workers swarmed a major new housing development. Just past the construction, the expansion of Centennial Boulevard was underway; the city just *had* to accommodate all those cars after all. Mesa Creek was a narrow, winding band of green snaking through a concrete world.

The new development gobbled up land to within five feet of the riparian area. In some cases, the two-foot-high, black sediment control fence reached into the forest, marking a stark boundary. "Here is where nature ends," it stated. The entire area to the north and east was bare dirt, freshly bulldozed, not a hint of vegetation remained. In less than a year, hundreds of new homes and a highway would dominate that section of the creek.

I dove back into the forest. The hackberry and honeysuckle were heavy with berries, the grass was waist-high and luxurious. I saw a milkweed dressed with a caterpillar of the tiger milkweed butterfly. In the uplands, chamisa flowered. There was yucca, prickly pear, cactus, currents, juniper, and gooseberry. In the afternoon light, each cottonwood leaf caught sun, transforming the light and launching it back into the sky as something wholly different. Fluorescent. Neon.

Further, I encountered an unhoused person in a tent. The thick forest wrapped him in, sheltering his tent behind a screen of vegetation. He had set his tent on a slight rise. The water alternately pooled and spread into wide flats around him, like a moat.

Still further, a power line crossed the creek. On the right bank, mansions dominated the hillside. I came across another encampment of unhoused men and it struck me how, in the Middle Ages, the rich and the rulers lived on the hills in the fresh air and sunlight while everyone else scrounged below. In far too many ways, nothing had changed.

Willows gave way to more cottonwoods, juniper, Russian olive, and even some pine. I came to a concrete spillway. Signs marked water pipes. A dirt road paralleled the creek then climbed toward the mesa. More unhoused people, their camps strewn with trash. I wondered how the people who count the unhoused in El Paso County could possibly find all the people I had come across in these tributaries. I would bet the surveys are missing hundreds of people, if not thousands, just within the Fountain watershed.

Higher still, the valley widened. More pine. The soils thinned and grasses dominated. There, I found what I was looking for. A beaver dam and pond. A bird enthusiast I had met near Colorado College had told me about an impressively tall beaver dam that shouldn't be missed.

The beaver had constructed the dam where the canyon narrowed. It struck me as an extremely unlikely location, jammed between two steep hill slopes, but there it was, at least fifteen feet high. The dam held a large pond of milky blue, algae filled water. The flow from the pond tumbled down stacks of sticks and logs threaded with willow branches. You could see that at some point the pond had been a lake, reaching the rim of the ravine where tire tracks flattened the grasses. But that was ages ago. A beaver lodge, dried out and long since broken open, hugged the side of the hill a good ten to fifteen feet above the current. When the lake was full the lodge had been out in the lake, demonstrating just how large the lake had been at one time. As it turned out, this towering beaver dam was the first in the series of eight progressively smaller dams, stair-stepped up the valley to the west.

We tend to think our personal experiences define reality. We tend to think that because the world looks as it does right here, right now, within our lifetimes, it must have always been that way. The beaver dam tells a different story

Once upon a time, this dry little valley, cut by a shallow, narrow stream, had been filled with water. Dozens of beaver families created a complex of lakes that, at various times, probably brought the water all the way up to the modern hilltop road, if not higher. These lakes allowed the water to seep into the ground, filling the aquifer, pouring forth downstream as dozens of rich springs that fed Monument Creek and ultimately the Fountain. Once upon a time, that valley had been a marshy paradise. One hundred fifty years of cattle grazing, timber harvesting, the reaping of beaver pelts, and urbanization has turned what was a lush landscape into a semi-desert. America is the author of its own problems.

Very few people living in Colorado today are aware of this land's rich ecological history. It is not just Coloradoans. Across the world, humans suffer from shifting baseline syndrome, an intergenerational form of amnesia in which we accept the current state of the world as normal when it is anything but.

When I was a kid, my grandfather would point to certain dry arroyos and talk about the fish he used to pull from, what to me, was nothing but a sandbox. Pick up a birding magazine from 1920 or 1950 and read about flocks of thousands upon thousands of birds that filled our skies. Now, we are impressed with a gathering of a dozen birds. Puebloans today will tell how winters were always mild and dry. National Weather Service data tells a different story.

It is not simply the whimsy of memory at work here. In northeastern New Mexico there is a dead, dry feature trailing the landscape known as Rio de las Truchas (River of Trout). The Spanish named it so because it was once a year-round stream rich with fish. When I inquired about the name at a nearby store, four men in boots and overalls assured me that the arroyo had always been dry. Always and forever. But that simply wasn't true. The American West is covered in landscape names that hint at the rich, wet landscape that existed when Europeans arrived.

Above the beaver ponds, Mesa Creek fell from the mouth of a concrete culvert. Above that, the water petered out in a matrix of small, cattail-filled wetlands just below a spread of athletic fields at the local middle school. I crossed the school grounds to West Fillmore Street, hoping the creek would continue further up. Instead, I came to Coronado High School, a few random square ponds, and more athletic fields. Then I arrived to a sprawl of condos and homes scatted over a spiderweb of golf links and tennis courts at the Kissing Camels, a high-end resort community with dramatic views of The Peak, Garden of the Gods, antennae-studded Cheyenne Mountain, the Cameron Cone, Blodgett Peak, and a wall-like outcropping of Dakota sandstone that curves to the north along the Front Range.

I had hoped to find the source of the tributary—and maybe I did. I could not make heads nor tails of the landscape and how the water flowed given the roads and houses. Instead, I wandered the golf course to a water treatment plant and still more oversized single-family homes where deer grazed on front lawns. Behind the homes loomed the fire-scarred, high-angle points of the Rampart Range, where a geologic fault marks the boundary between sedimentary bedrock and the pink granite so common in the Fountain watershed. The Pikeview quarry scar spilled across the hill slope, a raw rash slated for some type of restoration that may or may not include a mountain bike play park. The quarry operated from 1905 to the 1950s, supplying limestone for concrete used in the city's building boom. At one time, a village grew there. It began as a whistle stop on the Denver and Rio Grande Western Railroad. Later, the town of Pikeview built a school and a post office. A nearby coal mine, known for poor management and frequent deaths of miners, became one of the numerous sparks for the 1914 miners' strikes and the ensuing bloody Colorado Coalfield War.

I wandered around thinking there should be more. Yet there was no epiphany to be had. I sat on a bench next to the road and watched a man covered in tattoos enjoy a cigarette. I drank water then made my way back down the road to the Mesa Valley Open Space, the Catamount Institute building at Sonderman Park, I-25, and eventually to a bar on Nevada Street where I relieved the soreness in my feet with a cold IPA.

JACKSON CREEK

December

An unhoused man slept in the center of an oak below the nest of a Cooper's hawk. He appeared like a prisoner, trapped in a knitted web of branches, another Tolkien-esque scene. Music leaked from a pair of speakers near his head. A chickadee chattered from a bushy mahogany. Bushtits flocked to a chamisa. Three deer and a turkey strolled through the oaks. There was no snow.

I had parked at the Natural Grocers near the I-25. Magpies mobbed a dumpster behind the store while two employees hung out back, smoking, talking, waving their hands, and pacing. I mounted an eroding two-track and made my way uphill. Rotting erosion control netting covered the slope. At some point the incline had been seeded with native grasses and forbs; still, non-native species pushed in.

The noise in the verge was unnerving. A police helicopter

passed overhead. Then a helicopter belonging to a local TV news outlet. To the west, I-25 strung out along the edge of the mountains, jammed with cars, semis, pickups, and vans. Looking east, a four-lane parkway, also loaded with vehicles, rimmed the little creek. Beyond that, a massive shopping center and still more roads. To the north I could see yet another shopping center. It was late afternoon. Rush hour. I stood, marooned on an island of grass and oaks, surrounded by a sea of stores, roads, and traffic.

Robert McFarlane found a certain hope in these pockets of wild. "The weeds thrusting through a crack in the pavement, the tree root impudently cracking carapace of tarmac: these were wild signs, as much as the storm wave and the snowflake," McFarlane wrote in *The Wild Places*. He is right of course. Before came the wild, and the wild will remain when the asphalt is gone. On that day, however, on most days really, a desire for a better existence within my lifetime clouded my ability to take the long view. Deep-time-think-like-a-creek perspectives proved elusive.

Dozens of oaks; large, gnarled trees unfurled their branches into sheltering umbrellas. The oaks stood apart from one another, savannah-like, interspersed with knee-high grasses yellowed by winter. The oak bark was rough, thick, dressed in rusty green and orange mosses or algae. Some of the oaks were tremendously old, already large long before the sprawl boxed them in.

Jackson Creek sloughed at the base of a channel below the oaks, just a few feet from Jackson Creek Parkway where a stalled moving van blocked one lane of traffic. Three men and a woman all peered under the hood, arguing whether or not they could fix the problem or if they should call for help. The woman insisted she knew what was wrong. The men folded their arms and stood back as she reached into the engine.

The creek flowed from a culvert into a stack of hidden beaver ponds tucked beneath the road. Willow and cattail packed the banks. There was a drowned alder and several cottonwoods, one holding the nest of an eagle. I could see a shopping cart caught in the mud, a television screen dangling in the crotch of a still-living alder.

I crossed Jackson Creek Parkway and dropped back to the creek. To my left was a pond just below the Brakes Plus and a Goodwill. In front of me, a wide, tree-dotted green space spread out between the road and a housing development. Behind me, the growling road. I mounted a low slope and ran into an orange sign:

WARNING!
NO PUBLIC ACCESS
OR MOWING BEYOND
THIS POINT:
Wildlife Habitat
Preservation Area
Protected Under
Federal 404 Permit
No. 1998-30063
Possible Fines
Of $25,000 per day
And Imprisonment

My first thought was: WOW! How did they manage to get that many words on one narrow sheet of metal? My second thought was: Dammit. If it is not Private Property, No Trespassing signs keeping me away from the waters, it is the damn wildlife! Or, well, the feds. What was going on here that I could get a $25,000 fine and prison time for walking next to Jackson Creek?

The protected area was a mix of dry hills covered in oak and low areas wet from beaver and thick with cattail and willow. A mountain chickadee flew past, disappearing into an oak. I followed him off the sidewalk hoping for a better look and ran into an encampment of unhoused men. I turned around and followed the sidewalk along the edge of the wildlife area, keeping the creek to my right.

Behind the Goodwill, a puzzle of old ranch fencing spread down a hill. Most of it was barbed wire. Sheets of plastic had caught up in the wire and fluttered in the breeze like pendants. And there was trash. Trash everywhere.

I was confused as to what was the wildlife area and what was not. I slid down the slope. Apache plume and gooseberry grew next to the little pond. There was milkweed, yarrow, and the occasional Russian olive. A red-tailed hawk watched from a snag. Several Canadian geese and goslings plied the waters pushing past bobbing hunks of Styrofoam. Footpaths led from where the homeless slept to the edge of a larger pond where they took water or washed. These ponds were probably constructed many decades before for cattle. White PVC pipe scattered the grassy uplands of the wetland.

Not having $25,000 to my name—not even in my pathetic retirement account—I was not eager for a fine, so I searched for more warning signs. Seeing none, I picked my way through the wetlands, past a blue heron and a flock of red-winged blackbirds, to a series of long-established beaver ponds. Cold water seeped into my boots and up my pant leg. The blue heron did not appreciate my presence. Another one appeared, and they moved up the creek away from me.

The shopping center, the roads, and hundreds of ridiculously large houses encased the wetland. The houses were silly looking and tasteless.

A mile or so upstream I arrived at a road called Leather Chaps. I crawled over a fence and crossed the road to a cement trail that paralleled the road. A white woman in a blue coat and a Denver Broncos hat rushed over and threatened to call the police.

"I'm just looking at birds, ma'am." It was not a total lie. I kept a list of the birds I had seen in the wetland.

She grabbed my coat sleeve and pulled me down the trail to another sign, this one in red and white.

WILDLIFE HABITAT -
NO TRESSPASSING -
CALL POLICE AT . . .

Again she threatened to call the police. Again I told her I just wanted to look at birds.

"Do you know what no trespassing means?"

"Is your name Karen by chance?" I asked.

She pulled out her phone and I could see her settle in. I did not want a run-in with the cops. "You know what, Karen? You're right." I turned, walking down the path to my truck.

"My name's not Karen!" She shouted.

I came to another sign.

Preeble's Meadow Jumping Mouse
Jackson Creek Conservation Bank

The mouse, the sign explained, was an endangered species found only in riparian areas below eight thousand feet in elevation along the Front Range of Colorado and Wyoming. The area around me had been set aside specifically to protect this little rodent. A drawing of the mouse made by high school sophomore Braeden Holcombe in 2018 graced the text.

It took the US Fish and Wildlife Service (USFWS) from 1985 to 1998 to list the mouse as threatened. Getting there required multiple lawsuits from conservation organizations. It took another round of lawsuits to force Fish and Wildlife to do its job and designate protected habitat for the mouse. Even the thirty to forty thousand acres that were eventually designated were not enough for the mouse to thrive.

I found it ironic. Because we had driven this species to the brink of extinction by developing every inch possible, we had no choice but to lock up land and keep humans out. An extreme response to an extreme problem. The result, however, is to further alienate people from the land in order to protect the species. These are the constant ironies of an economic system that creates problem after problem, runs itself up against a wall, and then circumvents the wall by causing yet another problem.

Developers, in general, despise the Endangered Species Act (ESA). Admittedly, I also have my qualms with the law. Yet, it is the best and only tool we have to protect what little we have left. The ESA is constantly undermined for more economic greed because it actually works as a fairly effective science-based tool to tell us when we've gone too far. If you are pushing a species to the brink of extinction—whether it is a mouse, a grasshopper, or a large charismatic carnivore—then you have gone too far. You need to stop and do things differently. It is simple really. However, we live in a society that despises boundaries even when they make perfect sense. I mean, ours is the country where a huge number of people lost their minds because we asked them to place a piece of cloth over their face for a year to protect themselves and their neighbors from a deadly disease.

Frustrated, I followed the cement down past the houses, the auto part stores, the banks, the supermarkets, the liquor stores, tanning parlors and fast-food joints, surrounded by thousands and thousands of cars, and back to my truck, which I then added to the gut-wrenching traffic.

I turned on the heat then the radio. There was a major fire here and a tragic fire there and it was December. Another heat wave was coming to a place that should not be experiencing midwinter heat waves. A city was flooded. I turned off the radio and drove.

One ridge over from Jackson Creek another development was underway. There were spaces for hundreds more of the cookie-cutter, garage-dominated homes. Concrete curbs had been poured, streets had been paved, and the utilities were roughed in. Bobcats, bulldozers, and earth scrapers all at work. Orange pipes poked up everywhere. The fire hydrants were freshly painted. The entire infrastructure was in. The only thing missing was the houses. By the time you read this book, those homes will have been built and occupied.

Through the rest of the day, I worked my way up what remained of Jackson Creek, driving to where I wouldn't be seen, then setting off into the watershed. Return to my truck, get to the next spot, walk, and repeat. The creek ran through more oak and ultimately into an overgrown forest of ponderosa pine, the kind of overgrowth that will go up in flames one day soon.

Cattle grazed in some areas. No Trespassing signs screamed from every verge. I arrived to another stretch of wetlands where bulldozers laid out roads and crews set forms for soon-to-be-poured curbs and gutters. This was the reason we are not allowed to walk in the jumping mouse protection area.

I followed what was left of the creek through a high-end development called Colonial Pines. Jackson Creek's headwaters were a grassy gutter in a development of multimillion dollar, faux-English manor house style mansions tucked among fire-prone ponderosas.

SHOOK'S RUN

July

In the spring of 1913, a wall of water roared down Shook's Run. Accounts noted the destructive force of the roiling waters, but what caught everyone's attention was the water-driven trash and sewage sweeping away shacks, encampments, and small homes. All that trash and sewage complicated rescue efforts.

A flood on Shook's in the 2020s was hard to imagine, at least in its upper reaches. There was no water. Most of Shook's had been twice diverted in its upper reach coming off Austin Bluffs. Shook's was totally urbanized, its headwaters buried beneath late nineteenth and early twentieth century homes, streets, and public parks. A "run" is a type of small waterway, but "run" is not a term we use much in the West; it is more of an Appalachian word.

As I explored the various tributaries of the Fountain, I generally set off from where the tributary met the Fountain itself and walked upstream. With Shook's I did the opposite, starting instead from the Good Neighbor's Meeting House in Colorado Springs' Old North End. It had rained all night. The morning was humid. Drab pewter monsoonal clouds wrapped The Peak, but the rest of the sky was unambiguously blue.

I set off down the cement path, past a man on a bench sunning his belly. The trail curled a grassy parkway I assumed was the old creek bed. I walked through neighborhoods of Victorian and Edwardian homes sheltered in lofty elms and smaller ornamentals such as plum and mulberry. Flowers filled many of the yards. A woman threw sticks to her golden retriever. Two children hurled a frisbee. A man waved from a porch swing. Two joggers passed and a young mother pushed a stroller down the sidewalk, two infants deep asleep. The trail led from one park to the next, past a set of tennis courts and around a school where children played soccer in a field.

Eventually I found water. The creek appeared from a steel culvert running under East Cache le Poudre Street and spread into a shallow, sandy little channel before tumbling into a rock-lined passage ten or fifteen feet below the parks, roads, and houses. Trees sheltered the run, rendering the air cool and rich with the songs and calls of warblers, robins, pine siskins, and magpies.

"No Camping" signs appeared, tacked to metal posts or trees. I peered down into the run and saw several unhoused men, camps set just above water line. You could see how the rain from the night before had swelled Shook's, bending grasses and shrubs, pointing them downstream. I could not understand how the people camping down in the channel were not swept away. Surely their tents had flooded. Some of the encampments had clearly been there for months. It seemed a desperate and dangerous place to hide. And more rain was coming.

The trail wound through a jungle-like forest for a hundred yards or so. Shallow water, mud, and debris covered sections of the path. Green light cascaded through the leaves. A yellow warbler called. Then a Brewer's blackbird. I saw a Say's phoebe, a song sparrow. Swallows filled the air. It was hard to imagine I was in the middle of a city of seven hundred thousand or more people.

Shook's is named for two brothers from Iowa. Peter and Denton. They arrived in the area around 1868 looking to make rich off cattle. It seems that the Nuuchiu were not terribly impressed by the Shooks. They nearly got themselves killed up in South Park after encroaching on Nuuchiu hunting grounds. Later, in Black Forest, east of Colorado Springs, Peter barely escaped with his life when a band of upset Nuuchiu men came looking for him at the home of Amanda Husted. She and several other women fought a tug of war with the Nuuchiu men over Peter, preventing them from pulling him outside and killing him. It is unclear what the Shook boys did to the Nuuchiu, but whatever it was, it wasn't good. The animosity grew until the Shooks were forced out and returned to Iowa, tails tucked between their legs.

I came up from the dreamy forest through a chain of sere scrubby knolls and out to a line of railroad tracks, fences, jumbles of construction debris and a trash dumpster repair yard. The words "Good Weed" were sprawled across a building in large, neat letters. A sign on the house next to it announced "Bail Bondsman." Near there, about a half mile from the Fountain, I lost Shook's Run in a tangled maze of auto recycling shops, steel and iron recycling yards, a fortress-like enclosure of RVs adorned with Trump/Pence and Fuck Joe Biden flags, and then the Colorado Springs sewage treatment plant.

Paradise to paradise lost. I felt like Dante on descent.

I worked my way through the area, seeking a path to the Fountain, but I had no luck. Instead, I walked south, seeking Spring Creek, another Fountain tributary. The moisture-laden clouds moved down from the mountains pushing cool air. The sun faded and thunderstorms fattened to the east, swelling on evaporation from the prairie.

I followed the railroad tracks. East Las Vegas Street was too dangerous for walking. Still, there were people along the road, pushing shopping carts packed with belongings. Again, I was lost in a maze of roads, overpasses, railroad tracks, canals, power lines, homeless encampments, and dank ponds. The stench was mind numbing and the trash—literally thousands of pounds of trash—lay strewn along every route I attempted. "Route" being generous. There was no route. No way to walk. I pulled the N95 I had carried since COVID began over my face. It helped, but not much. I found my way to Spring Creek just as the clouds opened. My intention was to follow it back up into the neighborhoods, but I could not find a way to access the little waterway—and to be honest, I could not take the trash and the putrid miasma and turned around.

Rain drove the unhoused under tarps and plastic trash bags. I pulled out my umbrella and followed the tracks to Janitell Road bridge where I crossed the Fountain and descended an embankment along a string of barbed wire, onto another cement path paralleling the Fountain itself. Homeless encampments stretched for a mile or more up and downstream. The rain came in sheets. The Fountain's waters turned from a deep blue-green to a chocolaty orange. I walked upstream until I was soaked then sheltered under a bridge with dozens of still more Americans dealing with homelessness.

BEAR CREEK

June

From paradise lost to paradise gained.

That week, a soupy haze obscured downtown Colorado Springs. Smoke from Canadian wildfires dumped down the east side of the Rockies, obscuring The Peak.

Water poured from a trailer park into a narrow cement conveyance delivering directly to the Fountain. On the south end of Colorado Springs, multiple small, rancid waterways such as this empty into the Fountain, gurgling past fast-food establishments, auto body repair shops, storage units wrapped in barbed wire, lots crammed with cars for sale, and lots packed with RVs and boats. Car wash runoff ends up in these waterways. These creeks are not sewers, at least not technically, but they contain everything a sewer carries and more: oils, plastics, and needles as well as human urine and feces.

I crossed the five-lane road. A truck barreled down on me. I ran. A half-dressed woman porting dozens of plastic sacks blocked my way. "You're not going to get away with this!" She screamed. "I won't be your robot!" I stepped to the side and she swung the bags, missing. "You're microwaving my head!" She howled. "Brain eaters!"

I hit a trail into the lower reaches of Bear Creek Regional Park. Crossing under South 8th Street was like an epiphany: from a mess of obnoxious sprawlmart to a greening bliss in just a few steps. The tumult of the highways faded—it didn't go away—I don't think there is anywhere in Colorado Springs where you can escape the clamor of traffic, but it did fade.

A yellow warbler called from a gooseberry. A magpie peered from a tall cottonwood. Currents, elms, willows, and Russian olives appeared along the creek. The change was so stark I walked back and forth under South 8th Street several times, just for the experience of walking through what seemed like a door to another reality.

To my right, an expansive equestrian center covered the hillslope reaching just to the edge of Bear Creek. So close that, in a heavy rain or a spring snowmelt, horse waste flowed into the creek. Ideally, there would be a fifty to one hundred foot tree-filled buffer between the creek and the horse pens to catch and filter that run off, but there was not. North of the equestrian center, a circus tent was going up. To my left towered a massive erosional wall, testament to problems further upstream.

I sat and watched a western wood pewee pick moths from the embankment. It flew to a bare elm branch, gobbled the insect, and darted back for more. A white-haired woman with walking sticks approached. "Did you see the bear?"

I had not. She pulled her smart phone from her jeans and zoomed in to an adult black bear soaking in the waters about 200 yards upstream. I thanked her and hustled uphill. Before I found the bear another retiree approached.

"Have you seen the owls?"

I had not.

"They have babies!" After extracting a promise not to share the owl's location, she described in detail how to find them. Bear or owl? I cut off the path through a savannah-like field sprinkled with elms, to the tree the woman described. Two large adult owls, a male and a female, sat in a crook twenty feet off the ground. The tired parents snoozed, eyes closed. I snapped several pictures then sought out the babies. I could not find them so I jogged down to the creek, but the bear was gone.

Instead, dozens of children walked, hopped, skipped, and jumped down the trail toward me. They carried sheets of paper and compasses. "Does everyone have enough water?" An adult shouted. "Stay hydrated!"

They passed and I came to a stand of oaks. The broken, slurry song of a red-eyed vireo caught my ear. I stopped. The bird issued a staccato-like chatty call then crossed in front of me. Just above, a juvenile Cooper's hawk shouted for its mom. The little one did not like me around. I could not see the bird, but I located the nest high in the old scrub oak. Another young Cooper's called from about twenty yards away. The two babies shouted back and forth. I never saw the parents.

Another school group approached. The kids waved. They said they were on a scavenger hunt and one boy asked if I had seen an aster. I pointed into the grasses. "It's the little purple flower with the yellow middle."

Delighted, he raced off.

To my right, down by the creek, a girl shouted. "He threw a spider on me!" I could not see her, but I heard her. She forced an impressive glass-shattering screech from her little body.

"Jackson!" An adult yelled.

The girl screamed again and laughter warbled through the forest.

"Jackson!"

Yet another school group came down the path. I cut away, pushing through spiky locust to a broad, still pond mirroring the sky. The temperature dropped, the humidity rose, and a muskrat hurried away, paddling for the opposite shore. I had come to a series of beaver ponds tucked into the forest.

The first dam spread at least thirty feet across and three or four feet high. You could see the dam had been there for years as bright green willows grew from the mud the beavers had packed across the rim of the log and stick structure. I sat watching for the castor, but he or she never appeared. Eventually, I stepped out into the pond, balancing on logs, rocks, and stumps, picking my way upstream past several chokecherries to the next dam, this one smaller than the first. It was rimmed in a mudflat covered in coyote, cat, and beaver prints. A fox squirrel scurried down a tree.

As I moved upstream, each dam grew progressively smaller. A heron popped from a stand of flooded oaks, lifted toward me then turned downstream. The way in which the bird maneuvered the soggy forest was something to see. Its wings reached at least five feet across, yet it tucked and turned with ease as it navigated the trees.

At the Bear Creek Nature Center, a group of thirty-something fathers picnicked in the shade of a cottonwood. Strollers of sleeping infants surrounded the men, and they chatted in hushed tones, grateful for the break, sipping coffee and munching sandwiches. My kids were teens already, infancy long gone. I had been a single dad for years and remembered well what it was like to have those precious moments off. I used the bathroom, splashed my face, and hustled on. The day narrowed, and I had miles to cover.

Above the nature center, the paved road cut through a tall rock wall that had been blasted with dynamite. Three roads converged. Cars crowded the trailhead. Two men raced past on mountain bikes. A couple waved and called out good afternoon. Several young families walked up and down the lower reaches of the trail. One family used the iNaturalist smart phone app to learn about local plants. The kids raced up and down the creek, pointing the phone at a leaf or a flower then shouting to the parents. The family was still there when I came down several hours later, moving slowly, at the pace of discovery.

Past the parking area, the trail followed a steep incline along an old narrow-gauge railroad bed. To the left, a wall of giant rectangular granite blocks held back the sloughing hillside, placed at the time of the railroad.

David Burnham and I had discussed dropping our flies into those upper reaches of Bear Creek, but Colorado Parks and Wildlife put the kibosh on fishing, aiming to protect the last remnant population of genetically pure greenback cutthroat trout in the state.

The greenback was long thought vanished. Mining pollution, overfishing, and habitat loss led wildlife officials in the 1930s to declare the fish extinct. But in 2012, someone stumbled upon an odd population of trout in the upper section of Bear Creek. Genetic testing revealed the peculiar Bear Creek trout were actually genetically pure greenbacks. This was especially curious because greenbacks were not thought to survive in creeks like Bear or the countless other streams draining the east slope of the Rockies. Not to mention, Bear was nearly one hundred miles south of the fish's ancestral waters in the South Platte system. How did those cuthroats get there? The greenback probably owes its continued existence to a failed hotel.

In the 1870s, the Bear Creek route was a popular way to top The Peak. Hoping to capitalize on the increasing number of tourists headed to the summit, entrepreneur Joseph C. Jones constructed a nine-room hotel and an all-hours restaurant next to Bear Creek. He even offered telegraph service to Colorado Springs. It is unclear if the upper reaches of the Bear had a native trout population; it probably did not simply due to local geography. It's too hard for fish to mount the falls and cliffs in the creek. Jones aimed to change that however, expanding the offerings of his little resort to include high-altitude cold stream trout fishing for those who could afford it. Most likely, Jones gathered the greenbacks from somewhere in the South Platte watershed and ported them to Bear Creek in buckets by horse. The trout thrived. Jones's hotel not so much. Someone had carved the more efficient route to The Peak up Engelmann Canyon and he abandoned the lodge within a decade. Scatterings of bricks and nails and chunks of foundation are all that remain of Jones' dream.

And the fish.

The greenback is a beautiful animal. Rusty colored with the large black spots at the tail, two crimson lines across the throat, and red smears down the sides that appear as if swished with a paintbrush. The greenback's ability to alter its skin color to suit local ecosystems sets it apart from other western natives. The greenback population in Bear Creek is special because it is both genetically pure and genetically diverse. Since 2016, Colorado Parks and Wildlife has used the Bear Creek trout to successfully reintroduce the species across its native range in the South Platte watershed.

To the right, the slope dropped one hundred or more feet to the creek. The trail narrowed to just a few feet wide. The entire canyon was quite steep, producing a huge number of waterfalls in the creek bed. A large horseshoe shaped pipe poked from the edge of the trail, reaching into the creek. This too I assumed was from the days of the railroad. "You matter" and "Maria was here" were scrawled across the pipe in large, neat lettering. On top, someone had painted "Everything will be OK."

Several mountain bikers decked out in the latest gear flew down the narrow trail. After the bikers, a whole family passed on ebikes, laughing and teasing one another, plowing uphill. In a number of places, the Forest Service had placed gigantic boulders right in the center of the trail, presumably to block ATV and motorcycle access. Still, every now and again, I could see from deep gouges in the trail that a motorcycle or two had made it past the giant boulders and plowed up the path.

As I climbed, I could feel the smoke in my lungs. I coughed. My breathing was not as smooth as it should have been. Below, the city disappeared in the haze. The trail narrowed further, the wide canyon below, thick with conifers and interrupted only by outcroppings of the pink, orange, rosy Pike's Peak granite. A pair of chatty ravens played on the thermals.

NORTH CHEYENNE CREEK

February

Like Bear Creek, North Cheyenne Creek was a virtual sewer at its confluence with the Fountain. The last half mile of the tributary pushed through strip malls and car lots, nasty and rancid. I left my truck near Dorchester Park at the Colorado Springs Rescue Mission. Unhoused individuals and families filled the park. They sat in tents or lay on tarps in sleeping bags, huddled against the winter. A little girl peaked from one of the tents and waved. She could not have been more than seven years old.

I pushed on, up the North Cheyenne, into an upper-middle-income neighborhood built nearly on top of the creek constricting it into a narrow channel. A miles-long chain-link fence lined the bank, keeping people from the water. That section of the creek was all privately owned, and I had not gone more than a quarter-mile before a homeowner appeared on his deck, yelling. He thought I was an unhoused individual and railed at me about private property, respect, about getting a job, and that I should "just get out of here!" I waved politely and continued. He threatened to call the police. I waved again, turned around, and headed back to my truck.

Frustrated, I drove to a crossing near a junior high school and attempted to walk from there. Again, I met with an angry homeowner. This time, one with a dog. Again, I returned to my truck and again steered up the creek, now feeling a bit of despair. I had wanted to be out on the creek, moving through the forest, feeling the way the stream moved across the land, feeling the being-ness of the waters. This felt incredibly unjust.

At a turn out, I scrambled fifteen or so feet down to the creek, and began again. This was clearly better than facing angry landowners, dogs, and the potential of someone shooting me—a serious possibility in America of the 2020s. Still, a winding road cut the creek repeatedly. Before long, I found myself on the road, dodging cars, the drivers unable to see me around the blind curves.

For the third time that day I returned to my truck. Eventually, I parked at a wide asphalt lot rimmed with fences, signs, and a row of porta potties where Gold Camp Road morphed from pavement to rough dirt. I donned my Yaktrax and set off along the Seven Bridge Trail under that crisp blue, Colorado winter sky.

My father left the Navy in 1964 and immediately returned home to Colorado. With his brother, he bought an old miner's cabin among the ruins of Victor, once a city of thirty-five thousand people, then a ghost town of less than four hundred. They paid about $700 for the house. My brother and I spent a significant chunk of our childhood roaming the haunted gold fields, tailings piles, and crumbling buildings of the fallen city.

Victor and nearby Cripple Creek anchored Colorado's second Gold Rush in the 1890s. To get supplies and equipment to the high-altitude mines, workers laid a railway along what came to be known as Gold Camp Road. This was a "short line" train, hauling food, tools, and other supplies from Colorado Springs to Victor and Cripple Creek, returning with ore and minerals and often times bodies of those killed in the mines. In the late 1920s or early 30s, my uncle Bill's brother was one of those killed in the mines of Cripple Creek, falling to the abyss when a support plank gave way.

President Theodore Roosevelt rode the short line from Colorado Springs to Cripple Creek. He described the route as so breathtaking it "bankrupts the English language." Our family, driving up from Pueblo in our International Harvester Scout, four-wheeled Gold Camp to Victor. What I recall most were the tunnels. Three long, dark passages dynamited through the rock to make way for the train. Once inside the tunnels, my father honked the horn. The echo drove our mutt Toby bananas and the dog howled to the other side. At times, we parked before the tunnels and entered by foot in silence, listening for the voices of children. As the story goes, a busload of orphans was crushed when one of the tunnels partially collapsed in the 1930s or 1940s. When it happened depended on whom you talked to. The old lady Mary, owner of the antique store in Victor in the 1970s, told us that the kids had survived for days after the catastrophe before succumbing to the lack of oxygen. She said that if we took flashlights into the tunnel and looked hard enough, we could still see the handprints of the children on the stone. I have never seen any evidence that the story of the crushed busload of orphans was true, but it certainly unnerved me as a kid.

The climb up North Cheyenne from the parking lot was gentle at first, tracing the wide, graded narrow gauge railroad path. I saw hikers and mountain bikers despite the ice and cold, but there was surprisingly little snow for February at that elevation. That winter had been an anomaly among a string of anomalous winters. After several years in a row of below—and often well below—normal snowpack, most of Colorado had received a bounty of snow. Every river basin in the state stood well above average for February. Every basin, that is, except for the Arkansas River basin, which for some reason, had not kept pace. Bare ground marked most of the trail. Where snow did cover the gravelly soil, it was thin, less than an inch deep. Most of the surrounding spruce/pine forest was bereft of snow.

Winter. Stillness. Graffiti eyes on granite boulders. Carved names and symbols marked every aspen. Other hikers passed coming down, mostly older white people with dogs. I saw one man in his twenties, a lanky, bearded thirty-something in shorts, two middle-aged men dragging an uncooperative Chihuahua, and two high school girls training—one in shorts, but bundled around her torso. In a rare patch of snow, someone had carved a heart. A biting breeze rose then was gone. On and off, helicopters rumbled just beyond the ridge. I assumed they were all military. At one point, a Black Hawk passed, maybe two hundred feet above. The thump of the propellers rattled my head.

I passed in and out of the sun, but the higher I climbed the less light I had, the thickening forest blocking the sun and that indifferent blue sky. I crossed a series of well-built wooden bridges, the canyon narrowed and the trail grew steep. In places, the creek knocked the surface free of ice. In other spots, the water disappeared under the ice, the voice of the waters murmuring in a hollow tunnel. I could hear women somewhere off in the forest. "Wow!" said one, then they too were gone.

I resolved to go as far as I could before dark, to push well beyond the end of the trail, to scramble through the icy water and over boulders and logs to make up for the lack of walking along the creek in the city. I felt like I had cheated.

By that time, I had walked a dozen or more of the Fountain's tributaries. Every single one had proven a challenge. Not because of my will or my physical ability, but the barriers of private property, home ownership, cars, and roads. Even though I was then well beyond all that, winding up the trail into the mountains, I felt a certain exhaustion with it all.

I entered a land of rockslides and avalanches. You could see the cataclysmic remnants everywhere, great spreads of bare rock and impossibly steep hillsides of crumbling granite and fans of collapsed trees.

Well beyond the seventh bridge, the snow deepened, but only in the shadows. Where the sun hit, the trail was bare. Narrow-leaved yucca spread across the warmer south facing slope.

Eventually, I arrived where human footprints gave way to those of coyote, mountain lion, and elk. I stood in an aspen grove carpeted in knee-high winter grasses fringed in snow. Visitors had carved on every single tree in the grove, reminders of those who had climbed the trail. Some of the markings were old. Others made the previous summer. There were dates, phrases, symbols, and numerous initials.

I walked the grove with my notebook, scribbling the arborglyphs on page after page, until a breeze cut through my layers. After a day of frustrations, I was finally where I wanted to be, but the sun was about to set and I was done with the cold.

PATHWAYS

"A path is a prior interpretation of the best way to traverse a landscape."

–Rebecca Solnit, Wanderlust

A cordilleran flycatcher balanced on a narrow branch of willow. I had heard its drunken three-part call from under a bridge in Manitou Springs where I had been scouring the pink-orange gravels of the Fountain for signs of caddis and mayfly—trout food. The cold waters of the creek soothed my tired feet. Temperatures pushed one hundred degrees. Forest fire smoke from California, Arizona, Washington, and Oregon dumped over the peaks and down along the Front Range. Despite the heat, I wore a black face mask against the smog.

I trailed the bird. The flycatcher was the size of a tennis ball. He sported olive-green plumage, wings striped in black and white, and large eyes the shape of teardrops. He foraged for insects in the middle height of the willow. When he saw me, he dropped lower and closer, taking stock with his outsized eyes. Then he was back to lunch. I followed him upstream to a little park where he settled on a branch above a beaver pond.

Most likely this male had passed the winter in the forested canyons of western Mexico. I remembered seeing them in Durango and Mazatlán at Christmas, especially along the Rio Marisma below the Piaxtla bridge. In winter, they are virtually impossible to distinguish from Pacific-slope flycatchers and pine flycatchers, so I'd probably seen all three and not known enough to separate one from another. Come spring, this male would have set off north, skimming pine tops along the Sierra Madre between Mazatlán and Creel. He would have made his way through the marginally protected areas of Cascada del Basaseachi and Tutuaca, to the bootheel of southwestern New Mexico and the Big Hatchet mountains, where he would have flitted among the piñon and juniper, dressed in late-season snow, atop the layer-cake limestone cliffs of the uplift that created the isolated mountains.

From the Big Hatchets, I imagined this young male made his way among the Sky Islands of southern New Mexico to the Rio Grande Valley. He followed the big river north, crossing the Sangre de Cristo range somewhere in southern Colorado, perhaps near the towns of La Veta, Trinidad, or Walsenburg. There, the mountain chain breaks for several miles, offering easy passage from the San Luis Valley to the Great Plains. He would have followed the base of the mountains west of I-25, north to the village of Beulah west of Pueblo, the town of Florence, up along Turkey Creek, and finally to the Fountain and Manitou Springs. Here, on the eastern rim of the cordilleran flycatcher territory, he gorged and mated, his partner fashioning a cup-like nest of moss, grass, hair, and bark all bound as one with the silk of spiderwebs. Cordillera is Spanish for mountain range. This flycatcher is a mountain bird through and through. Come autumn he would set course for the Mexican highlands.

The same things that attract wildlife—water, food, shelter—attract people. For at least twenty thousand years, and probably much longer, humans have utilized the Fountain to navigate the landscape. While there is no comprehensive accounting of precontact Indigenous cultures in the watershed, meaty Clovis and elegant leaf-like Folsom spear points dating to twelve thousand years ago turn up in and around the Fountain. A major bison kill site, replete with awls, drills, points, and scrapers, sits below a series of low bluffs on one of the Fountain's eastern tributaries. I know of a collection of teepee rings on a private ranch just south of the City of Fountain. There are dozens or more of the stone circles situated on a rise with ample views of both the creek and the plains. The perfect vantage to track game and watch for threats.

The Nuuchiu, Tin-ne-ah, Numunuu, Hinono'eino, Tsistsistas, and Ka'igwu people all utilized the Fountain, the path of the waters easing routes between seasonal homes along the liminal edge of mountain and plain. The sacred waters of Manitou's boiling springs seem to have been a shared resource, a neutral ground for the various nations of the region.

Later, Euro-American colonial settlers followed the Cherokee Trail and the Trapper's Trail along the Fountain. All through the latter half of the nineteenth century, prospectors, hungry for wealth, followed the Fountain along the Ute Trail from Colorado Springs to the high-altitude gold fields of Victor and Cripple Creek.

The flycatcher disappeared upstream. I walked from the creek into Schryver Park, where a family of six picnicked in the shade. At the edge of Manitou Springs, the Fountain runs through a deep green canopy of elms and willows. The creek, lit by streaks of sun, glints from white-capped curls topping the flow. The billion-year-old granitic soils of the watershed carpet the channel bottom playing with the light and hues, the creek turning from blue to green to orange and pink, then blue again. Along the surface of the water, tranquil waves of cool air drifted from the mountains.

Giant, puzzle-piece like slabs of broken concrete—each about a foot thick, encased the creek banks. The slabs were meant to protect the riverbank from itself, channeling it, speeding up the water, and moving upstream problems downstream. Under Highway 24, a man sat in the shadows of the overpass.

In Schryver Park, beaver had ponded a rivulet seeping from

the soil. The aquatic rodent had placed an ingenious little dam underneath a footbridge. The diminutive pond was a rich gem of a wetland. A muskrat swam past. A family of mallards and a solitary teal picked at duckweed. A spotted towhee poked for snacks under a bush. The flycatcher darted from an elm to pick insects from just above the surface. I did not see the beaver, but fresh prints in the mud told me he or she was not far. Just below the footbridge, wrapped to an elm, was a Colorado Parks and Wildlife trail camera. Someone was watching the beaver. I knelt and made faces at the camera like an elementary school kid.

The beaver pond in Schryver could have grown large enough to flood the park, the parking lot, and possibly the road. Instead of busting the dam, however, CPW had installed a structure known as a "beaver deceiver."

The deceiver is a simple contraption made of pipe and wire. The pipe extends *through* the dam into the pond where a wire mesh covers the intake. The wire allows water to flow into the pipe and out of the pond while keeping the beaver from plugging the leak, which they are naturally inclined to do. The diameter of the pipe determines how much water flows from the pond in order to maintain a consistent size and volume. The system allows the beaver to retain their homes and allows humans to benefit from the critical watershed work beavers perform without threats to houses, buildings, farm fields, roads, and other infrastructure. Of course, I'd prefer to live in a world where keystone species like the beaver are allowed to do their own thing unimpeded, but that is not going to happen, at least not in my lifetime. The beaver deceiver is a good compromise, offering the sort of mutually beneficial relationships we desperately need to court with the rest of creation. That some good humans had taken the time and effort to install the deceiver instead of killing or relocating the beaver felt like an act of rebellion, an act of sanity in a nation where Wildlife Services, a federal agency, kills over twenty-six thousand beavers a year in nearly every state.

I crossed the creek and picked up a gentle gravel path snaking through a forest of deep green. At times, the path hugged the creek. Elsewhere, the two diverged, divorced by RV parks or homes. Through much of Manitou Springs, the Fountain has the feel of a waterway settlers hoped to bury. Literally. Not only does construction run right up to the edge of the creek, but the creek is locked into a cement and stone wall channel. In places, buildings were even placed *over* the creek, tunneling the waters. A sign tacked to a tree warned of flash floods. Another warning sign hung from an electricity pole. Another to a building.

This tendency to shackle rivers isn't unique to the American West. Humans refuse rivers the space they require. Then, when the rivers push back—inundating homes, businesses, and agricultural fields—people are stunned. Yet instead of learning and retreating from the floodplain, the response is almost universally to double down, totalizing the domination of waterways.

Which, of course, rarely works. Rivers have a life of their own.

I had set off early that morning from the confluence of the Fountain and the Monument in Colorado Springs. Summer edged the air, pushing it low and flat; cool at dawn, then scorching. Wildfire smoke hazed the sky, obscuring the sun.

I aimed to follow the Fountain upstream along an asphalt path sandwiched between the creek and Highway 24. I would walk as far as I could, find a place to sleep, then continue on to the town of Woodland Park, twenty-eight miles distant at the top of the watershed.

The Fountain and Monument met under a spaghetti of roads, highways, overpasses, interchanges, and railroad tracks near a soon-to-be-demolished power station and America the Beautiful Park, built atop the old Hispanic neighborhood of Conejos.

I wandered beneath the highways exploring various paths among the willows and Russian olives. Pathways turned to clipped urine-scented, trash-strewn tunnels through the vegetation, opening at the water's edge where three men sat, staring at the water. I hopped from stone to stone, moving down then upstream to the next trash-strewn path that would lead me back to the main trail. The grating drone of the traffic irritated my body.

Underneath an overpass, a dozen or more unhoused Americans gathered in the shade. One man had a shopping cart full of scavenged bike parts. He had a box of various tools and offered repairs to other unhoused individuals with bikes. Another man had a pushcart to which he had fixed a double-burner Coleman camp stove on a flat plank of wood. I had seen him up and down the Fountain for a year or more and, although gruff, he seemed quite popular. Other riparian dwellers called out his name and waved. He never waved back, but he encouraged folks to heat their cans of soup or water for instant coffee on his stove. I asked if he charged for the service. He scrunched his face and scowled. "Nah, man."

I crossed a footbridge over the Monument just above the confluence and followed a cement path under I-25 and then along the Fountain. I picked my way through a dozen or so tents and shelters. An angler, fully decked out in hundreds of dollars in gear, cast for trout at the base of a low pool. At the top of the pool, several men and a woman washed their clothes in the Fountain's waters.

The creek was thick with willows but there were no trees. In spots, the willows had been burned in ten- to thirty-foot-diameter smears. On the right bank, across from me, a crowded trailer park spilled along the creek bank at the base of a massive hill of old mine tailings known as Gold Hill Mesa. The trailers were unpainted, cracked, and patched with duct tape, random chunks of wood, nails, and rope. Cars, many of them clearly broken, packed the creek's edge. The scene was medieval in its squalor. On the hill, mansions towered above the trailer park.

Just past the homeless encampment and trailer park, I came to a beaver dam and a wide swampy area jammed with plastics, shopping carts, busted appliances, and other trash. It reminded me of places I had visited in Haiti. The heat squeezed the stench of landfill from the pond. I pulled the COVID mask over my face to cut the smell but immediately began to sweat into my own mouth. The path cut away and crossed Highway 24 into an older working-class neighborhood dotted with car repair shops, boat and RV storage yards, and storage units wrapped in barbed wire.

The path widened. It did not always parallel the creek and I found myself frequently diverted, working to stay as close to the creek as possible. I put in my ear buds to deaden, somewhat, the roar of the highway. Where the creek entered private property, I ducked into the willows, stepped into the water, and hustled to the next road. In two places, I felt too exposed to trespass and stayed along the path or street.

On one of these diversions, I stumbled upon a triangular little parking lot full of people living out of their cars, vans, and trucks. They roasted hotdogs together over a fire on the pavement. Crows, magpies, and ravens picked at piles of trash, reeking in the heat. I waved at one man and he waved back. The dashboard of his beat-up Ford F-100 held a display of two dozen some well cared for paper coffee cups. An impressive pile of newspapers, magazines, books, and clothes filled the passenger seat. Two small flags hung from the truck's antennae. One, the yellow Gadsden flag, stated DON'T TREAD ON ME. The other was a Trump/Pence banner.

The Fountain ran shallow, constricted into a funnel forty to fifty yards wide, crammed with trees. The Fountain's floodplain had been bulldozed for the highway, parking lots, and shopping centers. Our creek's new bank was made of simple construction fill. Signs also littered the creek.

NO CAMPING
NO LOITERING
CLIMB TO HIGHER GROUND IN CASE OF FLASH FLOODS
ADOPTED by so and so
DOGS MUST BE ON LEASH
PICK UP EXCREMENT

Tacked to trees, dozens of orange paper notifications spread along the Fountain, warning unhoused people to move on. Gifts from the Colorado Springs Police Department's Homeless Outreach Team (HOT), the notices ordered folks to remove their camps within twenty-four hours or face action. Each notice carried a list of official grievances against the squatter, as if anyone struggling just to survive day-to-day could care a lick about this ordinance or that. Most of the notices were fresh, posted and dated within the previous four to five days.

A woman had set camp about forty feet from one of the notices. I turned, walked two blocks to Colorado City's main street, bought two large coffees, and walked back to the woman.

"Coffee?" I offered.

"Too goddamn hot for coffee. But you're a fucking saint. Won't say no. Can't say no! I need a little get up and go this morning."

Thanks to the HOT notices, the woman had relocated that morning before dawn. It had taken three trips to get all her things. She was just one hundred yards or so upstream from her old camp.

"They want me out but they want me to go . . . where? They're playing whack-a-mole. Chase us out of one place and we show up somewhere else. Cause what else choice do we have?" She sipped the coffee. "I get it. We're an eyesore. We stink. We make the city look bad. But I don't got nowhere else to go. If they don't want us down here, they'd better build some fucking housing, huh? How about that? Build some fucking housing I can afford and I'll get off the fucking streets." It was the same justified rant I'd heard dozens of times up and down the Fountain at that point.

Not twenty feet from her camp, cars idled at a drive through bank. More cars lined up at the Starbucks next to the thriving little tourist strip that is Colorado City. Further upstream, visitors crammed the Timber Lodge, the Buffalo Lodge, and the Mecca Motel. One place offered a creek-side patio where visitors sipped coffee and tea, feasted on ham and cheese omelets, huevos rancheros, or steak and eggs. An unhoused couple with a small black puppy maintained a camp just below the patio.

All through Colorado City, the Fountain is confined to a hidden, narrow channel. It makes an excellent hiding place—or an excellent place for a city to hide those it does not want to have seen. That day, I counted more than three dozen homeless encampments between Colorado Springs and Manitou Springs. One Dickensian camp, just behind a Sonic, sheltered at least thirty people, including children.

From your car, you might not even know the Fountain was just a few feet from Highway 24, which parallels the Fountain from The Springs all the way to Woodland Park, then up and out of the Fountain watershed to Leadville and the wealthy playgrounds of the Vail Valley. Colorado Springs, Colorado City, and Manitou Springs have grown together, creating one long urban corridor strung out along the Fountain.

Moving along Highway 24 by car tricks the mind. It feels as if you are in a tunnel or a funnel perhaps. Instead of the open road, the highway is claustrophobic. This is true of any high-speed road. Driving alters our visual interaction with the landscape. For most of us, thirteen to fifteen frames per second is all the visual stimulation our minds can process. This translates into about seventy miles per hour. Beyond that, our brains are overloaded by stimuli and begin to close off, limiting visual inputs by dumbing down the world outside our rolling box. Houses, trees, fences, crosswalks; all blur forming a single wall in your brain, hence the sense of moving through a tunnel or tube. Crowded roadways amplify the impact on the driver. Surrounded by other cars, the mind narrows still further, focusing on what is directly in front—not bikes, not pedestrians, not wildlife, and certainly not dark creeks hidden in trees.

Traffic safety experts have noted this driver impairment since the 1950s. It is one reason why high speeds and crowded roads result in more accidents, injuries, and death. But our car obsession does more, impacting economies and our very understanding of the world around us.

Transportation planning 101: wider roads and increased speeds kill local businesses. For a number of years, I lived in the north valley of Albuquerque, New Mexico. My casita sat close to 4th Street, a road that had, once upon a time, been a thriving, walkable commercial district lined with dozens of locally owned businesses. At some point, the road was widened, car speeds increased, and the sidewalk narrowed—in some cases to barely a foot wide. Planners assured business owners that more traffic equaled more business and so most of them supported the road expansion project.

Just the opposite occurred. With sidewalks all but gone and cars moving faster, potential customers could no longer easily locate the tailor, bakery, tamale shop, or other small business they were looking for. Slowing down to find parking became a hazard. Customers could not get in and out of their cars and get into the local pet store or TV repair shop. Within a few years, 4th Street went from a bustling business district to a cemetery of zombie storefronts. Today, drivers whiz through the dead zone, unaware of the cultural and economic loss sacrificed to more cars and higher speeds.

In this sense, our car-dominated culture benefits national

chain stores at the expense of locally owned businesses and economies. If you can no longer walk or bike to a local business, you are likely to go elsewhere. If you drive but cannot slow down enough to find the small business you are looking for, or to turn into a tiny parking lot, you will naturally keep moving to a shopping center surrounded by wide roads and ample, large parking spaces. Economics is so often sold to us as if we are all "rational actors," but there is little rational when it comes to the economics of cars. We know that the most thriving of local business districts are the ones without cars. "If you're a small business advocate," a community activist once told me, "and you fight against walkable, bikeable cities, then you're failing small business."

Experiencing the world from behind the wheel even influences our judgment and perception of people and places. Driving cuts us off from the information we need to adequately judge and assess our surroundings. And it's not just the speed. A number of studies found that drivers tend to view less affluent and less familiar neighborhoods more negatively than people who walk or bike those neighborhoods. The inverse is true when it comes to more affluent areas. I think about this when I talk to people dealing with America's housing shortage. From behind the windshield, those individuals appear to most Americans as subhuman, targets of disdain and criticism. When you actually get out of the car and have a conversation, human beings unexpectedly look very different indeed.

It makes sense. Strapping yourself into a closed, three-thousand-pound hunk of steel and fiberglass removes you from the information you require to make fully informed decisions. "I like walking because it is slow," Rebecca Solnit wrote. "And I suspect that the mind, like the feet works at about three miles an hour. If this is so, the modern life is moving faster than the speed of thought, or thoughtfulness."

Cars reinforce our tendency to make quick judgments

that confirm long held biases. Driving, as opposed to walking, removes you from human-scale interaction, connection, and empathy. We are all going too fast to see, comprehend, appreciate, and understand the world around us. We are going too fast to give any thought to our place in the world, which, I suspect, is why so many people who live in the Fountain watershed do not seem to know there is a river there, often just feet away. I too prefer walking, precisely because it is slow.

Seemingly random footpaths cut from the main trail through Manitou Springs. I followed them through the riparian area, allowing the paths to choose me. Mostly, they lead out to apartments or a home. Sometimes they led to sheltered terraces adorned with plastic lawn chairs. I returned to the main path.

Clearly, this path was an afterthought. It crisscrossed the flow to avoid private property. It bent to the will of hotels, motels, RV parks, restaurants, parking lots, tchotchke shops, and homes crowding the creek. The path struggled to find its path. There were sections of the creek flowing through a canopy of trees and stretches where the waters rushed between cement and stone walls or tunneled underneath homes and businesses. In several spots, the path climbed away from the Fountain and became a sidewalk packed with tourists before dipping back down into the trees.

The path ended abruptly at the edge of a packed parking lot. I made my way through the penny arcade and a collection of mechanical airplanes, space ships, dragons, and giraffes. Children swarmed the toy machines, racing in and out of the arcade. Two heavily tattooed women in yoga pants and tank tops walked past. They each carried a snake. One of the reptiles was a giant yellow and white boa wrapped around the woman's neck, its curious head dangling to her ankles. She asked if I wanted to pet him. I did. She offered me a joint. I declined. A man with a guitar and a chained pit bull yelled at someone in a car. A truck eked forward in the traffic blasting *Outkast*. A group of kids danced and yelled to the driver to turn it up. A trans woman sang Willie Nelson next to a gurgling fountain. People passed, pushing popcorn, saltwater taffy, ice cream, and funnel cakes into their mouths.

The path rejoined the Fountain, passed through a park then disappeared into a road construction project on the west end of town. Men and women laboring in the heat snickered and pointed at the tourists and merry makers.

I found a new path and returned to the Fountain. This one was different, thin and ephemeral and, like the creek, it edged the road and the parade of cars. Back among the trees, the flycatcher called. It was the same slurred trill I'd heard hours before on the opposite end of Manitou Springs. The new path disappeared and I stepped into the creek, cold water filling my shoes. There was no in between: it was either walk in the water or walk in the road. The choice was not hard.

I'd come to Manitou just a few days after the collapse of a condominium in Surfside, Florida. At the time, eleven bodies had been recovered. One hundred fifty residents remained missing. Some speculated that sea level rise may have contributed to the structural breakdown of the building. Eventually, ninety-eight people would be confirmed dead. Several were never found. A direct link to sea level rise was never proven. There were many issues at play, but the connection between America's aging infrastructure and climate change was at least on the table for consideration. That day, temperatures neared 120 degrees Fahrenheit in the Pacific Northwest and British Colombia. Nearly two thousand people would die of the PNW heat wave before it was over—the deadliest weather event in Canadian history. The heat of 2023 and 2024 was still to come.

I peeked in one of the tourist bars. On the screen, children in Portland, Seattle, and Vancouver ate ice cream and played in the sprinklers. It was one big party, not an emergency. Some news reports mentioned the role of climate change in the heat dome parked over the PNW, but precious few. A different heat wave crushed Massachusetts. Siberia was quite literally on fire. An oil well in the Gulf of Mexico suffered a ruptured pipe. The ocean burned. In broadcast drone footage, tugboats squirted sad streams of water on what seemed the very gates of hell itself. In the Atlantic, storms built as if it were August not June. Hurricane Ida was still to come. The December Midwest tornado outbreak was still to come. A Texas ice storm was still to come. The Delta variant of COVID was on the march but had yet to reach the murderous climax it would hit later that summer.

My friend Frank linked me to a meme on Twitter. In it, Bart Simpson complained, "This is the hottest summer of my life!" Homer Simpson leans close. "No son, this is the coldest summer of the rest of your life!"

That week, the weight of the climate emergency was crushing. It felt like an apex, an inflection. But it was all inflection points anymore. Mitch, Katrina, the 2003 European heat wave, Sandy, Deepwater Horizon, the floods in India and Bangladesh, Haiyan. Every damn day was an inflection point.

But there, in the little mountain tourist haven of Manitou Springs, traffic stood bumper-to-bumper from one end of town to the next. Blissful tourists ate ice cream and cotton candy while packing the streets, bars, cafes, and shops. COVID raged and smoke filled the air, but I don't think I saw a single mask all day. It felt like nothing was wrong. Everything was just fine. Everything *would be* just fine. Nothing was out of place. Nothing except everything.

Above Manitou, a heavily bearded man walked down the road,

weaving between the cars. I heard him coming from the creek. He wore an orange winter hunting cap despite the heat and carried an overstuffed backpack. A mandolin dangled from his neck. He yelled at the cars.

He asked where I was from. Pueblo, I said. He told me he had lived in Pueblo when he was a kid. That was on the East Side. Near the Fountain. Then his family took him to Missouri for high school. "My Auntie is still down there." He asked how Pueblo was doing.

"Pueblo is Pueblo, no?"

He nodded. I felt as if he were assessing me, making sure I was safe before asking what he really wanted to know. I must have looked like I could handle it.

"So . . . is that big old alien spaceship still hanging over the creek? The one with the octopuses?"

"I don't know about that."

He asked if I knew about the vortex on the east side of Pueblo. I said I did not. He told me his homies called him "East Side Jesus." Then he quoted from Revelations. "The sun turned black like sackcloth made of goat hair. The whole moon turned blood red. The stars in the sky will fall to the Earth. Every mountain, every single mountain will be removed from its place."

He told me that these were the end times. I must have nodded agreement because he pointed at me. "See? Even people like you know it. Science people. Right? You're a science person but you still know it. Even you know it. We've killed off all the birds. We're done."

"Birds are powerful," I told him.

"That . . . that is exactly why they want to kill them all!" He put his index finger into the air and told me that he had come up from Missouri a few days before. He said he had family members on the mountain. He pointed towards The Peak. He said they had put his father in chains and then they put him in jail and then they killed him. He said they kicked his other family members out of their houses and stepped on them. "They were attacking my family! I had to come!"

Who were they? I did not ask. "What did you find?"

"They're all gone, man! They killed my whole goddamned family!" He cried. Then he explained how, just the other night, a spaceship appeared over The Peak, and a host of giant cephalopods poured from the ship like rain, pulled the birds from the trees, and ate them. Or crushed them. Or stepped on them. Maybe all of it. I couldn't be sure; he was talking so fast by that point I struggled to follow. Agony drowned his eyes.

The cephalopods came from New York City, China, Russia, and Saudi Arabia, and he had to get back to Pueblo to fix something, but I didn't understand what exactly he had to fix. He was angry. He pulled his beard and paced. "Then there came flashes of lightening, rumbles, peals of thunder and a severe earthquake. A great city will split into parts," he preached, again from Revelations. "We're gonna crush ourselves!"

He fell silent, stomped his feet and drank from a plastic water bottle. He seemed embarrassed. "It's too late, man," he whispered. "We're already too late." He apologized for taking my time. I wished him good luck. "We'll need it," he said, and East Side Jesus went downstream. I went up, walking in the creek through a culvert and under another bridge. When the creek narrowed, tumbling over boulders, the flow grew too strong for walking. I scrambled up a slope to a parking lot.

"You here for the falls?" A man asked. He wore a navy blue baseball cap that said "Vietnam Vet," a service ribbon dividing the words. His vest announced "Volunteer" and he seemed excited, happy to see me. He waved for me to follow, asked if I'd like to make a donation, then directed me up a short path to a woman with a bullhorn. The path was new, cement, and defined by a neat stone wall on either side. The previous path had washed out in the 2013 flood the woman told me.

Ahead, teenagers scrambled across the rocks and splashed in the Fountain. Behind the teens, the creek poured through a narrow cut in the red granite and decomposing sandstone, tumbling thirty or so feet into the sandy channel below a rough looking arched overpass built in 1932. Officially, the area was known as "Rainbow Falls." Locally it was known as "Graffiti Falls," and indeed, graffiti covered the lower support pillars and bridge arch. Much of the paint scrawled across the bridge in a messy jumble. But some of the artwork was extremely well done, particularly a growling pink dinosaur, the face of a green-eyed, crying black woman, and an olive crocodile sporting a crown. There were words and phrases: Rook, The Earth Without Art is Just Eh, We the People, It was the government, Fuck Shit Bitch, This, Trixie, Help, Fuck COVID.

You could see that county workers had tried to remove the paintings at some point but it was unsuccessful, the result being layer upon layer of incomprehensible color. "It's a shame," the woman with the bullhorn approached.

"I kind of like it."

She frowned. "Don't like nature much, do you?"

I shrugged.

Then, the sky opened. A frigid rain drove us to shelter in the little hut near the entrance. "Wow!" The Vietnam vet ran in last.

It was too crowded for me. I left the hut and made for the Fountain. "Don't get killed!" The veteran shouted.

"Thanks!"

I hid from the rain down among the willows. The Fountain rose, covering the footprints I had made in the red gravel not thirty minutes before. Lightning flashed. Peals of thunder echoed down the canyon. Perhaps, I wondered, East Side Jesus was not so crazy after all. I hustled back down the road and into Manitou. The rain was torrential by then, pooling in the streets, soaking my clothes. Tourists scrambled for shelter.

I stepped out of the rain into a bar, shook the water from my pack, and ordered a sandwich and a chilly, hazy IPA. Immediately, I caught a buzz. I watched the rain. The song *A Horse with No Name* came on the radio. I found it depressing. The sandwich was very mediocre. I was the only one in the bar wearing a mask. I felt like an idiot and took it off, telling myself I was fully vaccinated. Only the beer, at least, was good so I ordered another.

When the rain stopped, I crossed the street for an espresso to battle the beer. A piano sat in the middle of the sidewalk and a man sat at the keyboard playing Handel's *Water Music*. He was filthy and barefoot and spit crusted in the corners of his mouth. His long fingers flowed across the keys in practiced, masterful strokes. I was astounded at the speed with which he made the high keys trill. It was not quite the same as the flycatcher trill and yet I could not help but think of the bird.

I walked on. The sun poked through the clouds.

The sky cleared and the humidity poured from the cement and asphalt in right-hook like waves. The smoke returned. I dropped to the shaded path next to the Fountain. A small girl in an orange dress had stacked large leaves from a plant that reminded me of rhubarb. Her father watched from the shade. She picked one oversized leaf from the pile, took a small stick, placed the stick in the center of the leaf, and set the leaf into the current.

DISCARDED

"Anyone who has ever struggled with poverty, knows how extremely expensive it is to be poor."

–James Baldwin

It rained just after noon. I opened my umbrella and followed the cement path from America the Beautiful Park in downtown Colorado Springs to the edge of the Fountain. Thunder rumbled to the north. The Fountain pushed her banks, muddy and swift, swollen with rainwater.

Just below the park, dozens of unhoused Americans eked out a fragile existence between the water and the Interstate. Under a bridge, I passed six people heating cans of soup on a Coleman stove one man ported in a wheelbarrow.

There were more unhoused people under the South Tejon Street Bridge. Dozens. They waited for friends. They waited for an aid worker from the mission who would bring toiletries. They waited for the shelters to reopen. They waited for housing vouchers. They waited for paperwork. They waited to hear about jobs. They waited to hear about addiction treatment options. They waited to hear about mental health services.

A Colorado Springs Police Department van crept down the trail. A lifetime of unpleasant encounters with law enforcement left me skittish when it comes to cops. I pulled out my smart phone, ready to document police abuse of the homeless and spread it all over social media. Instead, the cops handed bottles of water to the unhoused folks living along the creek.

"You okay?" one of the officers asked me.

"I am," I said, surprised. "Thank you."

"Careful down here," he said. The van made its way north along the bike trail.

I walked south. Just past the Nevada Avenue bridge, a man pushed a shopping cart overloaded with bags and bottles, a stove, cans of soup, a sleeping bag, and buckets of knickknacks. The front wheels caught in a crack in the cement and the cart tipped, crashing to the ground, spilling the man's things across the path. Together, we gathered his stuff and got his cart upright. He told me how he was trying to get a phone so that he could get into transitional housing. He needed to have a phone both for the housing and for a job he applied for. But he couldn't get one. No one would cash his COVID relief check because he did not have an ID and he could not get an ID because he did not have an address and he couldn't get the address because he needed the phone.

We maneuvered the cart down the trail, then down an embankment to an eroding edge, overhanging the frothing waters of the Fountain about ten feet below. There, the man had carved out a home of sorts. He told me his name was Jerry. He'd hung a lantern in an elm. A small American flag dangled from a string stretched between two other elms and over his tent. He'd dangled Mardi Gras beads from all the nearby branches and had pounded a mailbox atop a post into the dirt. His set up was neat. Tidy.

"It's all I got," he shrugged. "At least for now. I figured, if I'm going to live by the creek I might as well make it nice. I keep my area clean. The cops appreciate that. They don't harass me. I hung that American flag up there to make the cops think I'm conservative. You know how they are."

Jerry saw the flag as a sort of protection. A shield. Sometimes, friends would write a note or a postcard and put it in his mailbox. A smile filled his face when he told me. "The cops said I could stay for now, as long as I keep my area clean and stay away from the tourists. But the tourists don't come to the creek. They don't wanna see anything dirty."

Stories matter. Listening matters more.

One October morning, I joined a crew of thirty-some people at a Loaf-n-Jug convenience store on the north side of Pueblo. It was Creek Week and folks all up and down the Fountain volunteered to clean various sections of the waterway. Ours was a mile long segment on the Fountain's east side.

Attached to the Loaf-n-Jug was the Riverside Bar and Grill. In high school, a female friend waited tables at the grill, serving drinks despite being underage. Closing up was her job so my friend Mike Montez and I picked her up on late Friday nights. As payback, she snuck crates of beer from the bar. We sat in camp chairs in the parking lot, drinking, talking shit, and pitching the empties over the edge, down towards the creek. I do not recall how long we did this, on and off for a least two years.

That October morning, I grabbed a pair of gloves, several trash bags and bee-lined it to where I knew my thirty-year-old empties would be. It was time to clean up after myself. The bottles lay, half-buried, on a slope covered in some sort of spiny weed. The labels had all worn away but I knew what they were: Miller Genuine Draft, Corona, Tecate, and Bartles & Jaymes. I cringed.

An older woman joined me. Combat boots encased her feet. She wore thick Carhartt pants and a conical rice hat that cast a shadow across her entire upper body. She said she was thinking of keeping bees and that she had planted her yard with native flowers. "Where did all these bottles come from?" She asked.

"Stupid teenagers, I guess."

"Well, I hope they had fun."

"I bet they miss those days." I opened a third trash bag and filled it. This could not possibly have all been mine . . .

We finished with the empties and turned to cleaning up an abandoned homeless encampment. Another woman and three middle school girls arrived. They were part of a local 4H club doing a community service project. "Drugs and alcohol," the 4H leader said to the girls. She scanned the bottles in the dirt. "That's how you end up homeless."

"I think it's a bit more complicated than that," said the prospective honey farmer.

The 4H woman cut her off. "We gotta shut down the shelters and that soup kitchen," she said. "We're just enabling them. Giving them money? That's got to stop. It keeps them from working."

She went on and on, wondering why people experiencing homelessness couldn't just get a job, why they couldn't just get an apartment. "There's plenty of empty apartments in this town!"

"I don't think . . ."

"You got to stop helping them 'cause it keeps them from getting work."

The bee-lady looked to me, helpless.

I shook my head. A lifetime of collecting stories told me that the 4H woman had never once listened to a person dealing with homelessness.

"Stories embody reciprocity," wrote architect Charles Hailey in *The Porch*. Hailey and his family lived, on and off, for several years in a small cabin on Florida's Homosassa River. A tiny, screened-in porch hanging from the house became a sort of lab for Hailey from which he explored the interface of home and the world beyond. "The edge of nature," he called it.

The family once sheltered several shipwrecked tourists on that porch. All afternoon, over streams of coffee and cookies, they exchanged tales of lives lived and experiences had: where they had gone, why, when, what they had done and how it all altered the course of their lives. They told each other how they learned this or that and why they chose to do things one way and not another.

These are the stories that help us make sense of the world. They draw us in and hold us because they emphasize community and connection. Relationships. Stories open doors to fresh ideas and new ways of understanding. Stories give meaning.

Reciprocity is the act of taking as well as giving back in equal measure. Stories then, Hailey holds, are a way of both seeing ourselves and allowing ourselves to be seen. Stories are a reciprocity of acknowledgment. Stories help us build relationships, share power and alter the narratives running about our brains through the experience of sharing. Stories are a way of saying: 'Hey, I'm human, just like you.'

Author, farmer, and environmentalist Wendell Berry pointed out that while humans and nature are two different beings, they are indivisible. How then, could one tell the story of a creek without the voices of its human inhabitants? These are after all, stories of place.

Estimates of the number of unhoused Americans varies from six hundred thousand to more than two million. Some 2.5 million American children experience homelessness at some point each year. Colorado has somewhere between ten thousand and fifteen thousand unhoused individuals. There are an estimated one thousand plus unhoused people in Pueblo, two thousand or so in Colorado Springs. These are surely undercounts. Firm numbers are hard to come by due to the different definitions of homelessness and the difficulty of getting an accurate count. In many cases, the problem is a straightforward unwillingness to know how large the problem might be.

There was a 6 percent increase in unhoused Americans between 2016 and 2020. Officially, about 25 percent of unhoused Americans are employed full-time. Another 40 to 60 percent are part-time employed or float in and out of work. My experience listening to people experiencing homelessness along the Fountain is that the percentage of unhoused people that are full-time employed hovers around 50 percent. These are working people unable to afford housing.

According to the United States Department of Housing and Urban Development, almost half of unhoused Americans lived outdoors. As of 2024 there were more people in encampments than there were in shelters. Outside, weather extremes impact the unhoused far more harshly than it does the rest of us. Heat waves, rain, cold, insects, flooding, and in the near future, wet bulb, a condition where excess heat and humidity cause the human body to literally burn up from the inside. Since 2015 there has been a marked increase in heat related deaths among the unhoused in Arizona and Nevada. Climate change will only make this worse.

—

Two cops sat vaping in a police car behind the Target in Pueblo. They ate licorice and drank sodas. They looked like sweaty sausages in an oven. It was a few days after the Creek Week clean up. "Can I help you?" The driver sucked his vaporizer and smiled.

I told them I was heading down to the creek to interview some of the people living there.

"We'll need you to stay out of there for now," he said.

"It's just too dangerous at the moment," the other cop chimed in. "They got animal control down there. Bulldozers too. You can look, just don't go past the sidewalk."

Crews from Pueblo Parks and Recreation, CDOT, and the PPD were on scene with Bobcats, front-end loaders, and dump trucks to clean out the riparian forest. They had given several days' notice to the people living by the creek before the cleanup began.

I thanked the officers and walked over to where an unhoused man corralled three shopping carts overflowing with possessions. I recognized him as Michael. I had listened to him several months previously. Michael sported holiday lights and several incandescent light bulbs on his vest and around his waist. The lights plugged into some battery pack in his pocket and he was lit like a Christmas tree. Michael said the city crews had been nice enough to help him gather his things and clear out, but he had been living down along the creek for so long he had no idea where else he would go. "Once they finish the cleanup, we'll all just move back down here anyway," he said.

Another man joined. He spoke rapidly and waved his arms around. I could not make sense of what he was saying. I asked his name but he did not respond. He had five dogs, all on leashes. The dogs danced around the man, wrapping him in the leashes. He skillfully dropped the leads, stepped from the web, and regathered the leashes. They wrapped him again and he repeated his escape. Then again. It was like a finely choreographed dance. He asked for help. Michael and I pushed his wheelbarrow out of the cleanup zone. He also had a children's bike trailer, stuffed with his things. The two men headed north, dogs trailing.

The situation along the stretch of Fountain running from behind the Target and Goodwill, from Highway 47 on the north, south to the Highway 50 bypass, had become untenable. The trash, drugs, fires, violence, and rabid dogs had business owners demanding the City of Pueblo do "something." Anything.

And it wasn't just the unhoused folks. Construction companies, trash companies, and independent contractors used the Fountain as an illegal dumping ground for construction debris and household waste. Part of the cleanup involved the placement of several giant boulders along the edge of the riparian zone to block trucks from dumping trash.

"They city gave everyone a warning but they didn't give them any options," a woman from Parks and Rec told me. "I don't understand why the city didn't open a temporary shelter. Just a week or two would have been enough."

This was an area I'd visited the year before with a crew from the Pueblo Rescue Mission. We had delivered backpacks full of food and hygiene products and information on where and how to get free vaccines for COVID, the flu, pneumonia, and Hepatitis. Some of the people living in this stretch had fenced off their areas. These were mostly clean, orderly. In one encampment, a vegetable garden flourished. But overall, the situation was nothing short of horrific.

While overloaded front-end loader after overloaded front-end loader crawled up out of the willows and tamarisk, two teams of animal control officers searched the area. They wore red shirts and black pants and asked me to stand clear. A rabid dog had bitten someone. Or two dogs. "There's kind of a pack running around down here," one of the officers told me. "The operators are having a hard time seeing," she said. "Not to mention the dogs, nails, broken glass, and the needles. We're pretty worried about safety."

I did not bother telling them I had been prowling around on and off down there for years.

The front loaders filled a waiting line of dump trucks. Plywood, mattresses, shopping carts, blankets, sleeping bags, busted and burned tents, and endless black bags of trash. The heavy equipment tore through the vegetation, carving out new, wide roads in the riparian zone. Usually, this would infuriate me. But that section of the Fountain's forest was such a disaster, there was really nothing else to be done.

I called Posada of Pueblo, a housing organization helping people get back on their feet. A woman told me they had a three- to four-year waiting list and that there was a whole mess of paperwork involved. The Pueblo Housing Authority had a three year wait. Mental health services? They essentially don't exist. Getting treatment for substance use disorder (SUD) is just as hard if not more so.

Inpatient drug and alcohol centers can be several hours' drive away—and expensive. Other detox facilities only accept private insurance—something no one living on the banks of the Fountain has access to. The few places that do accept Medicaid or offer free services are so booked out, someone seeking help would have to wait months, if not years, for treatment.

"It doesn't work that way," a woman named Bonnie told me. Bonnie had camped in her pop-up trailer down by the creek for three years waiting for housing. She survived off a small pension from the school district. "When you see a person ready to end their addiction, you don't tell them, oh, honey, we'll have a place for you in May or October or next February! No! You got to jump on that opportunity. You ready to get off drugs right now? Let's do it. Right now. Right now. Get them while they are ready. In two, four, six, eight months they'll be dead. I've seen it too many times."

Over the years, I'd spent hours and hours listening to stories from homeless people. Everyone I listened to focused on just how difficult it was to get on your feet.

"Do you know how goddamn hard it is to get a job?" Jerome lived in a drainage tunnel on the south end of Colorado Springs. When I met him, he had been trying to get paid work for over a year. No luck. "These places want you to have a permanent address when you apply. Permanent address? Like what, the drain under Nevada by the Wal-Mart? Right. Then you need a phone. You gotta have a phone to get a job, but then you hear people complaining because a homeless person got a phone. Can't win for shit. So to get a job you need a home, a phone . . . you need a car 'cause the bus system is total shit. You can't have any addiction, no mental health stuff, no gap in your resume, and on and on. Dude, we all got mental health issues. This is trauma, man, day in and day out. You may not have mental health issues when you land on the street, but you certainly will have mental health issues within a month. Oh, and a shower and clean clothes. Shower and clean clothes? Fuck, dude. I live on the fucking street. You want me all washed up? I told this one place I applied to that if they just let me keep some clean clothes at the store and let me hose off out back—like I was trying man!"

"What did they say?"

"No. Of course."

Jerome's eyes filled with the weight of it all.

"Get a job, you can't have a job, get a phone, oh look a homeless guy with a phone, get clean but walk five miles across town to get a shower—right. They make it impossible for us to get off the street."

What do we value? When it comes to people suffering through homelessness along Fountain Creek, what you hear more than anything else is exasperation. Exhaustion. The people living by the creek are tired. Local businesses are tired. Residents are tired. The police are tired. ER staffers are tired. Mission and shelter workers are tired. The situation has become so extensive and so intractable that everyone is pulling their hair out.

And yet it isn't complicated. Homelessness is a housing issue, pure and simple, and yet we refuse to build enough housing, we refuse to build enough treatment centers to help people get clean, we refuse to create enough mental health assistance. Compassion grows to exasperation, which becomes frustration then resentment.

Unhoused people living by the Fountain have a big negative impact on the creek, but what are the options? Get them out? To where? Push them even further to the fringe? Cities across the country are creating and enforcing laws against homelessness. Denver enacted a camping ban in 2012, hoping to push people experiencing homelessness out of the city. Instead, homelessness has only increased. In 2023, a Pueblo city councilor proposed a camping ban claiming, falsely, that there were enough shelter beds for all of Pueblo's unhoused. The ban became law in early 2024. Statements like that make clear that many elected officials have no clue just how bad the problem has become. Camping bans not only don't work; they are barbaric. To outlaw homelessness without providing housing is nothing short of performative cruelty.

Someone once pointed out that we treat the dead with far more attention, honor, and care than we do those that are alive and right in front of us. You cannot just push the dirt under the rug. Waterways have become places where we discard human beings we do not want to see, people that are somehow considered "dirty" by social norms. In this case, the "real dirt" is our treatment of our fellow human beings.

It is safe to say that most Americans believe that unhoused individuals and families somehow deserve their fate. Accusations range from poor economic choices to laziness to immoral behavior to crime and drug use. Even disabled people in America are blamed for their condition. Our society refuses to accept that we allow homelessness to happen. Our society has chosen to put as many barriers as possible in front of unhoused people and when they then "fail" to succeed, we blame them. Fault them. Label them as unworthy. Most of the people I see laying Byzantine barriers and a maze of demands in the path of homeless people would themselves not be able to overcome those barriers. Victim blaming is a national pastime.

Late April.

I wrapped myself into several layers of coats. A breeze blew out of the northwest forcing men, women, and a few children to huddle in blankets outside the Pueblo Community Soup Kitchen. They ate donuts and yogurt, downing hot coffee from Styrofoam cups. One woman did not like all the sugar. It made her shaky, she said. She would prefer some protein in the mornings but there was not another option.

Across the street, a blue and white trailer connected to a fire hydrant with a thick, yellow hose. A line of men and woman waited outside, eager for a shower. I walked over and introduced myself.

"We're from one of the Catholic churches." Wayne wore a thick brown and gray flannel. He opened it to show me a purple t-shirt that asked, "What would Jesus do?"

Wayne explained that the City of Pueblo and the United Way had joined to find money for the shower trailer. Once a week, they set up at different places around the city offering showers and haircuts to unhoused individuals.

"So? What *would* Jesus do?" I asked him.

Wayne smiled. "Well, I don't think he'd be preaching. Preaching doesn't do anyone any good. Acts of love says it all." He pointed to the trailer.

Wayne explained that his coalition had received enough money to purchase the trailer but not enough for operations and maintenance. The Pueblo Fire Department allowed them to use the hydrants, but the trailer ran, more or less, on donations from the community. "During the winter, the Methodist church downtown offers showers," he said, "but it's just not enough to meet the need."

Inside the soup kitchen, Helen Benevides fielded phone calls, receipts, and food orders. The lack of cooperation between the service providers for Pueblo's unhoused frustrated her to no end. "I got a million donuts but what I want is fruit. The shelter got boxes of apples that they can't use, but I can't get anyone to bring them over here and now they want money? Come on."

Blessed with an extremely foul mouth, Benevides ranted like a machine gun on full auto. “We serve around 150 people a day. It goes up and down but that’s the average. I feel good about the job I do. I’m living to make other people’s lives better. But it takes its toll on you, I tell you what.”

Benevides listed the things unhoused people need most: water, socks, sunscreen, tents, sleeping bags, bug spray, tampons, toothpaste, Band-Aids, and foot powder.

“We don’t really know how many homeless there are in Pueblo. The last official count was in 2019, but even that was considered an undercount. They did it at night for some reason and it was very inaccurate. “I’d guess there are more than a thousand unhoused people just here in Pueblo. Springs has more. Fountain too. Manitou and even up in Woodland Park. And more people show up each day. We’ve got a van outside right now, showed up yesterday. A mom, dad, and three kids. The dad has a job but they can’t afford a place to live. The mom had a mental break down. She is in crisis. I’m trying to get her a counselor to talk with. And without a home, they can’t get the kids into school. You’d be surprised how many homeless people have jobs. Real jobs, real money, but they can’t find a place to live.”

Benevides explained that many of the shelters and transitional housing programs require people to be off drugs and alcohol. However, she said, they are missing a step. In order to get clean, you need shelter first; you need the basics—a place to live—and only then can you start dealing with your addiction or mental health issues.

“They got it backwards,” she told me. “Housing first. You know, we’ve got two empty K-Mart buildings and an empty grocery warehouse over there on Prairie Avenue. Why doesn’t the city get people in there? ‘Cause they don’t care enough.”

There were solutions, Benevides told me, but they were complex and expensive and, as a society, she said, we simply don’t value human beings enough to solve the problem. "You're never going to totally end homelessness. Nobody is saying that's a realistic goal. But what we *can* do is massively reduce the problem."

Benevides railed against the externalized costs of not caring for people. From the perspective of the local governments and businesses, it was cheaper to put people on the streets. It saved the government money and kept taxes low. "But the need remains," she said. "The cost remains. So, who picks up the tab? Churches, volunteers, non-profits, foundations . . . our elected officials cover up their failings by relying on the generous people of this community who have a conscious." She pointed at the line up of people arriving for food. "These are human beings we're talking about here."

FLOW

"All men are equal before fish."
–Herbert Hoover

David Burnham gave a woot. I pulled the fish to the net.

I'd been meeting up with Burnham about once a month to fish different sections of the Fountain. We'd dropped flies all through Manitou, pulling in small, but aggressive, rainbows and brookies from the shallow pools in the middle of town. We hit every hole between Gold Hill Mesa and the regional youth sports park, where the bigger fish hung about. Navigating the trash and the encampments was challenging, but the fishing was worth it.

I slid the barbless hook from the fish's lower lip. We measured the rainbow at slightly more than twenty-two inches, then I held him in the flow until the sleek salmonid was ready to return to his frothy hole, just below the confluence of the Fountain and the Monument. The trout rested, then slid from my hands with a subtle bend of its muscled body.

Not long before the onset of COVID, a bearded army vet from Pueblo, Alan Peak, took to posting images of Fountain trout on Facebook. Followers were incredulous. Few imagined trout in the Fountain, much less a relatively healthy population of fifteen, twenty, or twenty-two-inch rainbows right in the center of Colorado Springs. Before long, other anglers, including yours truly, were posting Fountain fish photos on Facebook.

Peak thought the Fountain was a tragedy and he wanted the creek cleaned up. His idea was that if people appreciated the Fountain as a trout fishery, maybe the creek would get the respect it deserved as a vital waterway. He took to posting pictures of needles, trash, and homeless encampments alongside the fish photos. Before long, Peak turned up in newspaper articles, pushing his vision, a celebrity activist for the creek.

David Leinweber, owner of the Angler's Covey flyshop, (and later Colorado Springs city councilor) was one of the few not surprised by the fishy Facebook celebrities. "I always suspected that, with just a little support, the upper Fountain could be a small, but top-notch, fishery. The lower sections closer to Pueblo are too warm for trout but up here? We have opportunities," he told me.

The Angler's Covey sat on a flattened and paved pile of road fill between Highway 24 and the Fountain in Colorado City. In 2020, Leinweber signed a five-year lease with the city of Colorado Springs to rehabilitate a small section of the Fountain just below his shop. Fed up after a fire at a homeless encampment threatened his store, Leinweber fenced a quarter mile stretch of the creek and ejected the campers. Meanwhile, inside the shop, he took to raising rainbows in a giant tank provided by Trout Unlimited. "I'm going after a permit to put rainbows in this section of the creek," he told me. "Like the junior high kids up on the North Cheyenne."

Leinweber led me down a short, steep path to the water's edge, where his crew had cleaned out the trash and introduced rocks and downed trees to the creek to mimic a more natural system, habitat for the trout. Leinweber's goal was to create an outdoor classroom where local students and anglers could learn about aquatic insects, fish, habitat, and water quality. "We got to treat this creek better than we have," he said. "And it's going to take a lot of work."

—

The Fountain was never a trout stream. At least not for the rainbows, brookies, and browns snagged by Alan Peak, David Burnham, and myself since around 2017. It is possible that some sort of cutthroat trout—the Hayden Creek, greenback or yellowfin, or a now extinct species—inhabited the cold and bubbly upper tributaries of the Fountain prior to colonization. However, even that is debatable. There's no evidence for this. Remember, the hotelier hauled the greenbacks to Bear Creek in buckets from the South Platte River. Although the Fountain begins high in the mountains, for most of its trek to the Arkansas River it was traditionally a sultry, sporadic plains stream dominated by warm water Cypriniformes, a ray-finned order of fish comprising some 4,500 species including flathead chub, fathead minnow, longnose dace, central stoneroller, red shiner, sand shiner, and the like. Others, the green sunfish, Arkansas darter, and the black bullhead catfish, were also time-honored members of the Fountain's ecosystem.

For the flathead chub (officially a state "species of special conservation concern") the Fountain is somewhat of a stronghold. The fish's numbers are in decline statewide and while the palm-sized, pointy-nosed chub shows up in the main stem of the Arkansas River in small numbers, it has disappeared upstream of Pueblo Reservoir and has seen drastic declines downstream of John Martin Reservoir. The chubs overwinter lower in the Fountain system, from Piñon to the confluence, but non-native predators just downstream in the Arkansas hit chub hard if they venture much beyond the Fountain's junction with the Arkansas.

If the Fountain is somewhat of a fortress, protecting the chub from extirpation, or local extinction, it is an imperfect fortress. Flathead chub numbers in Monument Creek have dropped significantly since 2000. No one has seen chub in Monument Creek since 2010. The fish barely hangs on within Colorado Springs. The non-native trout are the likely culprits for these declines, munching minnows and fattening on chub fry. Where we find brown trout, we don't find flathead chub. Still, the biggest challenge facing the chub are the diversions, erosional channelization, PFAS, mercury, selenium, and, most significantly, human created structures blocking migration.

Alex Jouney, the Arkansas Basin Native Aquatic Species Biologist for Colorado Parks and Wildlife (CPW), compared the chub to Pacific salmon. Just as the ocean-going salmon makes its way upstream to spawn, so too do the chub and other native Fountain species.

The life cycle of the chub, Jouney explained, remains poorly understood. We know that they prefer to spawn in open water as opposed to the nest-like structures utilized by some species. Their buoyant eggs drift downstream with the current and hatch while drifting. Young chub are weak swimmers and rely on the current to keep them afloat until they are strong enough to manage. Once they are developed enough, they will migrate back upstream to their natal spawning grounds, thought to be along both Monument Creek and the Fountain in and around Colorado Springs. Migration typically takes place from March to August with the highest numbers of migrating fish seen in June and July.

But. Human created barriers placed into the Fountain over the years block migration. One CPW study found flathead chub moving up to 20.5 miles (33km) in the Fountain while the average trip is more like one to eight miles. Without the concrete barriers, Jouney thinks the chub would probably move much further on a regular basis.

More is known about the Arkansas darter, another finger-sized, mayfly-munching native that tends to prefer spring-fed tributaries, utilizing the main stem of the Fountain more for dispersal than year-round habitat. The darter migrates less or not at all. These fish spawn from late February to July depending on water temperature. They prefer cool, shallow waters flowing over sand or gravels, making tributaries such as Jimmy Camp Creek an ideal location. The pollution-sensitive darter seems to be persisting—but not thriving—in its tributary fortresses. The constant threat of dewatering hangs over many darter populations.

"We need fish passage structures for native species," Jouney told me. "We have to increase connectivity in the system for the chub and other natives to power on. My hunch is that if we alter or rework the barriers and restored connectivity all the way to Monument, we would see native fish populations rebound over time."

Meanwhile, in the muddy, orange-tinged waters south of Piñon Road and north of Pueblo, the little fish is thriving. "It's a killer system south of Piñon," Jouney said. "A system that works as it should." And it works because in that part of the Fountain, water flows relatively unimpeded.

There has been some progress when it comes to relinking fish habitat with more to be done. For years, the Owens-Hall diversion just north of Clear Springs Ranch blocked access to spawning grounds for the chub and other species. The dam fed cooling water to the Ray Nixon Power Plant, but it impeded native fish migration. Fisheries biologists observed desperate chub attempting to jump the diversion. Few succeeded. The masses of trapped, confused fish became a killing pool, a massacre, when herons and egrets turned up to feast.

Then, in 2015, Colorado Springs Utilities, CPW, and other stakeholders constructed a winding, six-foot-high, fifty-foot-long fish ladder at the diversion site. Known as a Longrie-Fectau fish passage structure, the modular, prefab contraption was set at a 2 percent grade that would allow the fish to zig-zag their way upstream to spawn. The passage mimics, somewhat, the rocky bottom of a creek, with stones and pools for the fish to rest in as they battle their way north. Subsequent research found that at least four native species successfully navigated the passage, making their way at night. More research is needed to get a better handle on the structure's effectiveness, Jouney said, but it seems to be working quite well, especially for the chub. "We are finding greater numbers of flathead chub above the fish ladder compared to before its construction."

Unfortunately, there are a slew of structures above the Owens-Hall diversion that are essentially Berlin Walls for native plains fish, the Chilcotte diversion being the most egregious. Jouney, CPW, and CSU aim to construct a fish passage at Chilcotte in 2024 or 2025. Then the next spot. And the next. Eventually, Jouney hopes, the Fountain's fish will be able to traverse as much of the riverine system as possible.

The fish passage structure doesn't just benefit the fish. From an ecological perspective, intact fish habitat encourages overall biodiversity, which helps the whole system to function. One of the oft-forgotten central goals of conservation is to keep common species common.

The State of Colorado steadfastly manages the Fountain as a "native system" to protect aboriginal species despite calls to make it more of a trout sports fishery. Yet conservation is about compromise. "A trout fishery in Fountain Creek in Manitou or upstream of there would be a great way for folks to get involved in caring for the Fountain," Jouney told me. "The main stem of the Fountain below Monument Creek, however, should remain a stronghold for native fish."

That said, Jouney and CPW do not advocate removing the trout from the Fountain. Not only is it unfeasible, he says, it just isn't worth the effort or the potential controversy. "I'm not too concerned about the urban trout," he says, "They're just barely getting by, they're not thriving. It's not the right habitat."

Jouney explained that my world record trout was not likely reproducing in the pools below America the Beautiful Park due to various habitat constraints. Most likely, the trout found in the Fountain lay their eggs in the upper tributaries—North

Cheyenne, Ruxton, Bear—where the fingerlings wash downstream with spring melt. The human-made barriers blocking both tributaries and the main stem of the Fountain keep the trout from returning upstream to better habitat. Although recent data shows the trout population on the upswing, the days of dropping a fly in the Fountain right in downtown Colorado Springs are probably limited. It won't happen immediately, but it is on the horizon. Trout prefer cold water. As the climate warms, the water warms. Trout numbers around America the Beautiful Park will most likely decline while native species that prefer warmer water will, ideally, thrive.

It's not just fish. Fountain Creek is a major natural wildlife migration corridor linking the Great Plains to the peaks of the Rockies. Nearly all wild animals—fish, birds, insects, mammals—move or migrate to survive. Some move up and down daily between ecotones, seeking food and water. Others travel hundreds if not thousands of miles back and forth between habitats depending on the season. Rivers are natural corridors funneling wildlife from summer to winter habitats.

One might think that the Fountain is rich with birds. And in a way, it is. But only in the sense that a half-emptied library might feel rich after thousands of books have been ripped from shelves and tossed to the bonfire.

Again, shifting baseline syndrome or "environmental generational amnesia," the diagnosis that what we today consider healthy, thriving ecosystems, are anything but. Species endure as a shadow of their former selves. Our idea of what is "natural" was forged in an already impoverished world. Since 1970, the world's wildlife populations have plummeted by an average of 60 percent. Once common animals have become rare. Once rare animals have simply disappeared. What we consider "normal" when it comes to wildlife populations would be thought of as degraded by our ancestors' accounting. My grandfather was an avid outdoorsman, an angler mostly, but someone who thrilled in seeing birds, pronghorn, and elk. I sometimes imagine him, brought back from the dead, standing in his yard in Pueblo, listening and wondering: where did all the birds go?

My children, much less my grandchildren, will never hear the cacophony of birdsong I experienced as a kid, just as I can barely imagine the wealth of bird life my grandparents knew, not to mention what people saw on a daily basis prior to colonization. Since 1970, the year I was born, one in four North American birds has simply disappeared. That is an estimated three billion breeding birds. Ponder that. There are three billion fewer birds in North America in 2023 than in 1970.

Bird populations are crashing worldwide. I first noticed it while tracking wolves and lynx in the Slovakian Tatras in 2014. The forest was silent, the sort of silence that screams. Without birds there was the feeling that something vital was missing from the landscape. At the time, I wrote: "A number of people in both Austria and Slovakia have told me this was normal, that the birds had moved on for the winter [it was October] . . . it was just that time of the year . . . but that didn't compute for me because I had seen plenty of birds through the autumn and winter in the 1990s when I spent a lot of time hiking the Swiss and Italian Alps."

I wasn't mistaken. A University of Exeter study revealed a significant drop in Europe's bird populations. An estimated 421 million individual birds disappeared from Europe between 1990 and 2015. Forest monocultures, agricultural intensification for biofuels, and outdated "cultural" hunting practices all to blame. The European Union's Natura 2000 Initiative proved woefully inadequate to deal with the disaster since it focused narrowly on protecting rare species instead of taking a whole ecosystem/habitat approach, thereby condemning the most common species to a death spiral.

I have watched, recorded, and photographed birds throughout the American Southwest for almost two decades. Since about 2015, I have seen that flocks are smaller, visitors to my yard fewer, and birds are generally harder to find. Western meadowlark numbers, for example, have dropped 37 percent. Piñon Jays that once flocked to my feeder by the dozens have all but disappeared, their population plummeting by some 85 percent. Tragically, few people other than active bird-watchers and researchers notice the change.

Urbanization and development, oil and gas operations, expanding farmland, buildings lit at night, and wind turbines all contribute to the decline in birds. Domestic cats are another challenge, killing millions of birds each year. However, by far the largest problem facing North America's birds is climate change.

Colorado is warming and drying out. The state's average annual temperature has increased 2.5 degrees since 1920 and is expected to increase by five degrees before 2050. Heat waves are more common, snowpack is declining and melting earlier in spring. Droughts wrack the region with increasing frequency, drying soils, and exploding forests. Wildfire season has expanded from three to seven or even eight months a year and there is simply less water in general. Wildlife populations struggle to deal with these changes.

Memory is unreliable. The tragedy of shifting baseline syndrome is that we've grown blind to the enormity of the loss occurring right before our eyes. We don't see it because we aren't paying attention.

One of the reasons for this book was simply to bear witness, to record as accurately as possible what I saw, heard, and experienced throughout the Fountain watershed in the early 2020s. Listing or otherwise recording the plants, birds, and animals I experienced forced me to pay attention. It forced me to notice the world around and to interact with it—and to find some gratitude and appreciation for something beyond myself.

I also felt that I owed a record to my children, grandchildren, and beyond. I owed them a record of the world as it was so they could better comprehend what has been lost, or what might be regained. Without a record of the past, without an understanding of history, we lack direction for the future.

In *Braiding Sweetgrass*, the Potawatomi biologist Robin Wall Kimmerer taught us to live for the other, to be worthy future ancestors. In the story of Skywoman, Kimmerer explained, the grandmother, knowing her progeny would inherit the world focused her time, not on herself and the whims of her own wants and desires, but rather on acts of reciprocity, a way of interaction with the land, the water and the future that helps define Indigenous. "For all of us," Wall Kimmerer wrote, "becoming indigenous to a place means living as if our lives, both material and spiritual, depended on it."

Running right at the edge of the mountains and plains, the Fountain facilitates wildlife migration. Yet, the Interstate parallels the Fountain from Pueblo to Colorado Springs, while state Highway 24 sits almost directly atop the creek all the way to Woodland Park. The interstate is a four- (sometimes five or even six) lane strip of cement and asphalt.

Road ecology is the study of how our transportation infrastructure shapes the natural world and road ecologists have likened interstate highways to a moving wall, a fence made up of three- to four-thousand-pound hunks of steel, fiberglass, and plastic careening along at seventy-five miles an hour or more, blocking wildlife movement from the Fountain corridor to the mountains. Few animals can make the crossing and although there are a few too narrow culverts allowing *some* passage and, recently, the addition of some wildlife fencing, I-25 between Pueblo and Colorado Springs and Highway 24 from Colorado Springs to Woodland Park remains a wildlife nightmare. CDOT data from 2022 list mountain lions, porcupine, deer, hawk, fox, raccoon, skunk, pronghorn, bobcat, coyote, elk, and more all killed by cars on I-25.

For wildlife, America's car culture has proven catastrophic. An estimated 350 million vertebrates die each year on America's roads. Deer, elk, moose, wolves, coyotes, bears, eagles, snakes, turtles, toads; for insects, the numbers are far higher. This slaughter has grown so atrocious that entire wildlife species are being driven, quite literally, to extinction. Roads are wildlife-killing machines.

It could be worse. Because the interstate parallels the Fountain instead of crossing the creek for most of its route, the impacts to wildlife are, while still horrific, less horrific than along the I-70 corridor in north-central Colorado. I-70 is an east-west running behemoth, bisecting numerous major migration routes, resulting in thousands of animal deaths per year. Four of Colorado's threatened native Canada lynx have been killed trying to cross I-70. Traffic can run so thick along certain stretches of I-70 that some wildlife avoids the moving wall all together, resulting in death from starvation, population decline, and lack of suitable mates. Several wildlife crossings are planned, but they are incredibly expensive and an engineering challenge. Still, they are worth every penny. The fact is that well-built and properly-placed crossings work extremely well.

A still bigger problem for the wildlife of the Fountain watershed are the utility scale solar power installations spreading across southeastern Colorado, eating up critical wildlife habitat just east of the Fountain south of Colorado Springs. Panels, access roads, weeds, lighting, utility lines, and security fencing all negatively impact both habitat and migration routes from grouse to plover, from raptors to pronghorn, from bats to burrowing owls, kit fox and black-footed ferret. Solar energy is touted as "green," and it might be, done in another way. But at utility scale it is anything but green. As of 2023, solar development has eaten up around

100,000 acres of southeastern Colorado with hundreds of acres impacted within the Fountain watershed. CPW has developed a list of best management practices for solar developments, but the benefit of those guidelines to wildlife seems minimal at best.

The Fountain exists, and will continue to exist, within a human-dominated Anthropocene landscape in which a million people and our cars, highways, parking lots, stormwater runoff, pollution, gas stations, unhoused compatriots, pipelines, strip malls, and cities shape everything from how rivers flow, to how wildlife moves, to what we drink and think, and how we comprehend the world around us.

By 2030, cities will cover approximately 10 percent of the earth's surface. Solar panels will cover millions of acres. Roads will devour still more. The State of Colorado aims to add over two hundred new lane miles to its roads by 2030, resulting in an additional seventy thousand cars on the road. This runs counter to the state's climate goals, wildlife protection goals, and transportation goals. And yet, as of 2023, that's the plan. If we want wild animals to survive—and I most certainly do—we will have to learn to live with them. Some wildlife can adapt to us. Chicago's coyotes, the leopards of Mumbai, and Manhattan's red-tailed hawks attest to this. But only to a point. For most species, survival will depend more on humans adapting to wildlife than wildlife adapting to us.

"It's a lovely, babbling brook," Kellina Gilbreth pointed to North Cheyenne Creek, "until it isn't."

We stood in crusty, ankle-deep snow in the purplish gloam of a January evening. The creek was low and iced over, but you could hear the gurgling hiss and whisper of the water sliding beneath windows of glaze and rime. I'd met up with teachers Gilbreth and David Eick, plus Jerry Cordova—the guitar-playing, stormwater education coordinator for CSU—at the edge of North Cheyenne Creek, just a few days after my attempt to mount the stream on foot. Like all Front Range creeks, this Fountain tributary could be as fickle and bombastic as the Fountain itself. After all, this was the creek that washed poor Ronnie White away in 1965. On September 13, 2013, it flooded again. A foot of water dumped from the sky in just twenty-four hours and the North Cheyenne burst its banks drowning seventy homes, a school, and sending local residents scrambling for sandbags.

"People think, hey, it would be really cool to have a house right on a lovely little creek. But then you have to deal with reality." Gilbreth, a tall woman with flaming red hair and an authoritative teacher's voice taught science at Cheyenne Mountain Junior High School on the southwest side of Colorado Springs. She also ran the Cheyenne Creek Conservation Club, otherwise known as Creek Club.

Creek Club, an after-school enrichment program, dated to 1996 when Gilbreth's predecessor, David Eick, rounded up a group of students who'd been exploring the creek on their own and were excited to learn more about their backyard brook. Colorado River Watch, and later, Trout Unlimited and CPW all jumped at the opportunity to support the early STEM program.

"Of course, we have the usual . . . you know . . . people who are scared of everything . . . trying to shoot us down," Eick said, his breath billowing white. Too many people worry about kids falling, getting a scrape or a bruise, he explained. "But how else are they supposed to learn?"

Eick was an admirer of Dr. Lloyd "Pappy" Shaw, a teacher, principle, and superintendent in Colorado Springs from around 1916 to 1951. He was all about science and getting kids outdoors. He believed children should know their own backyard, scrapes, bruises, cuts included. Shaw was also a sort of ethnologist, a collector of folk music and folk tales, and is widely credited with the revival of square dancing across the US.

The kids in Creek Club had the opportunity to grow proficient with basic watershed science. They measured streamflow, water quality, aquatic insects, pH, dissolved oxygen levels, and how to count fish populations, all while being active and outside. The kids also learned how to track and record their observations then submit data sets to CPW, helping to inform waterway management. They also kept it clean, roaming up and down the creek, gathering trash. In 2019, Creek Club took to raising rainbow trout in a giant classroom tank donated by Trout Unlimited's "Trout in the Classroom Program," a similar operation to the one running at Angler's Covey. The kids had hoped to raise native cutthroat trout but were turned down by CPW with the excuse that natives were too fragile. With all the human alterations to the creeks, native trout just weren't native anymore. A transformed stream required transformed fish species, a thought that struck me as both logical and incredibly sad.

Regardless, CPW supported the rainbow work and the kids dove in. I peered into the tank. Hundreds of trout fry schooled in black clouds of fins, studying me with curious fish eyes. Come spring, Gilbreth's crew would deposit the fingerlings into the creek. A few of those trout would end up in the pools below America the Beautiful Park, edging out the Cypriniforme natives, but most of them would stick to North Cheyenne Creek. When I asked Alex Jouney about it, he wasn't concerned. "It's a worthy trade off," he said. "The educational benefits far outweigh any damage the rainbows will do."

The temperature plummeted and we made our way back to the classroom. "I wish I could do Creek Club all day every day," Gilbreth said. "This is the kind of teaching that excites me as an educator and gives the kids interesting, real-world experience." The problem with teaching, Gilbreth said, wasn't the poor pay, but rather the way the system stifles creativity. "More than anything, I want to do cool and exciting things with the kids. The kids want to do cool and exciting things with their education.

None of us want to be stuck in the classroom." In 2023, Gilbreth left the junior high to take on the position of Middle and High School Content Specialist for Colorado Parks and Wildlife, leaving Creek Club to the next mentor and extending her outdoor science education reach statewide.

In May, on the last day of school, I rounded up my dad. We drove to Colorado Springs and met Jerry, David, and Gilbreth upstairs at the junior high. The classroom swarmed with purposeful pupils, scooping trout with nets from the tank, lowering them into buckets of creek water bubbling from battery-powered aerators. The seventh and eighth graders measured the junior fish, recorded water quality and temperature, and after my dad and I lifted the buckets into two wagons, the kids carefully hauled the fish down the hall, down the elevator, and across the street to the water's edge.

The creek rushed past, effervescent, not in flood, but swollen with snowmelt. A reporter from the *Gazette* turned up, as did some school district bigwigs, a representative from Trout Unlimited, some parents, and several CPW biologists clad in waders.

The snow was gone, ice long faded, the day warm and green and full of potential, as are all spring mornings. Sweetness hung over the water, a flower in bloom I could not see. The fish release took on a party-like atmosphere. There was singing, shouts, laughter, and a hell of a lot of picture and video taking. The focus of the kids impressed me most. They had taken ownership over the project. They had become loving mammalian fish parents. They took the science seriously. They took the trout seriously. They cooperated. And they were hilarious, cracking absurd joke on top of absurd joke. The kids are all right, I thought. Better than all right.

One by one, the students scooped the pinky-sized rainbows into plastic cups and dribbled them into pools and eddies at the edge of the flow. Some of the fingerlings disappeared instantly, headed downstream. Others hung on, adjusting to the new temperature, the rush of the creek, and the whole new world they were about to enter.

PALIMPSESTS

"A new future requires a new past."

–*Eric Foner,* Reconstruction: America's Unfinished Revolution

Mama looked at me and growled.

"Knock it off." JoJo gave a light jerk to the dog's leash and pointed at the ground. Mama sat, then growled again. "Sorry about that, sir."

"She still doesn't like me." I had met Mama several times at that point. She could be friendly but standoffish, and at other times, overtly hostile.

JoJo gave the dog a treat and rubbed her ears. "This is the kinda dog that would help some robber, then attack the cops. Huevón. But I had her since she was a baby. Can't dump her now. I love her, sabe? Come on, I'll show you where the white lady was."

JoJo Trujillo led me to the Fountain through a war zone of busted and shredded trees. You spend any amount of time by the Fountain coming and going at different times of the year and you see that someone is always mucking about in the riparian forest. Now, someone had used a bulldozer to mow decades-old cottonwood and elm, snapping them off several feet above the ground, leaving the fall like a box of dropped matches. It looked, quite literally, like the Ardennes, circa 1918.

JoJo was small, bent, and wiry with a mouth devoid of teeth.

His eyes beamed, mesmerizing. JoJo was seventy-one years old and had lived his entire life next to the Fountain on Pueblo's lower East Side. His mom was an Aragon from Trinidad. His father hailed from the San Luis Valley and his grandfather had worked at the steel mill for over thirty years. JoJo raised ten kids, not all his own, working as a cowboy and ranch hand. He was worn from years of toil. I had met JoJo and Mama the summer before, then kept running into them.

"I'll pay you one hundred dollars to spend the night down here." He scowled then laughed. "Well, I don't got no pinche one hundred dollars, but I wouldn't have to pay you anyway, white boy."

"Why not?"

"Because." He stopped. "You wouldn't live to see the morning."

Mama growled. I knew it was mostly bluster. From both of them. Still, a shiver raced up my spine, despite the heat.

In the middle of the creek, a woman bathed a dog. On the opposite bank, a fight broke out among the creek dwellers and someone threatened to pull a gun.

JoJo let go of Mama's leash and turned to face me. He made a cup of his right hand, squeezed the fingers tight, then slapped the palm of his right hand with the thumb of his left hand. "Do like this. If you don't, she will turn you into like this." JoJo closed his eyes, tilted his head back and let his tongue loll out.

"Dead?"

He nodded and picked up the leash. The first time JoJo saw the white lady, he was about seven years old. She scraped on his window at night and when he looked, she waved for him to come outside. JoJo thought she was in trouble and he woke his parents. His father pushed the couch in front of the door, turned on all the lights, and loaded his pistol. He sat in the room JoJo shared with his brothers until dawn.

The next time JoJo saw the white lady, he was with one of his brothers. They had walked home from their auntie's house on Goat Hill, crossing the Fountain on planks of lumbered wood. His brother panicked and ran. JoJo couldn't keep up. In painful detail, JoJo described the frigid touch of the white lady as she grasped at his arms and legs. I shivered again.

He shook his head. "That's when my friend's abuela taught me this." Again, he performed the odd hand gesture then forced me to practice it ten times before we went any further.

"But it's the middle of the day!" I protested.

He frowned.

"What about this?" And I made the sign of the cross.

His frown deepened. He shook his head. "You think that Catholic horseshit gonna help you? This is the real world, huevón. Do it again."

I repeated the hand gesture.

Around 1960, JoJo said, the white lady took two kids from the neighbor's house, tied them in a gunny sack and drowned them in the Fountain. Another time, she pushed JoJo's father into the quicksand. JoJo found him, exhausted, sinking, buried to his chest. He and his mother rescued him with a horse, some branches, and a rope. On one winter night, the white lady scraped the window. They called the police. They police panicked and shot the woman. JoJo grabbed my arm fixing me with his gray eyes. "The bullets went right through." He re-enacted the scene. "We ran for the house, locked the doors, and turned on all the lights. The cops spent the whole night in our house they was so scared."

JoJo said he had collected stories of the white lady from people who lived along the Fountain. He had a notebook. I asked to see it. He said it was buried in a box. He had packed his things. He would run out of money by Labor Day and the thought of being homeless frightened him.

"I'm old. Can't work no more. Never made enough to save anything." He said he might go to the towns of Trinidad or Raton where housing was cheaper. Or maybe his daughter would come get him and take him to Phoenix. "But I don't want to go to Phoenix," he said. "It's not home."

JoJo led me along the creek bank, pointing out the location of each sighting of the white lady until we arrived to a train bridge crossing the Fountain. 1931 announced a metal plaque on the abutment. He told me to make the hand gesture. I did so and we walked under the bridge.

"This is where she lives," he whispered and bent down next to Mama. A thin whine eked from the dog.

I shivered again, but it might have just been the sweat trickling down my spine.

"Tienes miedo?"

"Well, I'm not going to spend the night down here."

"Told you."

The absence of La Llorona in the Craigin manuscripts is curious.

Between 1902 and 1916, Francis Craigin, erstwhile professor of geology at Colorado College, conducted hundreds if not thousands of interviews with old timers—farmer settlers, Indigenous warriors, traders, soldiers, miners, explorers—and their friends and families, for a massive and comprehensive history of the southern Rockies. It was a visionary work of unclear purpose.

The Rocky Mountain Library, as it was to be titled, would be a series of thirty-six chapters or volumes covering the years 1200 to 1880 and, from what I could tell, would be comprised largely of oral histories. The volumes were to carry names such as *Chichilticalli and Its Inhabitants 1200–1400*, *The First Glimpse of Colorado 1541–1779*, *The First French Fort in Kansas 1736–1751*, *The Fabry Fiasco 1741–1742*, *Jimmy Camp: The Fancies and the Facts 1836–1865*, and so on.

After an ownership dispute involving a large meteorite found in Kansas, Craigin left his lucrative position at Colorado College, invested all his savings into his new endeavor, and ultimately failed to realize his vision. The Craigin Collection, despite the best efforts of mother-daughter historian team Dorothy Price Shaw and Janet Shaw Lecompte (not to mention the curators at the Pioneer's Museum in Colorado Springs), was a mess.

As Craigin travelled up and down the southern Rockies from central New Mexico to southern Wyoming, he collected oral histories on the inside of used envelopes, the reverse of old letters, discarded letterhead from an assortment of failed businesses, old petitions, the margins of newspapers, and even on the saved exam papers of his former students. Without a clear plan for his notes, Craigin stuffed the interviews into various accordion-type folders labeled, roughly, along his proposed volume outline. Much of his scribbling is illegible, inverted, upside down, snaking along margins with seemingly random arrows and even, as Lecompte noted, "superimposed upon other writing." The chapters he was able to assemble were sprawling first or second drafts, heavily edited with deletions, additions, pieces of notes cut, trimmed, and glued here or there, and other chunks, torn from the page and re-glued somewhere else.

JoJo's white lady was, of course, La Llorona, the tragic sometimes malevolent spirit of a mother who drowned her children in spite against a cheating husband. In other versions, she discovers her children accidentally drowned next to the creek bank and kills herself in grief. The story takes a variety of forms, but suffice it to say, La Llorona haunts creeks, rivers, and acequias from Colombia and Venezuela to Pueblo and Colorado Springs, including the Fountain.

As far as I could tell, La Llorona makes no appearance in any of the existing Craigin manuscripts. I'm not saying she isn't there, I just couldn't locate her if she was. I find this curious for three reasons. First, the tale of the wailing ghost is perhaps the most ubiquitous story in the region. Second, Craigin spent extensive time collecting stories in the Hispanic communities of New Mexico and southern Colorado. Finally, while Craigin has been labeled a "kook" and a "crackpot," he was a brilliant, curious man, notable, Lecompte admits, for his "attention to detail and absorption in small historical puzzles."

So why no La Llorona?

Craigin, unlike his immediate predecessor, historian Hubert Howe Bancroft, did not set out to write a sweeping high-level history of the American West. Instead, Craigin appears to have focused on average Jane and Joe, Josefa and José. Craigin sensed the end of an age. The old-timers were dying and he sought to seize hold of and immortalize the experiences of a quickly passing generation in a massive body of stories. As LeCompte noted, Craigin was intrigued by "irrelevant hooey" instead of the grand sweep and significance of Rocky Mountain history. Craigin sought genuine human experiences over myth. Craigin wanted human stories. He sought to understand what was important to the storyteller and how a regional culture developed from memories, and to understand how that new regional culture supplanted, intermixed, or was influenced by millennia of Indigenous cultures.

"Sex."

I attended Central High School in Pueblo in the late 1980s. My memory is faulty, but this is how I recall the first day of high school history. Mr. Frank Graves, a bald, somewhat rotund Army vet blessed with an infectious smile, stood at the front of the class. The first word out of his mouth was "sex." If there is any more effective way to catch the attention of twenty fifteen- and sixteen-year-old kids, I haven't found it. The uncomfortable, eager silence was deafening.

Sex, Mr. Graves told us, was the root of all history. It was not only what created us as a species and as individuals, but sex sent armies to field, settled long-simmering disputes, inspired the greatest of poetry, music, and visual art, pushed men across oceans, established, stabilized, and destabilized nations. And sex could, he said, if explored thoughtfully, create lasting and important relationships. I remember thinking: Tell. Me. More.

Like Craigin, Graves' version of world history and later American history, did not center on kings and queens, dynasties and dates. Instead, he pushed us to explore history from the vantage of those "little people" and he pushed a theory that it was the joy and suffering of the average person that mattered most.

In every class period, Graves read a story, often autobiographical, from a farmer, a factory worker, a miner, a soldier, a warrior, a bartender, an enslaved person, a laundryman, a maid, a clerk, a cowboy, a housewife—and he gave us a list of readings to explore at home that kept focus on these "little people." Graves' readings also encompassed the broad sweep of experiences. The focus never rested on the lives of wealthy white people only. We read Black, Indigenous, poor, Hispanic, Arabic, and Asian perspectives, among others.

Today, Graves might be drummed out of his position in some schools for even mentioning sex, and I have little doubt he would be labeled "woke" or even "un-American." In the 1980s, he was simply a fantastic history teacher.

"Who owns history?" Graves pondered. Who gets to choose what stories are told and why? What and who do we choose to remember, and who and what do we choose to forget? History, he pressed, is a powerful and potentially dangerous tool. Whoever owned history, owned the future.

After school, when we did not have soccer practice, Dave Atencio and I would drive just northeast of Pueblo, to a low rise overlooking the Fountain. We hunted fossils and arrowheads there. Baculite Mesa is a pile of Cretaceous shale created when the

Western Interior Seaway covered much of what is now the Great Plains, seventy to eighty million years ago. The rise is rich with fossils. Ammonites, gastropods, sand dollars, nautiloids, and, of course, baculite. Long after the land rose and the seas fell away, Indigenous Americans utilized the mesa for twenty to thirty thousand years or more. It made sense. From the crest, Baculite offers an expansive view of much of the Fountain watershed and far out onto the grasslands spilling east from the Fountain's floodplain.

The place had been picked over. Mostly we found tipi rings, manos, metates, chip stone from tool making, fire-cracked rock, and occasionally, small projectile points: Abiquiu, Armijo, Bear Creek, Cienega. I was not interested in collecting, just experiencing. I believed then and I believe now that the remains of the past belong to the land and should remain on the land. Memory exists for a reason. Removing something from a place, it seemed to me, harmed the memory of place. Taking artifacts is, at once, the destruction of a people's historic connection to the land and a desecration of the land's memory of itself.

Atencio felt different. He was an eager collector, and we engaged in frequent, heated arguments about what belonged to the Earth and what did not. At some point, I refused to return to Baculite unless he agreed to leave behind anything we found. We never went back.

In *The Porch*, architect Charlie Hailey offered that collections make a nest. "In one sense," he wrote, "it is a delicate membrane between what we own and what we borrowed, between what we can control and what remains out of our hands." Collecting, then, may represent nothing but a feeble attempt at immortality, exactly the point of Bruce Chatwin's masterpiece *Utz*.

One evening, after several hours exploring Baculite Mesa, Dave produced his collection to his father. Mr. Atencio was a Korean War vet who claimed to have once guarded over a UFO crash site in the mountains of the Colorado-New Mexico border lands. He had seen the body of an alien. "And it wasn't anything like you'd think," he assured me. "Impossible to describe." Mr. Atencio looked over Dave's collection then produced a box of his own artifacts, also collected from Baculite Mesa in the late 1940s and throughout the 1950s.

That was the moment I first learned what a Clovis point was and how to distinguish a Clovis from a Folsom point. The older Atencio maintained an impressive collection of ancient treasures in that box. I recall several of the Clovis points, a dozen or more Folsom points, and hundreds of other types of points, ceramics, and bone tools. That collection stressed me. Years later, while working for the University of New Mexico as an archaeologist, I called Mr. Atencio and asked if I could have the box. He promised I could come get it after he died. He said that he would put my name on it. My plan was to turn it over to my friend Dr. David Kilby, who was then completing his PhD with a focus on Clovis assemblages from across the country.

The thought of outliving my children terrorizes me. Mr. Atencio outlived his. When he passed over, my mom clipped his obituary from the Pueblo Chieftain and mailed it to me. I was living in Taos, New Mexico and immediately drove to the Atencios' home. The house was full of people I did not know. They had cleared the abode, emptying the basement. I asked about the box with the artifacts. I described it and told them it was mine. No one recalled the box. A woman told me they had hauled pretty much everything from the basement to the city dump. There was no one alive to claim what was in the house, she said, and they had to clean it out and prepare it for sale. My heart sank. The box of Baculite artifacts, some seven thousand, ten thousand, or even fifteen thousand years old, now lies deep inside the old Pueblo landfill.

Collections offer no protection against death.

Not long after Mr. Atencio died, I had lunch in Taos with wealthy and notorious collector Forest Fenn. Fenn wanted me to write an article for *New Mexico Magazine* about his infamous treasure hunt. Sometime around 2009 or 2010, Fenn claimed to have hidden a treasure chest worth millions somewhere in the Rocky Mountains. Soon after, he published a memoir named *The Thrill of the Chase*. The book contained a mystifying twenty-four-line poem. That poem, Fenn said, was a map to the hidden treasure. The hunt became an international sensation. Thousands of people set out to find the chest, at least five losing their lives in the hunt.

I was dubious about the unclear request. Other, far more capable writers had already written about Fenn, his collections, and his treasure hunt. I suspect he sought a hagiography. I declined. Bestowing sainthood on anyone is not of interest to me, excusing someone's unethical behavior even less so. I told Fenn his whole treasure hunt was ludicrous. He responded that the point of the hunt was not about the treasure, but about the experience of seeking and finding a treasure.

"Sure," I said. "For you. But for the treasure seekers, most of them at least, it's about the things. The money."

He nodded. "True enough."

"I have this image of you in my mind, sitting at home, giggling to yourself while thousands of folk run all over the West, obsessing about your treasure," I ranted. "It's kind of a joke for you, no?"

He was silent. I pressed him. "Is the treasure even real?"

He asked for the check and said he had to get back to Santa Fe. He paid for his own meal and left without saying goodbye.

In June 2020, a thirty-two-year-old medical student from Michigan found Fenn's treasure. Jack Stuef claimed to have uncovered the stash of gold nuggets, gems, and pre-Colombian Indigenous artifacts in Wyoming. The value of Fenn's treasure was estimated at $2 million. Fenn died three months later, aged ninety.

To this day, I believe Fenn's whole treasure hunt was an

elaborate hoax, one giant, masterfully played joke. I am unsure what role, if any, Jack Stuef played but I hope to one day hear the real story.

Collections offer no immortality. Even if they are stories.

Craigin fell into poverty. His obsession led to divorce in 1913. His second wife did not hang around long and he moved alone into a tiny cottage near the Fountain in Colorado Springs. He struggled with *The Rocky Mountain Library* until his death. As Craigin fought to assemble his masterpiece, he sold his own collections and a number of priceless books just to keep the lights and heat on. He begged meals from friends and old colleagues. He took to writing poetry, poetry so unwieldy he himself admitted that visitors fell asleep as he recited his work aloud. In 1936, Craigin moved into the Stratton, a home for elders haunted by poverty. He passed there on June 15, 1937 at the age of seventy-nine.

Soon after Craigin's death, his daughter Helen came to empty the cottage. Of the experience she wrote:

> Things were in great disorder in his house, and there were thousands of papers, etc. besides all his books; we looked as best we could, as we didn't not want to destroy anything he had written, but it was almost a hopeless task . . . we worked many days trying to save what he would want saved, but papers were piled high all about . . . finally we had two truckloads of papers hauled to the city dump.

Landscapes are palimpsests indeed. A manuscript written and erased, written and erased again, ancient scribbling still visible beneath the new. Today is built of everything that has come before. No matter how deeply you bury the past, it never remains fully buried.

In deep time, only Sinawav the Creator and Coyote lived on the Earth. The two had lived there so long, they had forgotten how they had arrived. One day, Sinawav gave coyote a bag of sticks and specific instructions to deliver the bag, unopened, to the sacred valley on the other side of The Peak. But curiosity got the better of Coyote and before he had crossed the second ridge, he stopped to take a look inside the bag. Humans—in other words, chaos—ensued. The sticks had become people, and they spilled from the bag shouting in languages Coyote could not comprehend. He tried to corral them, but the people raced away in every direction. A few people, however, remained. They were fierce and loyal and Coyote gathered them up, hauled them to the sacred valley and left them there. These were the Nuuchiu. Sinawav was not happy. "Coyote," he said, "you do not comprehend the problems you have unleashed upon the Earth." Sinawav condemned Coyote to wander the Earth at night, forever, on all fours.

The Nuuchiu people are one of the few Indigenous nations without a migration story. They were born at the headwaters of the Fountain in the Rocky Mountains—the Shining Mountains in the Nuuchiu language—and have been there since.

The Nuuchiu speak a dialect of Uto-Aztecan and spread along the mountain chain from central New Mexico to Wyoming, and from the Fountain to eastern Utah. Anthropologist Frances Densmore proposed that the word "Ute" came from the Shoshone word *Tsiyuta* or "rabbit hunters." The name first appeared in Spanish documents as "Yuta" in 1626. Like many Euro-American names for native nations, the word is somewhat derogatory, or at least it used to be. Nuuchiu, their name for themselves, holds many meanings that lend insight to how the Nuuchiu saw themselves. Soul. Spirit. Chosen People. The People. The Mountain People.

The Nuuchiu organized themselves into ten to twelve allied "bands" as anthropologists call them. Think of states or provinces within a nation but with fluid boundaries depending on the season. It was the Tabaguache band of the Nuuchiu who called the Fountain watershed home.

On a warm day in early spring, I stood in knee-deep snow on a ridge above Woodland Park. The light and shadows folded across the snows blanketing The Peak. The sun was intense but the air chilled. It was the kind of day where your coat comes on and off and on and off, and sunburn happens far easier than you'd think.

At my feet, the snow melted. You could hear it trickling over the rocks below the snow and ice. It ran down the slope, eventually arriving to the Fountain, either through the shallow aquifer or via the gutters of Woodland Park.

Often, I try to imagine how a particular place may have appeared two hundred, five hundred, a thousand, or ten thousand years ago. Who was here and what did they do and how did they interact with the land? I want to know who walked here and why. I want to see what they saw. I want to hear what they heard, to smell what they smelled, to know how they experienced this place. I long to know what this land has witnessed. I imagined dozens, possibly hundreds, of campfires trickling smoke into the sky, spread up and down the valleys, all along the Fountain, and out onto the plains. The forest would have been different. The grasses too. And it is worth remembering that it was all ever changing. The view would have morphed through the eons. What might be true in 1500 was different in 900, different still in 500BCE, and vastly altered since the waning days of the last glacial maximum. Ecosystems and the humans living within those systems were forever in flux. In fact, an ecosystem is not a "thing," but rather a "process." Culture holds the same ever-evolving quality, shifting year to year. Nothing is ever the same.

No one knows for sure how long people have inhabited the Americas.

In 1929, a road crew working in the Blackwater Draw area near Clovis, New Mexico came across a mess of giant, ancient bones. Edgar B. Howard, the University of Pennsylvania archaeologist who began excavations at the site, described it as "matted masses of bones of mammoth." Mixed in with the bones were large, thin, fluted, lance-shaped spear points. The points were beautiful, crafted from cherts, obsidians, and jaspers. These are the famed Clovis points—tools unique to the Americas and the type Mr. Atencio had gathered from Baculite Mesa. More than ten thousand Clovis points have been found across the country, dating to 12,800-13,500 years ago. At the time of the New Mexico find, there was no accepted human habitation older than Clovis. This led archaeologists to conclude that Clovis points were evidence of the very first humans in the Americas.

The Clovis First Theory holds that small groups of people made their way from across the Bering Land Bridge about fourteen thousand years ago, when sea levels were low enough to connect Siberia to Alaska. These people supposedly made their way south following a one thousand-mile, ice-free corridor along the Rocky Mountains, into the interior of the continent.

But since the 1970s, dozens of pre-Clovis sites have turned up throughout North and South America. The oldest accepted physical evidence dates to 15,500 years ago, but some sites hint at older dates. Radiocarbon dating puts the Monte Verde site in southern Chile at 14,800 years old and possibly 33,000 years old. The Pedra Furada in Brazil has yielded similar dates. The Topper site in South Carolina indicates human habitation going back twenty thousand years, as does Bluefish Cave in the Yukon and Cactus Hill in Virginia. Flaked stone tools approximately thirty thousand years old have turned up at Mexico's Chiquihuite Cave. Bones with cut marks found in Uruguay date to thirty-four thousand years ago—and so on.

All these sites and dates are heavily disputed within the archaeological community. It is unclear, for example, how the stone tools found in Mexico were made. Most archaeologists doubt they are human-made tools at all. The Pedra Furada tools may have been created by Capuchin monkeys. Apparent cut marks on bones might be caused by modern construction work or falling rock. They could also result from hungry animals. All these sites had been disturbed, making reliable dates hard to come by.

Enter White Sands.

New Mexico's White Sands National Park holds the largest collection of Ice Age human and animal footprints in the world. Much of the park was once a vast, shallow body of water surrounded by savannah-like forests. Archaeologists and geologists call this Lake Otero. During the Ice Age, New Mexico was much cooler and wetter than it is today, and Otero was one of many such lakes throughout the region. For more than two thousand years, humans and animals frequented this rich marshland, leaving behind multiple layers of footprints extending over several square miles. There are thousands and perhaps hundreds of thousands of these prints in the area representing mammoths, dire wolves, camels, giant sloths, short-faced bears, and other extinct megafauna.

Many of these prints were noted as far back as the 1940s and 1950s, but it was not until 2021 that an interdisciplinary team of researchers made a staggering announcement: the human footprints left behind in the lakeshore mud had been dated to between twenty-one thousand and twenty-three thousand years ago.

Unlike the other sites, the White Sands prints are undisputable evidence of human beings. The sediments in which the prints were found were geologically intact and the methods used to obtain the dates solid.

One of the many things that makes these ancient dates so astounding is that the prints were made at a time when the ice sheets were at their maximum. Sea levels were four hundred feet lower than today, and glaciers reached as far south as present-day Illinois and Missouri, blocking north-to-south movement for thousands of years. The ancestors of the people living at Lake Otero, then, must have arrived at least ten thousand to fifteen thousand years before Clovis.

Still, the long-debunked Clovis First hypothesis is taught in our public schools and appears regularly in the media. Of course, much of what we teach about American history is just plain wrong, much of it made up of deliberately warped mythological narratives. But narratives have shape and history is without shape. Nothing is preordained. There is a difference between history and ideology and much of what is taught in American schools is just pure ideology. As a result, when it comes to life in North and South America before 1492, almost everything you think you know is at best boring—and at worst, false.

"He who controls the past controls the future," wrote George Orwell in *1984*. "He who controls the present controls the past." There is a toxic yet vital debate underway in today's America about what should we and should we not teach our children about the past. The battle isn't really about teaching or even history. It is about power.

The stories we tell about the past matter.

For Indigenous Americans, how we think about the past is particularly relevant. Euro-Americans have long justified the genocide of Native Americans and the taking of land by denying or distorting Indigenous people's history. When colonizers imagine a people without history, that people's connection to both land and reality is severed. Destroying them becomes easier. Taking land and resources from colonized peoples becomes very nearly benevolent. After all, a human without history is no human at all.

Early Euro-Americans refused to see the link between Native Americans and the impressive mounds, monuments, and cities found across the continent. Instead, they claimed, these structures were built by Atlanteans, Nephites, mysterious giants, lost Israelites, Irish monks, or even beings from outer space. The modern "ancient aliens" craze is rooted in this historical justification for genocide and land theft.

I understood the science, but I wanted a better understanding of what the White Sands prints meant on a deeper level to Indigenous Americans, so I called up Kim Pasqual-Charlie to talk it through. Kim is a member of the Sky Clan and was the first female appointee of the Acoma Tribal Historical Preservation Board. Along with representatives of dozens of other regional Indigenous nations, Kim consulted and worked alongside the archaeologists uncovering the White Sands footprints.

"In our stories, we migrated from somewhere up north, but we never came over any Bering Land Bridge. For us, all Puebloan people were once the same, but we got in trouble and split. We wandered until we came to this place." She told me that the White Sands footprints connected many dots for her.

In the language of Acoma Pueblo (Keres) there is an ancient word for camel. "But how can we have that word if we'd never seen a camel?" For Kim, seeing tracks of ancient *Camelops* at White Sands—a species that went extinct more than thirteen thousand years ago—was a revelation. "We have that word because, at some point in our past, we had actually seen that animal," she told me. "We grow up listening to our traditional stories, but these aren't just bedtime stories. These are things that actually happened."

Indigenous stories have often been dismissed as mere folktales or mythologies instead of the wealth of historical knowledge they are. In fact, Native American origin stories are not in opposition to most Western scientific understandings of the peopling of the Americas. Indigenous stories frequently refer to massive walls of ice, strange giant animals, floods released by melting glaciers, rising sea levels, and the reappearance of lands in the throes of postglacial regeneration. The Cree people have a saying for "when the ice goes home," suggesting glacial retreat. The Salish of British Columbia have a mammoth song and mammoth dance. In the Osage oral traditions, there are stories of a battle between giant beasts, mammoths, sloths, bears, and dire wolves. These suggest that Indigenous Americans had, in the distant past, experienced at least one glaciation—if not more.

For Lyle Balenquah, an archaeologist from the Greasewood Clan of the Hopi Nation, the White Sands prints came as no surprise. "This is simply proof of what we were taught as kids. Science is verifying our own cultural history," he told me. "It is very significant in how we perceive our own history. As a scientist, I think the numbers are cool. But as a Hopi? Well, we don't attach numbers to our history. Dates don't matter as much as the relationships."

Relationships. This is key. The earliest arrivals to the Americas did not see themselves as conquering new lands. They were building fresh relationships.

I also called Dr. Joe Watkins, an archaeologist I knew who hailed from the Choctaw Nation of Oklahoma. "You're talking about two different worlds," Watkins told me. "On the Indigenous side, it doesn't matter putting dates. Philosophically, we were never anywhere else."

Only the Euro-American mind, obsessed with terms of ownership, possession, and conquest, fails to comprehend what Indigenous people mean when they refer to time immemorial. "It doesn't mean since forever," Watkins explained. "It means an entirely different way of being with the world. In the West, history has been a way of justifying yourself. There is an eagerness to find superiority and to define yourself in opposition to others instead of creating your own identity. But for Indigenous people, history is a way of recognizing connections and relationships, relationships with non-human people. The Western perspective is largely irrelevant. We Native peoples have nothing to prove."

Native stories and the human footprints at White Sands

are not the only line of evidence pointing to a deeply ancient Native North America. Recent genetic evidence demonstrates that human presence in the Americas dates anywhere from fifteen thousand to thirty thousand years ago. Some linguists have pointed to the incredible diversity of languages among Native Americans as evidence of a very early arrival in the Western Hemisphere. This controversial theory holds that languages diversify at a given rate and thus we can estimate when people arrived in the Americas based on that rate of change. The date linguists come up with is approximately thirty to thirty-five thousand years, far older than any archaeological evidence supports. While not totally dismissed among archaeologists, the linguistics theory has been widely seen as not plausible. Still, if the White Sands dates hold, the date of arrival fits closer to the linguistic estimate.

On the archaeological end of things, an increasing number of older and older sites are turning up because research methods and technologies have improved—but another big reason is that, finally, archaeologists are looking for them.

Dr. Paulette Steeves, a Cree-Métis archaeologist at Algoma University in Canada, told me that the White Sands prints are young in comparison to what is out there. Steeves has compiled an impressive database consisting of hundreds of credible sites throughout the Americas that are older than Clovis, and in many cases much, much older, perhaps going back fifty thousand or even one hundred thousand years. "It is mindboggling how much is out there," she said. "It's amazing." But the real treasure, says Steeves, is off the coasts: the oldest sites in North America may be under hundreds of feet of water.

During the Ice Ages, sea levels dropped, exposing hundreds of miles of new shore along both the Atlantic and Pacific continental shelves. Early migrants to the Americas most likely followed these ecologically rich coastlines, meaning that the earliest settlements and sites were flooded as the glaciers melted.

The question, then, of when the Nuuchiu arrived along the banks of the Fountain, is irrelevant. Sinawav and Coyote did what they did and the people grew in relationship with the land and the non-human relatives that lived there.

In *Trace*, author and geologist Lauret Savoy wrote "There remains no public agreement on slavery's impact, trauma or human cost." The same holds true when it comes to the genocide of Native America.

There is no consensus on how many people lived in North America on October 12, 1492, the day Christopher Columbus and his crew staggered onto the beaches of Guanahani in the Caribbean. In school, I learned that somewhere between five and twelve million people spread across the continent, living in small nomadic bands. This is most surely wrong. The sources for these numbers are unreliable, the motivation suspect. Scholars, utilizing a variety of methods to arrive at population numbers estimate anywhere from eighteen million to one hundred million people in North America on contact with Europeans and upwards of one hundred and even two hundred million between the two American continents. My own dive into this debate landed somewhere between forty to sixty million people in North America with slightly higher numbers in South America.

This matters for two reasons. First, by artificially lowering the original number of Indigenous people in the Americas, the extent of the absolute massacre and destruction of Native America is masked. A lower number lessens the need for accountability, introspection, and atonement for the darker corners of our past. It helps to absolve white America of the need to come to terms with the nation's foundational sin.

Second, the low population estimates are often ideological, reflecting the Euro-American drive for superiority, the idea that the United States is more "advanced" than other nations and cultures. When it comes to Indigenous Americans, historian Francis Jennings famously wrote, "Scholarly wisdom long held that Indians were so inferior in mind and works that they could not possibly have created or sustained large populations." And yet they did.

No large populations, no cities, no nations, no value. This is how we end up with the ancient aliens, Atlantean, and Nephite silliness. All these are baseless "theories" of the past born of racism, a drive to justify genocide and rewrite history in such a way as to deny the extraordinary diversity, power, and complexity of Indigenous America.

This isn't a question of good or bad, right or wrong. It's a question of who and what we are allowed to remember and who and what we are allowed to forget. In other words, it is about power and who is allowed to wield it.

To date, there is no comprehensive take on the pre-historic archaeology of the Fountain watershed, and large chunks of research remain unpublished. The Nuuchiu tell of violent invaders pushing into Colorado along the Front Range between 1200 and 1400AD. These were most likely Athabascan peoples, the fathers and mothers of the Diné, Tin-ne-ah, and Ka'igwu people. The Numunuu drove the Tin-ne-ah from the Front Range by the early 1700s. The mountain people remained in the mountains.

The Nuuchiu still live in present-day Colorado. But they have been driven from their home watershed.

First, it was the Spanish pushing into Nuuchiu lands. Next, it was the Mexicans. The southern Nuuchiu reported near constant attacks by Mexican land grant settlers across northern New Mexico and southern Colorado by the 1820s. The Nuuchiu pushed back, intimidating settlers along the upper Rio Grande and into the Taos Valley the way their families had been terrorized by the settlers.

After the United States invasion of northern Mexico in 1846–1848, the American army protected the Mexican settlers (newly-minted American citizens) from the Nuuchiu, allowing for further encroachment on traditional lands.

Despite all of this, the Nuuchiu sought calm and free trade with the settlers and the United States government, which officially classified the Nuuchiu as "peaceful." Yet the Americans violated every single treaty from Abiquiu in 1849 to the 1868 Hunt Treaty and beyond. Settler violence and disease took a toll.

It is the United States government or the United States Army that most often gets the blame for treaty violations and massacres of Indigenous Americans. This masks yet another uncomfortable reality. More often than not, it was the federal government and the army trying to keep the peace. It was the white and Hispanic settlers and miners, then pouring into Colorado by the thousands, who robbed and murdered the Nuuchiu, stealing their land. Then, when the Nuuchiu fought back, the settlers and miners called on the Army and Washington for help.

War spread up and down the Fountain and the Arkansas. At the confluence in Pueblo, the Nuuchiu attacked Fort El Pueblo early on the morning of Christmas Eve, 1854, killing fifteen men and taking a woman and two boys captive. It was the first, but not the last, bloodshed in the so-called Ute Wars.

Colonizers wrote of Nuuchiu families all up and down the Fountain watershed, wintering at Manitou, coming together by the hundreds in what we now call Garden of the Gods. Frank Waters, the half-white, half-Cheyenne writer and native of Colorado Springs, wrote how "bands of Utes kept coming down the mountains every year to pitch their smoke grey lodges near the new little resort of Manitou growing up around their tribal medicinal springs," and of Indigenous movement between plain and peak. "A band of Blue Cloud Arapahoes was crawling past to its encampment down the creek . . . heavily laden squaws and the ponies drawing still more dunnage lashed to spruce teepee poles dragging on the ground . . . Arapahoes and Cheyennes from out on the Great Plains, making for the mouth of the canyon [Fountain] at the foot of the high peak where every fall they gathered to drop offerings in the sacred springs [Manitou] and trade with the Utes."

In Colorado, gold became the most intractable issue. Miners flowed into Colorado seeking fortune. "Pike's Peak or Bust" the saying went, and the Nuuchiu retreated into the mountains in the face of the American onslaught, adopting a policy of isolation.

But not for long.

Fredrick Walker Pitkin waltzed into the Colorado Governor's office in 1879 under the slogan "The Utes Must Go!" Pitkin, who had declared martial law to crush a miners' strike in Leadville, was, by all accounts, a monster. "Your Indians are off their reservation annoying the white people," he wrote to Washington in October 1880. "Take them home or some of them will be hurt." When Washington protested, Pitkin threatened to raise an army of settlers to do the dirty work, reminding D.C. of the horrific massacre of Hinono'eino along Sand Creek in 1864. Pitkin's personal secretary William Vickers advocated for outright extermination of the Nuuchiu people. Pitkin again demanded their removal. The Meeker Massacre. The Battle at Milk Creek. Ethnic cleansing, genocide. By the mid 1880s, the Nuuchiu had been entirely removed from the Fountain watershed and most of their homeland, confined to two small reservations in southwestern Colorado. The Tabeguache Nuuchiu, the people of the Fountain watershed, the people of The Peak, had been forcibly relocated all the way to the Utah deserts.

Tony Morrison coined the term "re-memory," the idea that the past lives on in the present, that the past is alive with us right here, right now. And of course it is. Writing about the past is a way to shape the future. Writing honestly about the past is an even better way to shape the future. An honest history results in a present day that is easier to understand and creates the possibility for a more equitable and just future.

As I crawled under the bridge with JoJo, a chill shuttered my body. No, I did not imagine La Llorona would pour from the Fountain and strangle us with the icy mitts of a tragic ghost. It was, after all, the middle of a bright and clear one-hundred-degree day and I had JoJo and Mama on my team. Well, at least JoJo.

Still, I thought I heard voices beyond JoJo's tales, voices running like an undercurrent carrying that moment that I was there with them, carrying JoJo's life in the flow. Carrying mine alongside his. I sat back, closed my eyes, and listened. Simply listened. Mama moaned.

Of course, this land is haunted. How could so many memories and stories exist in one place without cracking the veil between then and now?

COMPASS

April 28: Fountain Creek Nature Center

Signs on the door requested: "Please Wash Your Hands. COVID kills. Masks required."

A school group stood against the fence, watching the parking lot turkeys chase the starlings from the feeders. The kids wore backpacks and carried water bottles. A teacher approached and asked if it bothered me the kids all wore masks. I told her it was none of my business but that I supported masking up and would do so if she wanted.

She told me that a woman had stood outside the school yelling at the kids who wore masks. "It was really traumatizing for them." She seemed to want my approval. I didn't understand why. I was just some random dude in the parking lot carrying a camera. "Did it get you?" she asked

"Nope. And I don't intend to get it either. You?"

She'd had COVID twice and said she still gets random headaches. She said she couldn't focus anymore like she used to. "I'm just trying to keep them safe. I just don't know what that means anymore." She directed two boys back in line and told everyone to stay hydrated then she led the kids to a deck overlooking a broad pond teeming with birds.

It was not until later that I realized the teacher sought connection. Acknowledgement. Reciprocity. Relationship. She hungered for someone to tell her she was doing her very best under the most difficult of circumstances. I had missed the moment and felt terrible.

I crossed the Fountain at a place I should not have. I stumbled and fell, barely saving my camera from the water. The breeze cut through my wet clothes like a knife. On the right bank I found a bench in a copse of budding elm. There were plastic flowers amongst the grass and song sparrows by the rim of the water. The sun broke through. I removed my jacket and shirt, spreading them on the bench to dry. I poured the water from my boots but left my pants on. Somehow, both my phone and notebook were saved.

It was a typical spring day in Colorado. The sun was there, burning and baking, drying my clothes. A line of clouds passed over. It was gone. A breeze rose from the ground. I shivered and stamped. The clouds floated east, the breeze faded and again it was hot. It was like that the entire day. Crows came to the elms, wings outstretched. They spoke in rolling guttural *rrrrrrrrs*, clicks, and sounds that, at times, seemed like human words. I spoke back to them, in English of course, asking what they were doing, what they had for breakfast, and where they would go next. They watched, heads tilted, milky quartz eyes analyzing. I tried Spanish, then French, and finally Finnish. That exhausted my language abilities. Then I wondered if maybe they might better understand a North American language. Hinóno'eitiit, Núuchi, or Cáuijógá. The crows preened, made their veer-cries and gurgles, then disappeared into the haze, inky blots on blue canvas.

I bit the bullet and pulled the wet shirt over my head. My arm stuck in my sleeve; I turned and smacked my face on a low-hanging elm branch. A thin line of blood grew across my cheek.

When I walked on, my boots squished and sqooshed like a sponge, and for some odd reason, I thought of Badger and Mr. Toad, characters from the river epic *Wind in the Willows*. There was a passage about fools and rivers. Later, I searched up the quote. "Independence is all very well," it said, "but we animals never allow our friends to make fools of themselves beyond a certain limit; and that limit you've reached."

Up from the elms, on the right bank, a prayer garden spread amongst the trees. Freshly cut trails unwound from a hut leading to plastic park bench after plastic park bench, each decorated in faded plastic flowers. A sign said: "Open to All Denominations" and there was a memorial for firefighters and paramedics. At the center of it all was a massive white cross, lined with stone benches. A woman approached. She wore a green vest and asked if I needed anything.

"Dry underwear?" I quipped.

She scowled then explained that this was a place for quiet contemplation, a place "to let God reveal to you your next mission, your assignment in life."

But the constant roar from I-25, less than half a mile distant, rattled my nerves. How could one settle physically, mentally, or emotionally with all the noise? The near constant gunfire from Fort Carson and the helicopters did not help. Quiet contemplation? "Do you sell earplugs?" I asked.

She scowled, then smiled and gently invited me back the next year to visit the yet-to-be-built Hall of Heroes.

Lines of multi-colored pennants festooned the entryway to the prayer garden on the interstate side, marking or denoting . . . something. It was unclear what exactly, but I think they were meant to mark off future parking areas, as if the owners expected thousands of pilgrims to arrive each week. They had bulldozed half an acre of grass, shrubs, and forest to make space for all the imagined future cars. Christian rock blared from the hut. I looked back across the Fountain.

If I were to contemplate God or my life's mission, if I were to reorient my internal compass, I would have to leave the obnoxious prayer garden. I needed somewhere quiet and wild. Or even semi-wild. Somewhere I could hear the voice of God on the leaves or in the ripple of a stream. I walked upstream and made another foolish crossing of the Fountain, pushing through cold, waist-high water, hoisting my camera, phone, and notebook above my head. No, it was not smart, but this time I did not fall.

In July of 2023, God cleansed the prayer garden in a flood and, if one can be sure of anything, God will do so again.

It had been a year and a half since I had visited the spot where I had tried to rebuild the beaver dam. My work remained but it was bent and broken, useless. The willow branches had washed away, and water poured through the vertical uprights I'd slammed into the bitter mud. Without the beaver dam, the brook had cut down through the sediments, eroding the banks. I walked up through what had been the pond. I could still hear I-25, the gunfire, and the helicopters, but a wall of elm and willow dulled the racket enough that my nerves calmed. There was a heron. This one massive, five feet tall if not more. She was noble, curious, erect. She studied me from little more than a yard away with eyes intense like a golden honey. I told her I would leave her alone, and I did.

The upper areas of the former beaver pond remained wet and swampy, enough for minnows to gather and enough for the great bird to come and feed. Still, the human destruction of the beaver's dam rankled. I felt a loss in my belly, butterflies, sick like just after a painful breakup. How, I wondered, would we ever put it all back together again?

Yellow-rumped warblers swarmed trailside elms in clouds of feathers. There were deer prints in the mud. I watched three enormous ravens wading in the creek above the diversion dam. In a meadow, the school kids erupted in howls of laughter and screams of joy. The teacher flapped her arms, turned in circles, strutted, and jumped up and down. It was like the dance of a sandhill crane. Three boys and a girl joined her, making caw sounds and dancing about. Then the rest of the kids joined in, squawking, hooting, and giggling.

You're doing the very best you can, I thought. And more.

VISIONS

"We abuse land because we regard it as a commodity belonging to us. When we see land as a community to which we belong, we may begin to use it with love and respect."

–Aldo Leopold, A Sand County Almanac

As the sun arced towards late morning, I shuffled into the shade next to Allison Schuch and downed half a liter of water. The burnt, tar-tinged stench of melting asphalt assaulted my nose.

We stood in the street in one of Colorado Springs' lower-middle-income neighborhoods, not far from where the Fountain runs under I-25. Kelly Bull, a smiling, energetic permaculturist, hopped about, pointing to the plants in her front yard, naming each in turn: echinacea, brown-eyed Susan, iris, hawthorn, and a diminutive peach. The lovely trees and flowers were not, however, the goal of our visit. It was the two holes in the curb in front of Bull's house that prompted the trip.

Back in 2013, Bull attended a workshop lead by Brad Lancaster, the guru of dryland water harvesting in the American Southwest. Since the early 1990s, Lancaster has transformed his neighborhood in Tucson, Arizona into a green, shady, and cool urban oasis, all by harvesting the scant rainfall of his Sonoran Desert home. In doing so, Lancaster also helped to create a close-knit community of neighbors and urban gardeners. His books are legend among the water conscious throughout the West. They are beautiful, simple, and accessible.

During the height of the COVID-19 pandemic, Bull and her husband packed up their Albuquerque house and, seeking better job opportunities, moved to Colorado Springs. They bought a small house in a quiet neighborhood and settled in.

Bull aimed to put Lancaster's designs to work. She set out improving the quality of the soil in her yard, adding compost, mulch, and "green fertilizers," plants that fix nitrogen in the soil. She scavenged pipes, tubes, barrels, and drains to manage the water on her own little chunk of Colorado. Then, on a steamy monsoon afternoon one July, Bull stood in the street watching hundreds of gallons of rainwater sluice by, overflowing gutters, and flooding the street. "I was like . . . what's the point of this?" She told us. "All that water just running off. I remember thinking: this makes no sense."

One of Lancaster's fundamental designs for harvesting urban runoff is the curb cut, a small hole or funnel in the street-side curb that allows stormwater to divert from the street to a tree- and flower-filled landscape with minimal human effort. A curb cut not only allows for efficient use of urban runoff, but it also allows pollutants to filter from the water as it soaks into the ground, keeping those chemicals and heavy metals out of nearby waterways.

Street runoff is toxic. There is zinc from tires, copper from brake linings, lead from gasoline and tire balancing weights, fertilizers, pesticides, pet waste, E. coli, cadmium from car paints, nitrogen oxide from vehicle exhaust, and a mind-numbing amount of microplastics from tires, and, well, pretty much everything else. Unless filtered, all that ends up in our creeks and rivers.

Urban water harvesting is less harvesting and more short-term borrowing. Water is not permanently diverted from nearby creeks and streams; it is simply slowed. Mellowed. Calmed. Street runoff is put to beneficial use, cleaned, then gradually returned to the system via the shallow local aquifer, thus reducing erosion and flooding. Think of it like a sponge that soaks up water and holds it, releasing it slowly. Water harvesting á la Lancaster is one of those rare win-win-win situations.

What does water want? It's a query journalist Erica Gies posed in *Water Always Wins,* a book begging for us to take climate change adaptation seriously. "What water wants," she answered, "is to slow down, and in that slowness, water forges its complex relationships with life in local ecosystems."

Lancaster, and now Bull, are part of what Erica Gies calls the Slow Water Movement, a crusade to restore natural processes to the ways in which we manage water. "When water stalls on the land, that's when the magic happens, cycling water underground and providing food and habitat for many forms of life, including us." Slow water doesn't flood. Slow water causes less erosion. Slow water feeds ecosystems.

It took the better part of a year, but Bull made her way through the Colorado Springs Planning, Utilities, and Engineering departments before obtaining a permit for the curb cut that would allow street runoff to water her flowering front yard. The curbs in Bull's neighborhood were not the same hard-edged, cubed design we see in most of the country. Rather, her curbs are rounded. The city engineer (who quickly understood the benefits of Bull's proposal) suggested that, instead of the traditional curb cut design, they drill two four-inch diameter holes through the cement to allow the water into her yard. The results were instantaneous.

Bull toured Schuch and me around the yard, pointing to where the water pooled, flowed, diverted, and fed her garden. "Flowers, trees, and suddenly the neighbors are looking at my yard telling me: I want that too!"

And it's no wonder. Colorado Springs' water use peaked in 2001. Most of the decline in per capita water use came from residents essentially abandoning their home landscapes. As the price of water rose, many allowed their lawns to degrade to dirt. CSU would prefer that residents transition to beautiful, drought resilient yards, full of native plant species instead of the ugly that is bare dirt. CSU has even gone so far as to offer classes to teach residents how to transition. As of December 2023, 150 people had completed the class, gaining access to free native seeds and high-efficiency irrigation nozzles. Still, a citywide curb cut program remains out of reach for the moment. The bureaucracy was on its way as Bull and Schuch were to find out.

Bull worked her way up and down the street like a door-to-door evangelist, convincing several folks to install curb cuts. She focused on those whose lawns had gone to dirt, and she generously offered to help her neighbors build their soil and choose appropriate native plants for landscaping. "What I'd like to see is a shady, spongy, cool, climate-change-adapted community full of trees and flowers. A place where we can meet as neighbors, have community dinners. I want this to be the type of place we all deserve to live in."

Soon after our visit, Schuch applied for a grant to help city residents with curb cuts and rain gardens. The district won the grant but immediately found itself embroiled in Colorado's complicated water laws. First, Schuch got a call from the State Engineer's Office, then CSU, then the city's stormwater office, and none of them were happy. As it turned out, developing a rain garden on your property is considered an illegal taking of water. That's right, moving water from the street into your flower bed is a violation of several state laws and regulations. In order to be compliant, Bull would have to have her property designated as an official stormwater facility, subject to annual monitoring and maintenance. Further, if she were to ever move, the designation and permits would have to be sold along with the home, potentially burdening the next owner and possibly reducing the value of her home.

"We're not giving up," Schuch told me. "We are thinking our workaround will be rain gardens that are fed from gutters versus curb cuts. The state engineers seemed to be fine with that . . . maybe. Let's see."

The idea of Colorado Springs as a sponge city isn't an original thought. In fact, it is the founding vision of the city.

When Rose Kingsley arrived to the outskirts of Colorado Springs in November 1871, she wasn't impressed. "You may imagine Colorado Springs, as I did, to be in a sequestered valley with bubbling fountains, green grass, and shady trees, but not a bit of it," she wrote. "Picture yourself a level, elevated plateau of greenish brown, without a single tree, sloping down about a quarter of a mile to the railroad track and Monument Creek."

Kingsley wasn't the first white voyager to find themselves underwhelmed or even dismayed by the Front Range piedmont. In 1852 Captain Randolph B. Marcy found it to be "barren and desolate wastes, where but few streams greet the eye of the traveler, and these are soon swallowed up by the thirsty sands over which they flow."

Dr. Edwin James of the 1820 Long Expedition wrote, "I do not hesitate in giving the opinion, that it is almost wholly unfit for cultivation, and of course uninhabitable by a people depending upon agriculture for their substance."

Early Euro-Americans labeled the plains The Great American Desert, a one-thousand-mile-wide wasteland and barrier to westward expansion. It is safe to say, they didn't understand what they were seeing. The prairie was, in fact, a diverse, biologically rich ecosystem where Indigenous Americans had thrived for thousands of years. The piedmont was particularly attractive to Indigenous nations due to its varied elevation-influenced ecosystems and ecotones offering bountiful food, reliable water sources, and shelter from the winds that course the great grassland steppe. Not to mention the healing waters of what is now Manitou Springs. But the newcomers didn't see this.

Kingsley, a British friend of the Palmer family, had been somewhat deceived by her soon-to-be hosts, General William Jackson Palmer and his wife, Queen. Palmer, often credited as the founder of Colorado Springs, was a Quaker and Civil War hero from Philadelphia. Palmer's vision for a future city on the piedmont was of a sort of tree-filled, agricultural oasis, a retreat for the well-healed sited at the base of The Peak. Alcohol drinkers, "fallen women," and penniless vagabonds need not apply. "Indians" might be tolerated, but only as nostalgic oddity; "Like the everlasting insignia of the wild earth's nobility," Frank Waters mournfully penned in the *Pike's Peak Trilogy*, a fictitious chronicle of Colorado Springs' birth.

An energetic entrepreneur and persistent promoter, Palmer sold his vision up and down the eastern seaboard and across the pond in London, enticing moneyed English migrants to invest in his oasis retreat and settle in the new city. And they did. For many years, Colorado Springs was known as "Little London" due to its disproportionate number of English settlers.

Palmer dreamed of a resort at the base of the Rocky Mountains. Colorado Springs would be a utopian refuge where the wealthy could escape the polluted, violent rot of the East Coast's industrializing cities and the blighted, coal-choked hellholes of Victorian England.

Unlike for his friend Ms. Kingsley, the piedmont was love at first site for Palmer. Riding up from Pueblo in 1869, the crisp mountain air drove the retired general to swoon. "I spread out my blankets . . . and slept soundly in the fresh air, until wakened by the round moon . . . when I found the magnificent Pike's Peak towering immediately above . . . I could not sleep anymore with all the splendid panorama of mountains gradually unrolling itself . . ." Palmer wrote to his wife, Queen, on July 28. The Front Range was a "paradise" he assured her. Queen, doubtful, bided her time back east until her husband could establish a home that suited her refined tastes. And still, Queen never quite took to Colorado. She found it dreary and downright miserable. Instead, Queen chose to spend most of her time on the East Coast or in England. Palmer, however, was convinced. The Promised Land lay along the banks of the Fountain at the base of Pike's Peak.

At the time of Palmer's arrival, the Fountain and Monument valleys were already populated by Euro-American and Hispanic settlers as well as the regional Indigenous nations. Pueblo had been a bustling agricultural and trading community for going on twenty years. Ranches, mostly sheep, but later cattle, lined the Fountain. A "grim collection of storefronts and houses [were] strewn up the mouth [of the Fountain] to Ute Pass." The trading post at Jimmy Camp thrived and Colorado City, built right on the Fountain, was already ten years old.

Palmer set to building his oasis. First, he purchased land at the confluence of the Monument and the Fountain, where the America the Beautiful Park lies today. He rounded up investors and established the Colorado Springs Company, selling "memberships" to what became the Fountain Colony, "founded as an unabashed exercise in pure speculative capitalism," geographer Curt Poulton wrote in his 1989 PhD dissertation. Yet, without irrigation, the colony would not survive. For an oasis, one requires water and with nary sixteen inches of precipitation annually, water was in short supply. We've already seen how the very existence of Colorado Springs lies in the extensive manipulation of water. The Ruxton Creek diversions and the reservoirs of Rampart and Catamount all had their roots in Palmer's bucolic wet dreams. "The founders were in the business of selling land and land with trees, lawns, and a steady supply of water was far more valuable than the dry and bleak mesa the first visitors saw," wrote John Harner.

"You go get the water where it is and you move it to where you want it to be. That's the Western way," historian Katherine Scott Sturdevant told me, echoing what I had heard at the Amara meeting.

Palmer's men dug the first irrigation canal in 1871, damming the Fountain and diverting the creek via a quarter-mile flume across the Monument. They dug lateral ditches along the main streets, wetting urban lots and public parks. By the end of 1872, some six hundred cottonwoods had been planted along the freshly plated streets. When Christmas 1873 rolled around, Palmer was sitting pretty with some four hundred investor/settlers signed up. The colony grew dramatically.

Palmer's company sunk several wells, pulling drinking water from the Fountain's aquifer. Private investors also burrowed for water, boring a dozen or more additional wells. The original irrigation ditch was expanded and Prospect Lake appeared in 1890, although not out of thin air. The Colorado Springs Company sought a reservoir doubling as water storage and public amenity. Water sung along streets, bubbled under sidewalks, coursed culverts, freshened air, and pushed rows of cottonwoods into the sky, all while greening yards, cemeteries, and parks alike. Without the El Paso Canal, Colorado Springs would not have survived, much less mushroomed as the resort getaway of Palmer's reveries.

It is, perhaps, a bit challenging to imagine a sort of log cabin Venice at the base of The Peak. And yet, to an extent, it was—minus the gondolas and St. Mark's. Water was everywhere, the city like a sponge. If Rose Kingsley had returned to Colorado Springs twenty years after her initial visit, she would have indeed found the sequestered valley of bubbling fountains. Palmer had a dream and he made it a reality.

For a moment, at least.

America's history is chock-full of people like Palmer, utopian dreamers yearning to break from the dank, avaricious, disease-ridden centers of laissez-faire capitalist America. At the time of Colorado Springs' birth, American cities from the Atlantic to the Mississippi River were overcrowded with extreme and widespread poverty, wracked by labor wars, disease, and malnutrition, lacking social safety nets and social services, and burdened by entrenched social stratification. Jim Crow and race-based terrorism plagued the South. It is no wonder so many people came West.

Yet everything Palmer sought to escape ultimately followed.

On a sticky, rain-soaked afternoon, I sat with a cluster of unhoused Coloradoans under a bridge listening to stories of life along the Fountain. One man, he called himself Bird, told how he'd snuck into the Pioneer's Museum to wash himself in the bathroom, how he'd put on the one nice shirt he keeps in a Ziploc, and how he then toured the exhibits to avoid another afternoon in the rain.

"Bullshit!" A woman called out. "No you didn't." She told me not to trust him, that Bird was always making up stories. But I'd seen the Palmer Exhibit too, and Bird wasn't lying.

Bird suffered anxiety. He had a jumpy knee. He'd chewed his fingernails until they were infected and bloody. Someone had bandaged his fingertips, but he continued the gnawing and he struggled to talk for the mouthful of fingers.

Still, he told me that one particular section of the General Palmer Exhibit had stuck with him. It was a letter, written by one of Palmer's employees. The letter extolled Palmer's virtues, telling how the Quaker warrior and entrepreneur had directed a construction team to reroute a road in order to avoid nesting birds . . . or perhaps butterflies. . . . Bird could not recall which. I couldn't either.

"That's nice," Bird said. "That's just really nice. We got to have more things that are just nice like that, you know?"

Everyone nodded except one large man who sat, elbows on knees, smoking. He shook his head, ditched the smoke, and stood. "There's nothing nice around here." He walked into the rain.

Bird pointed. "See?" And he put his fingers back into his mouth.

Somehow, the end does not justify the means. Palmer may well have loved the land and the natural bounty of the West. He may well have been a tolerant friend of the Nuuchiu. Rerouting a road to protect birds or butterflies is nice, really nice, but did he ever wonder if the road should be built in the first place? When your whole enterprise is geared around exploitation, utilizing just the methods you'd hoped to escape . . . well, somehow the end might not justify the means. The means create the end.

Much like Zebulon Pike, Palmer approached the American West with an astounding amount of hubris and stuckness of the brain. Pike failed to relinquish his Enlightenment understanding of the Rockies, even when the reality didn't match the dream. Prideful in his ignorance, he wasn't open to the insecurity of not knowing, of being vulnerable, the space where we can actually learn. Palmer suffered a similar condition.

Palmer thought he had "the answer," but he never really even asked the question. In the process of creating Utopia, did Utopia even need to be created? Of course it did. He was sure of it. Instead, he just created more problems. Lasting problems.

Archaeologist David Wengrow and the late great anthropologist David Graeber posit that this sort of mental "stuckness"—the type suffered by Zebulon Pike, anti-vaxxers, and climate change deniers—is a relatively recent Western cultural condition. In the sprawling and vitally important 720-page book *The Dawn of Everything*, Wengrow and Graeber point out that, through most of human history, human beings were creative, experimental, and flexible in how they organized their societies and economies. If conditions changed, so did they. If something didn't work, they made something new. Cultural evolution and adaptation was relatively easy and rapid, even in densely populated, so-called "complex" societies. It is only in the past four to five hundred years that we've lost, as a collective whole, the ability to vision or dream of social and economic systems that are different and better than what we've created.

Palmer's reverie ultimately failed because his fundamental come-from was stuck in the same process it sought to escape. What is the deeper problem then? Palmer, like Pike, came from a culture of entitlement, pride, domination, control, and exploitation. A culture of hubris. He ignored the wisdom surrounding him, believing he already had all the answers. With hindsight we might ask what can we learn from the fatal flaw in Palmer's vision so that we can avoid the mistakes of the past. Dreams and visions are powerful motivators, but they might better be approached with a bucketload of humility.

When the rain ended, I walked up from the Fountain towards a dry hotel room. More rain was coming and while Bird and company slept in the downpour, I'd sleep dry, in a bed with a nice, warm meal in my belly, and maybe a beer or two. I passed the blighted storefronts, encampments, and trash along the streets, reeling in the irony of Palmer's vision.

I received an email from a hydrologist. "Still writing that book about the Fountain?"

I told him I was and that I'd like to continue our conversation. He asked that I not use his name or any physical description of him. "Let's just say . . . I have some unorthodox opinions when it comes to water and restoration, and I worry about my job."

The hydrologist was also a Slow Water adherent, although he would probably use another term, something humble like 'logical.'

"Look," he told me, "If Colorado Springs was seriously committed to taking full responsibility for its storm water, around 50 percent of the urban environment would need to be transformed into wetlands and open space. Now, to be fair, that's not just Colorado Springs. That's every city, everywhere."

We met for beers in Pueblo on a February evening. It was the kind of harsh, cold night that made me wistful for the ninety-five-degree day when I'd met Kelly Bull. The discussion grew in intensity and we forgot to eat, beer lubricating the back and forth. I asked how he came by that number. Fifty percent is a hell of a lot of land base. The hydrologist ordered another beer, pulled out a pen, and set to scrawling equations across a napkin. Then another. Then another. My eyes glazed, and by the time he got to the fourth napkin, I was ready for another beer.

But, the idea was relatively straightforward. For every square foot paved with impervious surface, good water management demands an equally sized piece of land to deal with the water. More or less. Although he acknowledged that the 50 percent number would vary somewhat, depending on the local and regional climate—deserts versus rainforests—he held firm that Colorado Springs, and almost every city everywhere, should be at least half green space: protected wetlands and waterways, parks and urban meadows filled with native grasses. "Imagine a city like that. Green and cool and beautiful. A city that works for water, works for people too."

This was a vision Kelly Bull could agree with.

The hydrologist was not the only one to make the 50 percent claim. With all the pavement and cement we have used to construct our cities, we've given water no place to go. As climate change heats the atmosphere, the air above us holds more water. Increasingly, when it rains, it pours, dumping near Biblical deluges, the type of rain that would send a wayward Moomin father scrambling for an oak. The type of rain that might drive you to start all over. "And start all over we should," he said. "Wait 'till you hear my thoughts on stream restoration," he said.

"I can't wait."

"Okay . . . we'll come back to that."

The hydrologist pulled out his smart phone and swiped through an endless string of videos of recent floods of mythical scale: water bucketing into the New York subway, the inundated streets of Brooklyn, torrents washing through southern California, Houston half-drowned, cars washing down urban streets in Spain, Italy, Greece, Libya, India, China.

"We went and paved over everything, then we wonder why it floods. It's not complicated. Springs is the largest urban area in the Fountain watershed. They have no choice but to transform. It's going to have to become a sponge city."

Most urban planners simply shake their heads at the idea of a "sponge city" where 50 percent of the land base is green space. "Politically impossible" and "economically foolish" are terms I've heard, alongside more colorful language. "That would destroy our tax base" and "drive up home prices." And so on. They aren't wrong exactly, much of the way we have structured our cities makes smart land use challenging at best.

"Where would new housing go?" I asked.

"Infill. Build up, not out."

Protect your rivers and creeks. Build up. Turn 50 percent of your city into green space. We're not talking anonymous glass and steel high rise structures. We're talking densification that links people, builds community, increases productivity, and yes, manages water far better than we have. Ending parking and setback requirements and minimum lot size requirements, reducing zoning restrictions, increasing public transportation options, and adding duplex, triplex, and fourplex developments that fit with the character of the community. If we build smarter there is more room for green space. If we build smarter, we can help restore and protect the Fountain. Suddenly, an affordable sponge city of bubbling fountains and shady trees isn't so far-fetched.

Colorado Springs has had some success with urban revitalization efforts. In early 2023, crews set about the construction of several new apartment complexes right downtown. Colorado Springs has something to build on, the Old North End neighborhood for example, a reference point for dense urban neighborhoods in the traditional style of the city. To be sure, the Old North End is out of the price range of 90 percent of Colorado Springs residents, which only demonstrates just how attractive those tree-filled, mixed-use neighborhoods with properly designed off-street sidewalks and bike routes can be. And again, like Bull said, we all deserve to live like this. Not just the wealthy. Everyone.

In 2018, after losing yet another stormwater lawsuit—this one brought by the EPA, Colorado Department of Health and Environment, Pueblo County, and the Lower Arkansas Valley Water Conservancy—Colorado Springs ramped up efforts to install stormwater detention ponds throughout the city at a cost of $460 million over twenty years (paid for by taxpayers not developers). As of late 2023, $125 million had been spent on around seventeen projects with another seventeen or so in the planning stages.

"Pond" is a euphemism. These are far from the sponge city wetlands the hidden hydrologist envisions. Instead, they are sterile, rock-lined basins surrounded by clipped grasses, devoid of the trees, shrubs, cattails, and other species that create a vibrant wetland ecosystem. This is intentional, of course. Urban water managers don't want Mother Nature taking over wetland maintenance. They fear natural urban ecosystems as too complicated.

While inadequate—the city attorney warns of future storm water lawsuits—these "ponds" are for sure better than nothing.

It is progress. Stormwater Manager and Colorado Springs born and raised Richard Mulledy pointed me to North Douglas Creek, where severe erosion threatened I-25, several houses, and even the railroad tracks. Nearly $5 million and four years later, city crews had repaired and improved a concrete culvert and smoothed twenty-foot-high erosional cliffsalong the tributary to the Fountain. They flattened and widened the creek bottom, and planted hundreds of trees, sowing the understory in native grasses. Still, all this work and expense are but one stitch in a patient requiring one hundred thousand stitches.

People like Kelly Bull and Alli Schuch however, envision a more effective way forward. Instead of pricey sterile storm-water retention buckets, Colorado Springs might instead create a grant program to help homeowners and renters with curb cuts and landscaping. Imagine a hundred thousand or two hundred thousand yard-sized, inexpensive, flower-filled retention ponds spread throughout the city, slowing and cleaning stormwater runoff while cooling and beautifying neighborhoods. It is an admittedly utopian vision, but one that is eminently attainable—and harkens to Colorado Springs' founding vision.

The thing about the future is that, while you can't predict it, you can create it. First though, you have to dream it. Only then can you build it.

Visions for the future of the Fountain abound.

In 2020, the Lyda Hill Philanthropies offered the Fountain Creek Watershed Vision and Implementation Plan, covering about seven miles of the Fountain and Monument Creeks, centered on America the Beautiful Park. The detailed $800,000 plan is crammed with dreamy renderings of a maybe-future for the creek where children float in tubes, kayakers roll in pools, and anglers net healthy trout.

Another vision, one that attracts my praise in particular, is for the creation of a Fountain Creek Regional Trail, an unpaved, vehicle-free biking/hike/horse pathway running the length of the Fountain from the confluence in Pueblo to Palmer Lake and Woodland Park. While the trail is far from complete (it ends at the Pueblo Mall and doesn't pick up again until Clear Springs Ranch, then peters out again after three miles, then reappears at the Fountain Creek Nature Center . . . the section from Manitou to Woodland Park would prove a massive, expensive chore), several dozen miles have been completed.

At some point, Colorado's then-Senator, Ken Salazar, turned up at the Manitou Springs skate park with his own vision. "The Fountain Creek Crown Jewel Project." The plan, which a local reporter pointed out, "has no funding nor an exactly defined improvement area," imagined a state park running the length of the Fountain from Ute Pass to the confluence in Pueblo. "This ribbon of water could unify communities," Salazar dreamed. A Vision Task Force was created. Then . . . well, nothing.

Unfunded, ill-defined, and lacking leadership, the Crown Jewel vision is nonetheless an important one. It is one of the few ideas that takes account of the whole watershed, aiming to manage the watershed as a complete entity instead of keeping the Fountain divided into a jurisdictional jigsaw puzzle of competing values, visions, and interests.

In January 1890, John Wesley Powell, the famed one-armed explorer/scientist and head of the young USGS, famously infuriated the US Senate by calling for a cautious watershed-based colonization of the American West. Powell was one of the unique people who could be comfortable with not knowing, with asking the right questions and allowing the answers to come in due time.

Powell called out the greedy, Gilded Age, Manifest Destiny-driven land and water rush as a disaster in the making. Instead,

Powell advocated a more cooperative, community-centered settlement pattern based on the natural flow of water. A watershed, he said, is "that area of land, a bounded hydrologic system, within which all living things are inextricably linked by their common watercourse and where, as humans settled, simple logic demanded that they became part of a community."

Watershed divisions, instead of the random square-ish borders we ended up with—borders that have made it nearly impossible to manage water effectively and efficiently the past 150 years—he posited, might instead bound Western states.

I certainly don't have all the answers, but for those serious about dealing with the myriad issues facing the Fountain and seeing the creek thrive, a whole watershed approach is likely the best option. Visions such as those laid out by Palmer, Powell, and Salazar might be resurrected and integrated with visions such as those of Kelly Bull and the hidden hydrologist. Healing the Fountain is not just about the creek itself. It is about development, infrastructure, transportation, housing, and how we conceive of the river as a "thing" or a "being." A relative. It's about relationships.

There has been talk of creating a single watershed-wide management entity with taxing and regulatory authority comprised of the various interests within the watershed, from municipal, to ranching, to environmental, and so on. That is, admittedly, a hefty political lift, unlikely at the moment to say the least. If this ever came to pass, however, the Indigenous nations of the region, particularly the descendants of the Tavá Kaa-vi Nuuchiu, should likewise have a voice in the management of the Fountain watershed.

As of 2024, the most obvious candidate for a watershed-wide governing entity is the Fountain Creek Watershed Flood Control and Greenway District. Of course, the name will have to change to something less burdensome—the Fountain Creek Authority or the Fountain Creek Watershed Alliance—as well as the mission and structure of the organization. A watershed-wide entity may require an act of the Colorado State Legislature, or even Congress. Certainly, in tax-adverse Colorado, funding will prove the most controversial aspect of any such vision, but the free ride is over.

CULVERT

January 4: Waldo Canyon to Cascade

January. The emptiest time of the year.

I slunk to the creek and waded through a culvert. The ribbed, steel tube was just wide enough for a tall man like me to pass with only a slight bend at the waist. I inched forward like the cold, sluggish Fountain turning at my ankles.

The water was down and you could see the smooth rocks and gravels beneath the surface. Jagged windows of ice framed the flow and smears of snow hung under the trees. Even through my waterproof fishing boots the frigid water bit hard. Above, Highway 24 moaned and growled. Car after car. Truck upon truck.

I had been intimidated by this section of the creek. Here, in the canyon between Manitou Springs and Woodland Park, highway engineers had imprisoned the Fountain between four east and westbound lanes. They had allowed the creek no more than twenty to thirty feet across, and built the highway so that the waters ran fifteen to twenty feet below the traffic, nearly a tunnel. There was a sense that, if they could have, the engineers would have stuffed the Fountain into one giant, lifeless culvert, funneling the waters away to make room for more pavement. But they didn't. Or couldn't. The result being that the trees—cottonwood, elm, willow, Russian olive, and juniper—poked above the road, creating a wall of green down the center of the highway.

Highway 24 is a ridiculously dangerous road; the speeding, the tailgating. It is narrow and winding and, in the winter, icy. It is incredibly unfriendly and impossible to walk or bike. It is the type of place that screams: No Humans Allowed! No wildlife either, for that matter.

In the summer, I had walked north from Rainbow Falls with Amy Brautigan, ex-military and a watershed management student, working part-time for the Fountain Creek Watershed Flood Control and Greenway District. Amy, like me, wanted to know the Fountain intimately. She wanted boots on the ground, hands in the waters, and she too had walked much of the Fountain at that point. We had hoped to make the trek from the falls to the village of Cascade but the car-choked road and the monsoon-swollen creek set us back. There was no trail along the creek, just the highway. We waded through the knee- and sometimes waist-deep water. It was a warm and cloudless day, and I had checked the forecast every hour through the morning, watching for any signs of more rain. In the mountains, you can be sitting next to a trickling brook under a clear blue sky and seemingly out of nowhere, a flood arrives, signaling rain higher up. You never saw the storm, but you experienced the consequences. It took several hours to push one mile upstream. We scrambled over logs and other debris, taking care with each step. Exhausted, soaked, and hungry, we reached a culvert near Waldo Canyon and turned around.

Now, in winter, with the water low, I aimed to connect one of the missing links in my Fountain trek by walking downstream from Cascade to Waldo.

I exited the culvert along a slip of fine, orange gravel. I saw prints of deer, coyote, bobcat, mountain lion, and even beaver. None of the tracks were very old, but they had solidified in the winter air, hardened like stone, real until a thaw arrived.

Ahead spread an odd, shackled, and thin oasis. The Fountain's forest was thick with knee-high yellowed grasses, shrubs of current, mountain mahogany, and of course, the trees. I was surprised. I had not expected a rich little forest stuffed in the center of the highway. Even the traffic noise, although ever present, was more subdued than I had imagined. I felt somewhat cocooned, held, wrapped into a thing far larger and more important than myself.

For several hours, I ambled downstream. Where French Creek met the Fountain, I flushed a flock of bushtits. There were at least thirty of them, darting through the shrubs, chipping and twittering in their soft way. Their presence struck me as odd. Bushtits feed largely on beetles, ants, bees, and spiders. But there in the dead of winter, at 7,500 feet in elevation, what could they possibly feed on? Still, there they were.

Bushtits create rather remarkable nests. Utilizing spiderwebs as anchor material, the male and female construct a gourd-shaped nest that dangles six to twelve inches from a tree branch. The nest is filled out with plant material and stuffed with a cozy agglomeration of the found feathers of other birds as well as animal fur. They are extraordinarily well camouflaged with grasses, leaves, and sticks. If you live within bushtit range, you have probably walked right past a dozen or more of these nests. I listed the bushtits in my notebook, drank warm coffee from my thermos, and walked on. The cold air sunk into the channel. It smelled acrid and metallic, biting into the skin of my face. My cheeks tingled and I could see my breath. I pulled my wool cap low.

Over the next several hours, I counted two hairy woodpeckers, five Steller's jays, a raven, a chickadee, two wrens, and a slew of dark-eyed juncos. In a pool not quite a foot deep, a Townsend's solitaire dipped. You could see it was a solitaire by the white rings about its eyes. As with the bushtits, the bird's presence surprised me. The Townsend's typically drop to the lowlands for the winter. Later, I would see a brown creeper and, I think, a northern goshawk. The raptor careened past at chest height, skimming the tips of mahogany. I was convinced I had caught sight of the chest stripes, the white eyebrow, and the deep orange eyes, but I couldn't be sure. The bird was far too fast to follow.

Of course, in the canyon between Manitou and Woodland Park, the creek is squeezed far too thin. Still, animals were clearly moving through this green tunnel. The prints on the gravel bars attested to that reality. The birds too. The wildlife movement up and down this section of the Fountain makes the culverts under the road all the more important, allowing wildlife to move without being killed by cars.

In such a heavily urbanized watershed, it may come as a surprise that wildlife continues to move up and down the Fountain, utilizing the sinewy oasis to access safer or more productive habitat. Still, the very real tracks along the gravel bars and in the lines of snow testified to the Fountain's continued ecological importance.

Light gray clouds rolled down from the mountains and I caught a whiff of fresh snow on the breeze. I sat next to a coyote print and tried to sketch the track into my notebook between bites of sandwich. I have never developed drawing or painting skills, although I would like to one day. For my children, it came easily. They taught themselves, uninhibited by worries of perfection. I scratched out the sketch, finished the chilling coffee, packed my things, and moved on.

Just above Waldo Canyon, another culvert funneled the Fountain from the highway center. The culvert was smaller, narrower. At its mouth, Amy Brautigan and I had stopped the previous summer. I had connected my route, but I felt, as I always do at the end of a trek, that I should go on. As if I do not want to stop. I do not ever want to stop. Nevertheless, I had arrived. What else was there to do? When the snow fell—soft, light flakes tumbling like feathers from the gray—I turned and made my way back upstream to Cascade.

HEALERS

"To love a place is not enough, we must find ways to heal it."

–Robin Wall Kimmerer, Braiding Sweetgrass

Summer Lajoie was a smiling, talkative, young mother with a soothing voice and contagious smile. I met up with her at the Cavalier Park playground in Woodland Park where I'd sat with my father a year or even two years before.

That morning, I'd trudged the sandy creek bed from the Fountain's confluence with Crystola Creek, which trickles from a mosaic of high-altitude wetlands. There was no water in the Fountain. Just the pink sand. There was, however, water in the Crystola. It ran, one or two feet wide and four to five inches deep. Where it met the Fountain, the Crystola vanished into the gravel, becoming something else. For about thirty feet down from the meeting of the two creeks, the sand and gravels of the Fountain were moist, but that was it. From there, the sediments were dry for nearly six miles, to where water appeared again, trickling from the gravels like magic near Green Mountain Falls.

Out of curiosity, I dropped into the Crystola Roadhouse for an ice-cold Budweiser because the sign outside announced Bud as the specialty. It was early but dark inside. Four morning drinkers watched me from the shadows. The bartender set the mug in front of me without a word then disappeared into what I assumed was the kitchen. I smiled at the four in the corner.

They did not smile back. Without warning, Metallica exploded through the room, stinging my ears. The Bud was warm and awful, and I tried to rinse the taste away with water and some sharp cinnamon breath mints my son had abandoned in the truck weeks before. Then I left.

Not far up from the Roadhouse, a Walmart Supercenter, and its gargantuan parking lot, sprawled smack in the middle of the Fountain between Crystola and Woodland Park. How Walmart was able to obtain a permit from Teller County and the City of Woodland Park to build in the middle of a frequently flooding Fountain is beyond me. Although the Fountain ran dry most of the year that high up, Walmart nonetheless constructed towering retaining walls on the side of the building facing the main channel. It was another one of those land use decisions I simply could not wrap my head around. Well, of course I could. It wasn't about the land or water. It was about money.

ATV and motorcycle tracks scarred the creek bed. The sediments were soft, like an enormous red sandbox. Six-foot-tall used dump truck tires and great slabs of rebar-encrusted concrete lined the edge of the creek bed as useless erosion control at some point. The banks rose in twenty- to thirty-foot cliffs above the alluvium. They were steep and rapidly eroding. At one point, not that long ago, the Fountain had been up there, level with the forest floor. Now, after years of overgrazing, timber harvesting, vehicle impacts, and road construction, the Fountain had dug itself into a cavernous channel filled with construction debris.

It wasn't just the giant tires and concrete. There were car-sized blocks of cement, cinder blocks, pipes, chairs, asphalt, and hunks of random steel that may have been peeled from ancient automobiles. In several places, the creek had been mined for sand and gravel. It was a war zone of sorts, something you might find after a bombing run.

I scrambled up an embankment, the concrete carapace shifting and sliding under my every step as if I were Sisyphus in a video game, forever twisting and leaping from one sliding slab to the next as the ground beneath gave way. Jump, slide, step, twist, jump, slide, jump . . . the memory of a severely broken ankle crept into my mind and I dropped to all fours, holding on until the slope stabilized. Then, I crawled on hands and knees to the top and pulled myself out of the creek bed by a dangling mountain mahogany, only to find myself trapped between a construction company, a Guns+Ammo store, a gravel operation, and dozens of No Trespassing signs. I slunk back to the creek bed and worked my way to the Safeway and then the park. By the time I found Summer, I was in a foul mood.

It was understandable, she said. "Our society can be irritating." She asked me to find a comfortable place to sit. I threw down my pack and chose a bumpy granite slab with a slight depression just the size of my butt. The slab was one of many, making up an elevated, circular planter with a bonsai-like ponderosa at the center. "Now. Close your eyes and breathe gently," she said. "Let's refocus."

I closed my eyes. Minutes passed and Summer spoke again.

"By 'irritating,' I don't mean just annoying in the general sense . . . politics, greed, bad music . . . these are annoying. What I mean by 'irritating' is the way our culture literally creates physical irritation in the body. It messes with our nerves. It jars our cells and even our DNA. Modern life is not just annoying; it is irritating in a way that actually causes physical and mental harm."

I continued to breathe.

"The constant noise and visual stimulation keeps us on edge. You go into a café, a bar, a restaurant . . . you know, a place where you'd normally go to relax. But you can't. The stereo is blasting, the TV screens keep your brain from settling. That's just one example. Pollution, cars, ugly parking lots, ugly buildings, ugly trash . . . these all have very real impacts on our bodies. On our physical selves."

I told her what I'd seen walking up from Crystola Creek.

"The reason that experience irritated you and put you on edge is because it was ugly. The natural world is inherently beautiful. You walked through destruction, so of course that impacts your nerves and your brain. You suffered a minor trauma just seeing the ugliness that was done to the creek."

Dr. Bill Fleming taught watershed management at the University of New Mexico, where I did my master's degree. Fleming ranks right up there with Frank Graves as one of the most impactful teachers in my life. He was one of those unique individuals for whom science and art blended seamlessly. After several weeks studying watershed restoration techniques—some serious hard science stuff—I'd asked him how we could know for sure that we had done the right type of restoration. "Beauty," he answered. "If it's beautiful, it's right. That's how you know."

"But isn't beauty in the eye of the beholder?"

He didn't think so. For Fleming, like Summer, beauty was an objective truth we know in our hearts.

Summer waved a hand at me. "So now we are going to shift. We'll move from ugly to beauty. Close your eyes again. Just breathe to start."

I allowed my eyelids to relax. The chill from the stone crept through my pants and into my skin. The breeze tickled the hair on the back of my neck. The air trickled through the five days of stubble clinging to my face. My feet tingled; my hands dried of sweat. A spotted towhee called and at the playground, a girl explained the rules of a game to her friends. Even through my eyelids, I could make out the shift in shadows as the draft bent the pines and spruce. Then, unconsciously, my lungs emptied and I sucked in an enormously satisfying breath. My whole body slumped and I couldn't help but smile.

"That's right," Summer said. "That's just right. Your nervous system is calming. Let's take another minute or so."

Within seconds, my body pulled in another large breath.

Then another. A peaceful grogginess overcame me. A sleepiness . . . as if the blanket of sun spilling across the grass were itself alive and beckoning me to just lay down. Rest. Nap. Heal.

"We all carry so much. Too much," Summer said. "Once we start letting it go, our bodies become aware of the deep exhaustion that we mask with our frenetic lives."

I started to explain something. I don't remember what. Summer cut me off.

"Whatever your reaction is, it's okay. Don't judge. Just feel."

Knowledge of the medicinal powers of the natural world spans continents, cultures, and centuries. The 2,500-year-old *Corpus Hippocraticum* is imbued with concepts of nature medicine, and the way in which the wild alleviates physical and mental suffering. Even in hyper-religious Medieval Europe, God was understood to reveal himself (or herself, themselves) in sylvan woodlands. People understood animals and plants as symbols of God with healing properties all their own. From Finland's *Kalevala* to Taoist poetry to Native American prayers, from Emerson (*Water*) to Rosella di Paolo (*Prueba de galera*), and from Wordsworth (*Tintern Abbey*) to Tupac Shakur (*The Rose That Grew from the Concrete*), human beings have found the wild in all its forms, large and small, to be the solace soothing the turgid beast within.

It wasn't until the 1980s that research into the *why* of nature's healing powers began. Around 1982, Tomohide Akiyama, Japan's Secretary of Forestry, coined the term Shinrin yoku or "Forest Bathing." As Summer explained it, the Japanese had practiced the tradition of Shinrin yoku for centuries. Akiyama sort of formalized the exercise, codifying best practices for achieving the most satisfying and beneficial result. Shinrin yoku became more of a science with organized classes and certifications for teachers.

Summer had received her certification as a forest bathing professional just before COVID and she taught classes throughout the region, at schools, community gatherings, and at the various nature centers up and down the Fountain watershed.

"It's a science, but also a heart practice," Summer told me. "People are looking for answers, but, as valuable as science is, it can't offer answers to matters of the heart and if anything, a river, a creek, that's a matter of the heart. We just have to remember what we already know."

In the 1920s and 30s, Belarusian scientist Boris P. Tokin learned of the power of phytoncides, or airborne essential oils excreted by plants, specifically trees. These compounds, Tokin discovered, reduce blood pressure and increase your immune system's ability to fight off infection. A simple walk in the forest has instant, measurable health benefits. And there was more.

A host of studies highlight the benefits of sunshine and negative air ions (eases depression), expansive landscape views (balances heart rate and reduces blood pressure), and birdsong (reduces stress and anxiety). Japanese researchers have documented a broad range of physiological benefits, measured in study participants after several days enhanced by forest bathing. An increase in anticancer and antivirus cells, an increase in the number of hormones and molecules that reduce obesity and soothe diabetes. Shinrin yoku, forest bathing, also results in a drop in blood glucose.

Study participants reported feeling more relaxed. They had more energy and could hold focus on difficult tasks longer. Others talked about how their migraines were either reduced or eliminated. One of the biggest benefits of Shinrin yoku came to those suffering anxiety, an all-too-common problem in our irritating society.

"I find the most benefit comes around water," Summer said.

I opened my eyes, excited about a sudden connection I'd made. "When I was a raft guide, clients would have the most profound experiences in just three or four hours on the river," I told her. "It seemed like every week I'd have at least one customer break down and cry, literally cry, because they . . ."

"They were feeling a profound, physical sense of relief in their nervous system," Summer interrupted. "The negative ions, the sun, the long views, the sound of water. I'll bet you had a lot of laughing on your raft."

She was right. Every single trip down the Colorado, the Roaring Fork, the Ark, or the Rio Grande came filled with frequent bouts of uproarious laughter.

"We don't laugh enough," I said. "I certainly don't . . . or haven't in a long time."

"Your nervous system has to calm and your heart to open to genuinely laugh."

I thought of my son, Ilan, a hyperintelligent old soul, on fire with sensitivities. In many ways, Ilan takes in too much. He feels too much. The information from the world comes in far too fast for him to process and he can become overwhelmed. We call this his superpower because his caring empathy is off the charts. He feels things I may never see or notice. Poverty hits him particularly hard. He doesn't just see poverty and feel sad about it like I do. Ilan *feels* poverty. It touches his nerves. He sees it and knows what it's like, even though he's spent his entire life in a middle-class situation. And, at his young age, he struggled to handle what he felt in his body.

If anything grounds my boy, it is water. Any water. From a hot shower to a swimming pool to a frigid mountain creek. Water pulls him like a magnet and always has. He calms instantly. We jokingly called him "water boy" in our family, but the balancing effect of water on his system is very real and it helps him make sense of the world.

The Fountain, there at Cavalier Park was empty. Summer led me down to a copse of chamomile and mullein. The grass grew waist-high, yellowing. Black-eyed Susans poked from the spaces between the wired riprap boulders handcuffing the creek. We sat again and listened.

"The memories we have of being on the land or near the water are collective. They aren't just your own personal memories." For Summer, a river, a creek, a stream, a brook, a run . . . moving water was alive and carried personhood. She jumped to the channel bottom, brushed aside a crescent of sediments, and began to dig.

The cup-shaped depression filled with muddy liquid. The Fountain seemed dry, yet still it was there, just below the surface. I scooped the water into my palm and the hole refilled.

"When you spend time with a person, you build collective memories. It's the same with the creek," Summer said. "The creek knows we are here. It has a memory of us being here before. It knows us. You are a memory of water."

Summer described the chemical process of drinking a cup of water and how, when we excrete that water through sweat or urine, it takes something of us with it. When we put our hand or foot in the water, it takes something of us with it. Molecules, cells, and our DNA. This is how water remembers.

Water enters and exits all sorts of beings—horses, elk, cows, birds, coyotes, wolves, fish—binding us together, transforming knowledge, building relationships through a memory of experiences just as you might with a girlfriend, a boyfriend, a cousin, a father, a grandmother . . .

"It's not just consuming water that does it." Summer pointed at the puddle in my palm. "You're shedding memory of you into that water and that water will eventually makes its way through soils and sediments and gravels to Manitou, Colorado Springs, Pueblo, Kansas, and the Gulf of Mexico. And then it returns. One day you might be fishing downstream and when you dip your hand into the flow the creek will say . . . hey . . . I know this guy. I already have a relationship with him."

I thought of all the time I'd spent in and near the Fountain and its tributaries, how I'd walked in it, fished it, hunted it, dug in it, peed in it, repaired beaver dams, sweated in it, skipped stones across its width, gathered trash, scattered seeds, and floated flowers. If the Fountain had a memory of me, it was a long memory. For me at least. A flash in the pan for a river, but not nothing.

Summer watched me pondering. "Don't try to wrap your brain around it. Just feel."

"He came down a hillside covered with stumps into a meadow. At the edge of the meadow flowed the river. Nick was glad to get to the river. He walked upstream through the meadow. His trousers were soaked with the dew as he walked. After the hot day, the dew had come quickly and heavily . . . Nick looked down the river at the trout rising. They were rising to insects come from the swamp on the other side of the stream when the sun went down. The trout jumped out of the water to take them . . . as far down the long stretch as he could see, the trout were rising, making circles all down the surface of the water, as though it were starting to rain."

This is how Nick Adams returns to the world.

PTSD ate at Ernest Hemingway on his return from World War I. As a combat ambulance driver on the Italian front, Hemingway played an active role in one of the bloodiest wars in human history. All wars are stupid. World War I stands out as an exceptionally vapid waste of humanity. Not only did Hemingway bear witness to the Great War, but he himself was wounded a number of times. The fictionalized account of Hemingway's healing, *Big Two-Hearted River*, is a masterpiece of nature writing. On the surface, the story appears a straightforward recount of young Nick Adams out on a solitary fishing trip. Beneath the waters, however, flows a tale of the restorative power of rivers.

Henry David Thoreau hoped to achieve a sort of heart-bonding with nature. "I went to the woods because I wished to live deliberately . . . and see if I could learn what it [nature] had to teach . . ." goes the oft-quoted Thoreau line. Nick Adams sought the same: the peace, the balance, the simplicity, discipline, connection, comforting permanence that is nature itself.

To heal, Hemingway . . . Nick . . . is first forced to confront the agony of his PTSD—"shell shock" as they called it in those days. Nick traverses the burned-over town of Seney, he encounters fire-blackened grasshoppers and an impenetrable swamp, the bog triggering memories of youth hung up on barbed wire or struggling through an inundated Alpine plain, slumping one upon the other as Austrian gunners mowed the young men with bullets like so much grass.

The symbolism is stark. His wounds ripped open, Nick comes to terms with the depth of his trauma. Denial no longer an option, Nick must choose between healing or losing his hold on reality. It is only through the interaction with the river that wounds heal and Nick rediscovers his place in the world. "He did not need to get his map out. He knew where he was from the position of the river."

Rivers play an outsized role in our lives.

There is no shortage of books, poems, and songs about rivers, creeks, and streams. What Olivia Laing calls "The vast disordered library of river literature signals the power of moving water as thoroughly as does the wearing down of formidable mountains by those same waters." The healing power of water flows through that vast disordered library.

It seems to me that every river-borne author speaks of the power of rivers to salve broken spirits and sooth troubled minds. John baptized Jesus in the Jordan. The Maclean family left for the creek when they couldn't solve their problems, seeking the "healing effects of cold waters" in the pastoral classic *A River Runs Through It*. Karai Senryū, the Japanese poet, came to terms with his mortality on the banks of a creek before his death in 1790.

Now, the wintry wind-
but then let your buds blossom,
river willow.

Likewise, John Graves, a veteran of the brutal Pacific Island fighting of World War II (he fought alongside my uncle on Saipan), sought healing on Texas's Rio Brazos. He also sought to understand what America had become and where it was going. "You could drink the truth in its purity," he wrote, "if you went to the source." Graves's *Goodbye to a River* is a soothing antidote to its contemporary, Kerouac's frenetic *On the Road*.

So too, many of the unhoused individuals along the Fountain will tell you of the medicine that is the creek and how it calms their mental and emotional agonies.

Laing put it best. "There's a mystery about rivers that draws us to them," she wrote after walking the length of England's River Ouse. ". . . for they rise from hidden places and travel by routes that are not always tomorrow where they might be today. Unlike a lake or a sea, a river has its destination and there is something about that certainty with which it travels that makes it very soothing, particularly for those who've lost faith with where they're headed."

I met up with Alli Schuch and David Woolley for beers at Mash Mechanix Brewing Company in downtown Colorado Springs. Woolley had taken up a large, long table with boxes, vials, jars, Ziplocs, envelopes, ties, and an array of seeds. It was the Wednesday before Creek Week and Woolley aimed to have packets of native plant seeds ready for participants, the idea being that we could scatter the seeds along the banks of the Fountain as we collected trash.

Creek Week took off in 2014 when Schuch, then a volunteer for the Fountain Creek Watershed District, organized a cluster of community members fed up with the trash spilling along the Fountain and its tributaries. Initially, Creek Week was a dozen or so volunteers gathering junk at two or three locations over a weekend. Before long, this blossomed into a nine-day effort each October, involving thousands of volunteers, schools, businesses, state agencies, and local governments at dozens of locations from Pueblo to Woodland Park. One Manitou Springs elementary school, for example, saw its 350 students cleaning waste from about two miles of stream bank. It has grown to be one of the largest, if not the largest, river cleanup events in the country. In the six years I've participated in Creek Week, the various crews I worked with had gathered somewhere between one thousand and two thousand pounds of trash *per day*. The result being that around twenty thousand pounds of trash pulled from the Fountain by volunteers each year, somewhere around 145 *tons* since the effort began. By 2023, Creek Week had grown beyond the trash cleanup to encompass picnics, native tree planting, educational activities, music, art installations, and, of course, beer.

To celebrate Creek Week, the Fountain Creek Brewshed Alliance fashioned the "Impactful IPA," a collaboratively created concoction from several Fountain watershed breweries. The goal was to raise money for watershed restoration efforts through sales of a yummy brew. Beer is mostly water, the Brewshed Alliance points out. No clean water, no beer. This message resonates in Colorado, a state famous for its intimate relationship with beer and home to a deep history of brew culture. "The best drops for your hops," goes the alliance motto.

I'd met Woolley, a self-described "seed librarian," while watching a kestrel hunt along Bear Creek that spring. After attending a lecture at Colorado College by seed-saving guru Bill McDorman, Woolley started the Manitou Seed Library in 2012. He began with heirloom vegetables and medicinal herbs, trading seeds and seed saving secrets with other aficionados throughout the region. His skill set grew, and by 2018 Woolley turned his focus to native plants, wildflowers, trees, shrubs, and grasses.

On the table before us stood jars of white prairie clover seeds. They were tiny, round, and brown, somewhat like radish, I thought. There was also mountain Bahia, a star-like yellow flower. Seeds of the nettleleaf hyssop, a fuzzy, purple, cylindrical flower filled one jar while Bigelow's aster, golden buckwheat, and various yarrows filled envelopes scattered between pints of beer. There was butterfly milkweed, a fibrous forb topped in miniature red-orange blooms, Rydberg's pentstemon, the medicinal wild bergamot, and one of my favorites, the bee plant, a bright showy cleome that grows up to five feet tall. A favorite of hummingbirds, the bee plant is the oft-forgotten member of the three—actually four—sisters: corn, beans, and squash, the basis of many Indigenous North American diets. It is odd that this fourth sister is left out when discussing Indigenous agriculture because it ties the other three sisters together, particularly in what is now the American Southwest.

As a young archaeologist exploring the Four Corners region, my mentors from the Crow Canyon Archaeological Center taught me to look for the pink-flowered cleome as a way to locate ancestral Puebloan sites. The flower was utilized so widely by the ancient Pueblo people that it continues to cluster in and around towns and villages one thousand years after the inhabitants moved on.

My love of this flower extends beyond its beauty. The bee plant is edible, high in nutrients such as vitamin A, iron, and calcium. The seeds are perfect for porridges and breads. But its real power lay in how it perfected the sisterhood by attracting nectar-slurping insects and hummingbirds to the Puebloan gardens where the animal relations pollinated squash blossoms and bean flowers. Corn is pollinated by the wind.

Woolley hosted monthly "Seed Saturday" events around the watershed, inviting experts to trade and novices to learn. He presented in schools and to community groups. Seed saving was Woolley's hobby. He was also an artist, writer, father, and employee of the City of Fountain. I asked how he managed everything. "Well, as hobbies go, seed saving is pretty inexpensive, but fact is, I couldn't do any of it without my wife. She's not just accepting of my obsessions, she gets excited too!"

Together, and over pints of Impactful IPA, the three of us doled seeds into the envelopes, mixing the species and adding a spoonful of sand to each envelope. The sand helps to spread the seeds more evenly.

I told Schuch and Woolley about my fruitless attempt to rebuild the busted up beaver dam in the middle of winter, and how the experience left me confused. What was something concrete I could do to give back to the Fountain? There is power in action. There is healing in doing something, anything, to make things better, especially when you are making things better for someone or something else. Far too often, I felt powerless. If something as simple as picking up plastic cups and throwing down native seeds could help lighten the load, then more of it, please!

On another morning, Jerry Cordova led me on a tour of Colorado Springs' stormwater drains. It was probably not how most people would spend a weekend morning, but nearly every Colorado Springs street gutter drained to the Fountain, and Cordova wanted me to see what he'd been up to.

Jerry Cordova was a stormwater specialist with the City of Colorado Springs. Gregarious, intelligent, optimistic, funny, and consumed with an infectious joie de vivre, Cordova spent several nights a month creating music in bars and cafés with his multi-instrumental band *Spur*. Stormwater specialist, but what he really was, was a community organizer, working to help people protect the Fountain. He created opportunity for action.

We crossed the street just up from Mash Mechanix to a humble square hole in the street that drained rainwater and snowmelt. But it wasn't just any humble stormwater drain. This one had two things going for it. For one, a giant painted mermaid framed the box of the inlet, a portion of the sidewalk above and the manhole cover below. She sported blue hair, a shiny purple tail, and a slinky white T-shirt that said, "Only rain down the drain." The artwork, by Eliz Selby, was part of Cordova's Storm Drain Art Program.

"The thing is," he told me, "Most people simply aren't aware the street is connected to the creek. What ends up on our streets ends up in the Fountain. If we can bring awareness to that simple fact, I tend to think most people might think twice about dropping trash on the street or letting their oil pans leak."

I wasn't so sure. But Cordova was an optimist after all.

We toured several other drains, each decorated by a different artist. In one, a school of mermaids bathed in a creek against a backdrop of snowy peaks. Another was a close up of an osprey's head, yellow eyes watching. There were more mermaids, these sipping teas, giggling, and reading from books in a bright, watery room. I found it strangely erotic.

"Never in my life have I associated mermaids with Colorado," I told Cordova.

He grinned and shrugged. "Who's to say?"

There was a painting depicting the Garden of the Gods, another, the Colorado state flag, one of jagged, icy peaks, and another with a globe, octopus, and two fish.

The second thing going on was harder to see. We walked up the street to another party of Colorado mermaids clustering a storm drain, this one marked by a circular plaque: "Gutter Bin—Stormwater Filtration System."

"When we are out on Creek Week, picking up all that trash?"

"Yeah?"

"Well, I'm thinking how we cut down on all that trash in the first place." Cordova opened an undersized manhole cover and I peered inside.

The Gutter Bin is one of those ridiculously simple and ingenious items that has you slapping your head wondering why you didn't think of it in the first place. Essentially, it was an oversized coffee filter for street runoff. The filter, developed by Frog Creek Partners out of Wyoming, collected plastics, cigarette butts, broken glass, plastic bags, needles, and more from the streets. The bin, hidden within the storm drain, catches the junk while allowing the water to flow through, meaning cleaner water and no street flooding. Once a year, city crews empty the bins.

Gutter Bins cost anywhere from $600-$1,000 dollars, Cordova said, and they last up to twenty-five years. In Denver, twenty-two thousand such bins have removed around 4.5 million pounds of trash each year that would otherwise end up in the South Platte River. That is over two hundred pounds of trash per year, per Gutter Bin. For those of us cleaning up each year along the Fountain, the result is a huge reduction in workload, not to mention all the benefits to the creek itself.

A few days later, out on North Douglas Creek, I joined an older gentleman named Stephen. We were part of the CPW sponsored Creek Week cleanup crew, and we had come across a vast abandoned homeless encampment. The amount of trash was, frankly, appalling. Most curious were the thousands, yes, thousands, of empty plastic tortilla bags blowing up and down the creek bank, trapped in rocks and covered in leaves. We hung a black trash bag from an elm, donned our gloves, and set to work. The task ahead was intimidating. A biologist from CPW joined and kept us preoccupied with tales of her recent trip to Hawai'i.

At one point, I came to a pile of used needles. The Creek Week protocol is to avoid handling any biohazards. Instead, we were to drop a map pin using our phones, then text the pin to the group leader. She would in turn send the "hazmat" crew to each pin to collect the needles or whatever other biohazardous waste we came across. When I dropped the pin on my phone map, the mystery of the tortilla wrappings became clear. Just across the creek stood a tortilla factory. The campers had evidently found a way to get a hold of the tortillas and get them across the water to the encampment.

Hours passed. By early afternoon, we had cleared the forest, hauling up dozens of bags of trash, loaded shopping carts, and busted tortilla crates we'd filled with junk. Stephen and the CPW biologist headed off to get the truck to load the bags. I walked back and forth across the bare and brittle autumn forest, scattering Woolley's native seeds and a bag of gramma grass seed, gifted from another friend.

In spring, Summer introduced me to Tamara Herl, a forest bathing specialist with flowing silver locks living on the banks of Fountain Creek above Manitou and just below Highway 24. Herl operated a retreat center for nature healing. She fashioned Earth alters of aspen leaves, flowers, and willow catkins. She created masks of Fountain clay, bark, sage, found flicker feathers, and squirrel and mouse bones she'd pulled from the forest floor. These she hung in trees. Sentinels. That May, I walked with Herl down a mile-long, three-foot wide loop path her husband had cut through the riparian forest.

"What I do," she explained, "Is provide space. I mean, people can take space on their own, but they don't. So I allow people the time and the place to listen to what nature has to say. I create the space that allows people to hear the voice of the creek."

"What does the creek say?"

She led me to a log jutting from a sea of willow. "Sit." She pointed.

I sat. The Fountain gurgled across from me, tumbling between stones, down a hole in the sediments, fashioning a vernal chorus of echoing swoosh, and, at times, slurping and sucking.

Herl told me of a friend struggling with the ebbs and flow of life at middle age. She was down and wondered what she was worth and why her life went down this path or that, and why she continually hit bumps in the road. How, just when things settled, another challenge, a whole new drama would arise. "She was tired. Fed up. Both with herself and her world." Herl told me.

The woman had come earlier that spring. She'd walked the loop. She'd mediated at the Earth alters. She'd sat on the log. A yellow-rumped warbler appeared. The bird grasped onto a stout branch of willow and sat, perfectly still. Content. At peace. After several minutes, a stiff breeze kicked up and the warbler grew agitated and flew up then returned to the willow, this time to a thin stick of a branch that could hardly support its weight. The bird bounced and flapped, struggling to find balance and to hold on in the blow. Then it returned to the stout branch, finding purchase, calming. She watched the bird for minutes . . . hours . . . she didn't know how long. It watched her back. Then it pushed up, hovering, feeding on minuscule gnats. When it landed again, it returned to the same unstable little branch and struggled to settle, flapping its wings, jumping around. And so, the warbler returned once again to the stout branch.

Herl's friend studied the warbler, following this pattern as it repeated it at least a dozen times. She lost track of time but at some point, the heart, as Summer would say, made clear what the brain struggled to deduce. The experience of the bird on the two types of branches was a metaphor for what life chooses to do with us, Herl said. We seek stability, but the winds of life have different plans and we are forced to adjust. At times our own ambitions take us far afield, and when we return, grounding can be hard to find because we aren't the same person we had been before. Human beings, like rivers, are anything but static. We are forever in flux. The experience of the bird on the two types of branches was more like real life than anything else. Herl's friend looked around at the remains of a recent flood of snowmelt.

That's the "Ever-ending-Earth" I thought. The world is unreliable. Life is a process of ups and downs. Knowing this intellectually is one thing, Herl said. Understanding this view of life at a heart level integrates it into our physical bodies, sticking the knowledge to our nervous systems, and even our DNA. To understand a river is to understand life itself, with all its complexities, contradictions, and beauty.

"Whatever your take on it, she found incredible relief," Herl explained. "It wasn't just a bird on a stick, right? It was a whole new understating of how life works and how she might approach the future. Her own future. This is the language of nature. The language of the creek. I believe that if we would *only* stop, listen, and feel, we'd find priceless wisdom around every corner. But *only* if we listen."

Sentient life, personhood, does not need adhere to our own preconceived notions. We need a way to talk about, think about, a creek that isn't based in our own values that sees water as nothing but a commodity to be exploited.

"We only exist in relationship to others," Summer told me at one point. Families are created by relationships. Nations are created by relationships. Beingness lies in relationship. Arguably, we can't even exist as individuals. Robin Wall Kimmerer, the Potawatomi biologist and author, explained that "in Indigenous ways of knowing, we understand a person (which may include a river or a place) to be a person because of her relationships."

Kimmerer has written extensively on the ways in which Native American languages hold values and ways of speaking of the more than human world. Indigenous languages, she says, such as those of the Nuuchiu and Hinonoʼeino, recognize that life extends beyond how we think about "life" in the Western World. Humans, animals, and plants are alive to be sure, but so too are rocks, wind, stars, mountains, and rivers. This "being-ness" is reflected in the very grammatical structure of many Indigenous languages. To be is to be alive. This is strikingly different from the English language where nouns are rendered as static. A river in modern English is simply a "thing." An item. But in many Indigenous languages, Kimmerer points out, a river is not a noun but a verb. It is "being" a river which connotes action and agency. A miracle, much like a human.

Words create reality. Our ways of speaking create our ways of understanding the world. If we speak of something as alive then we see it as alive and interact with it as if it were alive. If we speak in terms of relationships, we have relationships.

Kimmerer advocates for a "grammar of animacy." A new way of speaking about the world around us. We are in a phase now where we've altered the world so profoundly that our words and concepts mask our understanding of what lies before us. Not only did I seek a new way of being in the Anthropocene, I hungered for a way to vocalize it, to conceive it, and to speak it into that reality.

The question of whether rivers are alive or not is an inquiry that transcends science, demanding a change in how we understand the world. Brother, sister, father, mother, uncle, aunt. The river is me.

At the time of my visit, Herl was new to the land. She'd moved from Colorado Springs after years in public education. As we walked, she asked what I noticed. What called to me.

I named the willows and the pine. I named the creek and the bright spring grasses. I named the robin and an early butterfly.

"What more?" She pushed.

"Beavers!" I said.

"What do you mean?"

"Once upon a time there were a hell of a lot of beavers on this land." I pointed out old dam after old dam, beaver cut tree stumps, and we traced the edges of what had been an assemblage of ponds, one upon the other.

"There was a flood," Herl said. "See all that?" She pointed to a bramble of collapsed willow, aspen, ponderosa . . . all piled against a thick stump. The Fountain turned, curled, and cut down through ancient pond sediments, shoving the eroded material towards Manitou Springs.

"What should we do?"

"Beavers," I repeated.

RESTORATION

"In short, a land ethic changes the role of Homo sapiens from conqueror of the land-community to plain member and citizen of it. It implies respect for his fellow-members, and also respect for the community as such."

–*Aldo Leopold,* A Sand County Almanac

Yes. I have a thing for beavers.

At one point in my life, I became intoxicated by a collection of dusty maps of the Colorado-New Mexico borderlands. I'd picked the maps off the shelf of an antiquarian bookstore in the western Colorado town of Durango. Never mind that frayed charts from days gone by are endlessly fascinating in and of themselves, what caught my attention on those specific maps were the hundreds of tiny, blue, sperm-like symbols spread across the charts. They turned up in meadows, below cliffs, in caves, and next to streams. These were symbols for aquifer-fed springs, where rivers are born and reborn. They were plotted by military, and later, USGS cartographers. I carried photocopies of those maps with me on hiking and backpack journeys, aiming to hunt down as many of the springs as possible. I had little luck. Ninety to 95 percent of the springs had dried up.

When you imagine the American Southwest, what comes to mind? If you are like most, sweeping expanses of desert backed by snow-packed peaks takes hold of your imagination, an "arid wasteland" as Justice Scalia so stupidly put it. Yes, the red buttes of Monument Valley, the Sonoran saguaros, the dunes of Death Valley, or the dunes of the San Luis Valley framed by the icy Sangre de Cristo range, are real enough. Perhaps you imagine sage-studded altiplano stocked with sheep and patrolling cowboys. This is also real. Above all, what you imagine is the aridity, the big dry. This isn't incorrect, but there is a hell of a lot more to the West than that.

"Here is a land where life is written in water," penned the 1979 Colorado State Poet Laureate, Thomas Hornsby Ferril. And indeed it is. Prior to the extermination of western beavers between about 1820 and 1860, the American West was vastly different than today. It was a wetter landscape, rich in ponds, lakes, marshes, year-round streams, and expansive aquifers feeding thousands upon thousands of bubbling springs spread like jewels across the land, springs such as the ones dotting my delicate maps. Remember shifting baseline syndrome? The way the West looks now and the West of the popular imagination bears little resemblance to the West of five hundred years ago. We've mentally adjusted to a vastly altered and I would say cheapened landscape. We think this is "normal" when it is anything but. Imagine the American Southwest of 1492 as sort of a soggy Shangri-la.

And why was the West so wet? Yup. Beavers.

Estimates are that somewhere between 15 and 250 million beaver ponds bejeweled North America prior to 1492. In *Eager: The Surprising Secret Life of Beavers and Why They Matter*, Ben Goldfarb estimated that beaver ponds once soaked at least 234,000 square miles of North America, an area, he points out, larger than the states of Nevada and Arizona combined. Without hyperbole, the 2018 *Eager* is one of the most important books of the twenty-first century.

Beaver families can inhabit the same ponds for centuries, adding to their dams and canals as they go. Dams can grow to be hundreds of feet long and dozens of feet high, storing truly massive amounts of water, soaking many square miles. Beavers and their dams have been around long enough and spread extensively enough that they have influenced the evolution of countless species, not to mention the entire North American landscape. Beavers and watersheds evolved together over forty million years. Beavers quite literally shaped the continent more than any other non-human animal. Beavers are so integral, it could be argued that without beavers, it is impossible for a river to function as it should. Without beavers, a river isn't a river.

Of course, it wasn't *just* the slaughter of beavers (the "Furpocalypse" as Goldfarb calls it) that dried out the American West. Overgrazing by horses, sheep, and cattle certainly took a massive toll on the water cycle, as did the diversion of waterways for agriculture, the clear-cutting of ancient forests, and the purposeful draining of wetlands. Millenia of Indigenous landscape stewardship (not always perfect, but generally so) was undone in a matter of decades. Still, it was the extirpation of *Castor canadensis* that truly unwound the water from the land and the past from what became the present.

My love for beavers is based in my infatuation with wetlands. Wetlands tend to be the most productive and dynamic ecosystems the world has to offer. Whether you're talking water storage, replenishing aquifers, pollution removal, nutrient cycling, flood control, forest fire mitigation, or wildlife habitat, wetlands have something for everyone. Moreover, they are beautiful. I love nothing more than to pull on my waders and prowl a marsh with my camera.

In 1998, I worked as a rural community organizer for the New Mexico Wilderness Alliance, spreading the gospel of public lands conservation to dubious ranchers and hostile county commissioners across the Land of Enchantment. That summer, I revisited what had been a barren, overgrazed chunk of range in Catron County, a section of the state known for violent attacks on environmentalists. The ranch was owned by a multigenerational gaucho I'd gotten to know during the vicious fight to reintroduce the Mexican wolf, or lobo, to its historic range in southern New Mexico and southeastern Arizona. He'd been skeptical of the wolf but had left enough of a door open to learning that we had some rich conversations, and I came to have a better understanding of the rural fear of the wolf . . . that had much more to do with the federal government than the lobo.

Deep arroyos had spread across his land, several springs had dried up, and his grass production was down. He and his ancestors had overgrazed the land to the point that they were about to go under. He knew he needed to change, but he wasn't yet sure what changes to make.

The rancher was skeptical of doing things different, but he was desperate and at least willing to try. When two beavers turned up, he ignored the advice of his father and the pleading of his brother, and allowed the beavers to stay. The water-bound rodents did what they do, constructing several small dams, slowing the water, catching the sediment, and raising the water table. Sagebrush and cactus soon gave way to cattails and sprouting willow. After just two years, the gaucho saw his grass production improve despite an expanding drought, and he wanted to know how he could get more beavers on the ranch.

"Beavers are ecological and hydrological Swiss Army knives," scribbled Ben Goldfarb. In the right circumstances, beavers are capable "of tackling just about any landscape-scale problem you might confront. Trying to mitigate floods or improve water quality? There is a beaver for that. Hoping to capture more water for agriculture in the face of climate change? Add a beaver. Concerned about sedimentation, salmon runs, wildfire? Take two families of beavers and check back in a year."

As I see it, beavers are not just the past, they are the future. Goldfarb put it this way: "Our ability to restore degraded land and water depends on our ability to close our eyes and gaze into the past, to see North America as the ponded, puddled, ecologically functioning marshscape it once was and, with a little ingenuity, may yet become again."

When I revisited my Catron County acquaintance in 2009, twelve- to fifteen-foot cottonwoods shaded his section of the creek, large duck-filled ponds spread across the landscape, the grass was tall and green (for a rancher, more and better grass translates to better income), and his ugly arroyos, while still ugly, had not expanded, rather, in many places, had begun to heal. The rancher credited rotational grazing he'd learned from the Quivira Coalition and the return of the beaver for his success. He also gave a cautious nod to the lobo, noting that the wolves kept the elk and deer moving, thinned the herds, and improved hunting. From rancher to "beaver believer," as Goldfarb labeled those of us who see the busy rodents as a way towards a better future. Before long, that rancher was spreading the Castorian Gospel to his neighbors, an evangelical for the healing power of beavers.

When it comes to the impacts of Colorado Springs' development on the Fountain watershed, Dr. Brian Mihlbachler has had a front row seat. "I'm right on Monument Creek and from my office window, I've got a view east across I-25," he told me. "I've watched the city spill north. The whole watershed has changed. We call it hydro-modification. That's when the watershed's flow pattern is altered by an increase in water volume, the frequency of runoff, and new sedimentation. Things like that. And . . . let's just say the modifications have been . . . major."

Mihlbachler, the USFWS Natural Resource Manager at the United States Air Force Academy, came to the job in 2000. His focus was protecting the threatened Preble's jumping mouse, a riparian rodent with a ridiculously long tail, huge hind feet, long hind legs, and the ability to jump upwards of four to five feet.

Preble's was the beast whose protected habitat I'd accidentally stumbled through on Jackson Creek. The mouse is endemic to riparian corridors in Colorado and Wyoming only. It is found nowhere else in the world.

I met Mihlbachler, a tall, long-legged biologist nearing retirement, at his office tucked among ponderosas in a lonely corner of the rambling Air Force Academy campus. "When I first started this job, I actually didn't think much about Monument Creek. It was in pretty good shape back then, so I focused on protecting other mouse habitat, mainly the uplands bordering the creeks. But that all changed with the rapid development on the other side of the interstate."

It was a sweltering morning in early September. Mihlbachler and I hopped in the truck, cranked the air conditioning, and toured the back roads of the Academy, seeking beavers. They weren't hard to find. Mihlbachler was doing everything he could to move beavers in and keep them. "You know," Mihlbachler said, "when the mouse was first listed in the 90s . . . in some ways it really wasn't about the mouse, it was more about habitat loss. The rarity of the mouse was Monument Creek talking to us, saying something isn't right. If we had listened to the creek then, we might have saved ourselves tens of millions of dollars and years of struggle."

We looked at one another and shrugged at the same time.

Historically, the Monument, much like the Fountain into which it flows, was an intermittent stream flowing only at certain times a year. But, as with the Fountain, development in the Town of Monument and effluent from two sewage treatment plants turned the Monument into a year-round waterway.

Because the Academy sits on prime Preble's habitat, the Endangered Species Act obligated the Air Force to protect the mouse's home. The Air Force has a conservation agreement with the USFWS to monitor, protect, and restore Preble's habitat. The agreement means that the Academy can do infrastructure repair and maintenance work without extensive ESA analysis and Mihlbachler has Air Force funding for Preble's research and monitoring, habitat protection, and restoration work. Yet, since 2000, the erosion problems turned up all across the Academy, problems the Air Force did not create.

As he watched Colorado Springs sprawl north, Mihlbachler noticed the once-functional Monument Creek and its east side tributaries (75 percent of Monument Creek's watershed drains through the Academy) were falling apart, eroding and dewatering before his eyes. "We went from a natural hydrology to too much water almost overnight."

The system was collapsing.

Once again, the culprit was the impervious surfaces spreading through the developments across the interstate. "They sent way too much runoff to the small tributary creeks and blew them out into huge ravines." More runoff, faster runoff, larger flooding events, and increased sedimentation all degraded the Monument and its tributaries. In just a few years Black Squirrel Creek, Black Forest Creek, Monument Branch, Middle Tributary, Pine Creek, Elkhorn Creek, and Kettle Creek were down cut with all the new water from the sprawl, creating near canyons where healthy, stable creeks had once thrived. All that erosion threatened roads, bridges, and damaged Preble's habitat as well as that of bats, butterflies, birds, fish, and amphibians. The development also increased the frequency and severity of flooding along the Monument. With the creeks dug so far down, their ability to interact with their floodplains disappeared. Floodwaters no longer spread out to dissipate energy. Instead, the water funneled into ever-deepening channels that in some cases worked like a fire hose to further exacerbate the problem.

Because the Air Force had funding for the mouse, and all the erosion harmed the mouse habitat, Mihlbachler was able to get consultants and contractors out to stabilize eroding channels and creek banks and, eventually, begin full-scale habitat restoration work. But it was expensive, typically running more than $1,000 per foot.

Recently, the City of Colorado Springs has helped the Academy with the creek restoration costs, contributing hundreds of thousands of dollars to Air Force projects or performing work on the Academy on their own. "There's a growing recognition that protecting and restoring the watershed within the Academy provides significant and multiple downstream benefits to the city," explained Mihlbachler. As development progresses in the county and Town of Monument, similar recognition and partnerships will be vital to protect and restore Monument Creek and its watershed.

We parked the truck near a field of smooth brome, side oats grama, and needlegrass. Late season sticky aster dotted the buttery grasses like purple buttons on a golden shirt. I walked to the eroding edge of a creek and peered down. The water was a good twenty feet below me. A ponderosa had collapsed into the arroyo, undercut by spring floods. We walked along the cliff's edge, Mihlbachler pointing out the creek's original floodplain and where the erosion was the worst. "It's a canyon down there," he said. "This is just ten years old. Seriously. Ten years ago, there was no canyon here. People have to see it to believe it."

Mihlbachler stopped to look at the invasive brome. I continued to edge the ravine. "If you need to pee," he called out, "Please don't pee in the creek. I don't need any more water down there!" He laughed.

Large-scale mechanical river restoration work is ridiculously expensive. Well, we choose to make it expensive. Most of the time, cheaper solutions are available, so Mihlbachler looked to beavers. Several families already inhabited the upper reaches of the Academy, but there weren't enough of them to make a difference given the enormity of the problems. So, Mihlbachler took to importing beavers, taking several slated for removal from the South Platte in Denver and several from areas being developed around Colorado Springs. Once roaming free at the Academy, the beavers did what beavers do. At the time of my visit, there were 160 dams scattered across the Academy. Restoration crews had also constructed several BDAs (beaver dam analogs) to attract still more castors. Unfortunately, late summer floods in 2022 and spring floods in 2023 blew out many of the structures including some dams.

"It's hard for them to get a foothold when these creeks are so flashy. The lack of cottonwoods and other trees is a serious problem when it comes to reintroduction because they need trees for forage and dam construction material. Still, we're making some progress and trying to be proactive, rather than always being reactive with intensive mechanical restoration." The floods of spring 2023 likewise ripped out some of the more recent restoration work, adding still more cost to an already expensive project. We pulled over and watched crews in bulldozers redo work they'd completed just six months before. One crew followed behind, spreading native grass seeds and covering them with erosion control netting.

"It's really not a question of what the creek says," Mihlbachler said, "but rather, are we listening? If we'd paid attention to what the creek and the mouse was telling us twenty-five years ago, we'd be doing a heck of a lot better now."

Another Beaver Believer is Jerry Mallett.

Mallett was, like me, a Pueblo kid, although he'd lived the bulk of his life in Colorado Springs. He is also somewhat of a legend, although he would laugh at such a label. Long before I met Jerry, I knew of him for his decades of conservation work as the Western Field Representative for The Wilderness Society and a co-founder of the stream protection nonprofit, American Rivers. More recently, Mallett helped to found Colorado Headwaters, a diverse collection of water protection advocates from across the state. Their goal is to work with the state, feds, and private landowners to protect and restore Colorado's mountain streams and wetlands. One of the group's primary tools? Yes, you guessed it.

"I guess I don't need to list out all the abuses the Fountain faces," Mallett grumbled when I called him up.

"No, sir. I think I've got a decent handle on that."

"Well, you should, being from Pueblo. But a lot of people in Pueblo don't even know the Fountain is there."

I could almost hear him shaking his head through the airwaves.

"Well, it's a mess," he continued. "They're spending millions and millions on mechanical fixes and while their hearts are in the right place, the fact is, beaver can do it better and cheaper than we ever could."

But.

It's not as if you can just go grab yourself a beaver and do with it what you please. My water-boy son hates when I say this but . . . it's complicated.

With 97 percent of major Colorado rivers and 61 percent of smaller streams considered partially or completely nonfunctional as riverine-riparian systems, the active reintroduction of beavers to as much of their ancestral habitat as possible might seem an obvious, effective, and cost-conscious way of repairing watersheds. However, beavers, like wolves, are so similar to humans we find them threatening. Beavers are controversial. In a 2021 article, the president of the Colorado Farm Bureau said that beavers can "certainly be a nuisance if they're in the wrong place."

While beavers do not "take" water (they merely slow it down), many farmers worry that beavers may indeed impact water availability downstream and that they will alter the timing of irrigation flows. Farmers are also concerned that evaporation from beaver ponds could result in a loss of irrigation water and that more trees and shrubs in the riparian zone would drink away their water. Then there is the interstate water treaty with Kansas that obligates the State of Colorado to deliver a certain amount of water to the Colorado-Kansas border each year.

As a result, those working to reintroduce beavers or perform any sort of extensive upstream restoration have been forced to navigate a maze of state rules and regulations. It wasn't until 2023 that Colorado lawmakers began working on legislation that would clarify what is and what isn't allowed when it comes to watershed restoration in Colorado. The 2023 restoration legislation was born of a bipartisan effort that hoped to meet the needs of as many Colorado water users as possible. The Colorado Healthy Headwaters group is comprised of academics, conservationists, federal and state agencies, and municipalities and irrigators. Unfortunately, the final law was watered down, limiting the types of restoration possible. The result was still more complexity (sorry, Ilan), but at least it offered a bit of clarity.

Goldfarb rightly points out that we must learn to live with beavers if our collective goal is to protect our water resources far into the future. Beaver-human relationships are managed relationships. Kind of like a marriage. With effort, curiosity, and kindness, we can coexist with *Castor canadensis*.

Still, for me, this reaction, although understandable from a very narrow perspective, is yet another demonstration of how we have collectively twisted ourselves into knots when it comes to water. Instead of altering the way we use water to match the workings of a healthy watershed, we instead insist the watershed remain in poor condition in order to meet our desires. Then we fork over extraordinary amounts of money to slap tenuous temporary Band-Aids all over that broken watershed. To me, this is proof of a sort of social insanity.

Mallett introduced me to Jackie Corday, a conservation attorney based in the western Colorado town of Montrose. Corday, a former water resource manager with CPW and the head of the Colorado Healthy Headwaters group, spent several years researching the pitfalls and opportunities of what is called "process based restoration," the idea that we can return a creek or river to a natural state by focusing on the natural processes and functions of the whole the system.

In 2022, Corday authored *Restoring Western Headwater Streams with Low-Tech Process-Based Methods: A Review of the Science and Case Study Results, Challenges and Opportunities.* The American Rivers publication found that low-tech, low-cost approaches to restoration are faster and generally more effective than expensive mechanical fixes. In locations where beavers cannot be reintroduced, Corday proposes BDAs, hammering vertical posts into the creek bed, much as I had done in my furious dam repair efforts a winter or two before. The vertical posts catch wood and other debris coming down the flow, mimicking a beaver dam, allowing debris buildup, allowing the water to pool and deposit sediment, and, if possible, jumpstarting a potential beaver home.

"Right now," Corday said, "much of the best beaver habitat is on private lands high in the watershed, so we need to develop relationships with landowners before we can get to work in many cases."

The Keystone Ecosystem Initiative is a Fountain watershed focused outgrowth of Colorado Headwaters. The idea behind the initiative is to utilize inexpensive, low-tech, nature-based solutions to help the watershed, with the focus on reestablishing historic wetlands throughout the system. Where beavers are not currently present but were historically, KEI hopes to relocate so-called "nuisance" beavers (the ones damming irrigation canals and street culverts) and encourage natural recolonization, or as a last resort, construct BDAs.

In arid regions, mountains are "wet islands" or "water banks." When allowed to function properly, mountains produce water (mostly from snow) and store it in high-altitude wetlands and aquifers. That stored water eventually makes it to the lowlands, where the majority of people and agriculture exist. Without mountain water banks, life in the lowlands would be hard pressed.

"We want to slow the water down high up. We want to rewater dried up wetlands, refill the aquifers, and get the system working as it should," Mallett explained. "If you're going to restore a watershed, you've got to start at the top of the watershed. For us, the mountains. Anything you do downstream without first getting the headwaters in shape is . . ."

He paused. I waited, somewhat expecting a frustrated rant. Instead, I got a deep sigh.

"Well . . . we can be smarter," he said.

In 2019, the Fountain Creek Watershed Flood Control and Greenway District approached the Barrs about a possible restoration project. An assessment study had identified the Barr Farm as under threat, a restoration project that stabilized the banks would protect the property, the District said, and reduce overall sediment load in the creek by more than one hundred thousand tons a year, making both the City of Pueblo and irrigators on the lower Arkansas happy. The Barrs agreed and in 2020, the $10.2 million projcct got underway.

The restoration work utilized heavy machinery and logs harvested from the 2018 Spring Creek fire, near the village of La Veta in southern Colorado, to create interlocking "toe wood structures" and "riprap" boulders to stabilize the bank. The bed of the creek was reshaped to create a better floodplain. Then, the District planted nearly two hundred thousand willows, one thousand cottonwoods, and fifty-some acres of native grass and shrub seeds to lock the restoration work in place. Unfortunately, it did not end there.

"I mean, they did a good job," Justin Barr told me in 2023. "But it's more like a Band-Aid than anything else."

Critics point out that the District is a hamstrung organization burdened with far too many responsibilities and no sustainable funding source to do its work. Initially, the District received $50 million under Condition 6 of the 1041 permit for the Southern Delivery System (SDS) and has been working hard to maximize those limited dollars. The SDS funds are specifically intended to offset impacts from return flows into Fountain Creek, where the District has land use authority—in the one-hundred-year floodplain south of the City of Fountain, to just north of the City of Pueblo, and this money is for the development of new projects only.

Two problems in particular stand out. One, the District received enough money for a few important projects but not enough money for the necessary maintenance and monitoring once restoration work is complete. If something goes wrong post restoration, as happened to the Barrs, there is not much the District can do.

Second, as we have seen again and again, the real problem lies upstream in the watershed, not in Pueblo County. Colorado Springs, Manitou Springs, Fountain, Monument, Palmer Lake, Green Mountain Falls, Woodland Park, and the military bases all cause problems that hurt folks and ecosystems downstream. Until those upstream problems get solved (and "solving" would require the necessary political will to require developers to go beyond the minimum runoff requirements as well as demanding businesses and homeowners to do their part—something Kelly Bull is all about), no amount of well-designed, well-executed multimillion dollar restoration projects in Pueblo County will hold for long.

"Upstream is where they should be spending all this money," the hidden hydrologist told me over beers a few days after my initial visit with the Barr family. "Solve the upstream issues and the downstream problems will eventually fix themselves. They've got it all bassackwards."

"I feel bad for Alli," Dr. Barr said referring to Allison Schuch, the Executive Director of the District. "She has her heart in it. But it's a tough job. It is impossible for her to do the right thing. She inherited a huge problem that she didn't create."

In early 2023, Justin noticed some of the restoration work coming undone. "The work didn't go far enough north to be effective," he told me. Then another, potentially larger problem, appeared. The sump that waters the Barr Farm stopped working. The sump was, essentially, a ten- to fifteen-foot-deep pit dug next to the Fountain that filled with water seeping through the gravels. A pump forced the water uphill to irrigate the Barr's crops. The Barrs hold some of the oldest water rights on the Fountain, dating to the HR Steele appropriation in 1865. The water right decree requires the sump be within one hundred feet of the creek and not more than two hundred feet from its historic location. Prior to the restoration work, the once-reliable sump was sixty feet from the flow. The restoration work changed the course of the creek and in the two years following, the Fountain migrated about three hundred feet west. The sump almost completely dried up.

"We're having trouble irrigating our land now," Justin said. "That means lost production; lost income . . . we need the creek back on this side of the floodplain." He sighed.

"Look," Dr. Barr leaned forward. "If the Fountain is going to be a river from here on out, it's going to require constant human intervention because it is a human creation. It's just not a natural system anymore."

I have yet to meet a single person that has anything bad to say about Allison Schuch. That's probably because she is so goddamn nice. And she gets stuff done. What everyone *does* say about Schuch is that they feel bad for her. That, as the Executive Director of the District, she has one of the most complex, complicated, frustrating, and unenviable jobs in the Western United States.

The District's power is incredibly limited. The Barrs and the hidden hydrologist were both correct: without authority beyond the one-hundred-year floodplain in the approximately fifty miles between the City of Fountain and the confluence, the District's ability to have a watershed-wide impact is almost nonexistent. Yes, the District can provide input when it comes to land use decisions, but it is frequently ignored and the board makeup—overextended elected officials—doesn't help the matter. Watershed professionals, local advocates, and conservationists may be a better fit to take an active role as board members with decision-making power.

The District has completed over twenty watershed studies, plans, and Master Plans, fourteen restoration projects, eleven years of Creek Week cleanups. They've also done some impressive community outreach that includes the creation of the Brewshed Alliance, a collection of over twenty conservation-minded microbreweries in the watershed that host monthly Liquid Lectures about the Fountain watershed. Funds raised through beer sales at the lectures support the District outreach efforts. It was the Brewshed Alliance that created the Impactful IPA I'd shared with Schuch and Woolley over seed packing for Creek Week.

Still, Schuch wrote in the 2023 strategic plan, "the District has identified at least a billion dollars in other project work needed across the watershed." But they're almost out of money.

The type of restoration work undertaken by the District has been limited to Pueblo County due to the SDS fund restrictions, and it is the polar opposite of the kind of work Mallett and Corday propose. This makes sense given the work Colorado Headwaters hopes to do at the top of the watershed, where issues have not yet compounded into the disaster areas found downstream in Pueblo County. For the District, beavers, BDAs, and one-rock dams simply won't cut the mustard. It takes some serious heavy equipment for the District to complete its projects.

In 2015, a flood realigned the Fountain just north of the Pueblo Mall. The creek migrated east, gouging out a sharp curve that threatened the Highway 47 bridge. This sort of stream migration is totally natural and nothing new. Still, the Colorado Department of Transportation (CDOT) flipped its bureaucratic lid and, in a near panic, drove front loaders, bulldozers, and dump trucks into the Fountain for an emergency "fix." They straightened the creek channel for a mile just north of the bridge. Of course, when you remove a river's ability to move naturally, you end up with a broken channelized system that down cuts, resulting in still more erosion and fresh threats to the bridge and other areas downstream. CDOT and the District collaborated to design a proper fix for this stretch in 2017, to the tune of $6.6 million (the District paid $4.5, CDOT contributed $1.5). Once again, a project was completed with no long-term maintenance plan.

A similar problem developed along 13th Street in Pueblo, in turn threatening the 8th Street Bridge. Restoration costs? $2.6 million. Another $2.3 million went to save the Piñon Bridge north of town. Four million dollars more has been approved in the 2024 budget to fix the fifty-foot cliff undermining Southmoore Drive in the City of Fountain and so on. When Dr. Barr says Alli Schuch has inherited a huge problem, he isn't exaggerating.

Most of these projects involve some fairly standard river restoration techniques: move the main stem of the creek away from the eroded cut bank, reconnect the water with the floodplain, reshape the cut banks so they aren't so steep and erodible, install several tons of large boulders (riprap) and/or toe wood structures to "lock" the creek in place, cover the bare soil with biodegradable erosion control netting, and finally plant thousands of native cottonwoods and willows to stabilize the soils, create resilient riparian habitat, and reduce future erosion. It's not as simple as it sounds but it's also not terribly complicated. It is expensive, however. And time consuming. And, as Justin Barr pointed out, the work doesn't always hold, even under relatively small flood events. The District's restoration projects haven't yet faced anything close to 1965, 1935, and 1921. This also concerns Jay Frost, still awaiting some sort of fix for The Great Wall.

Not only have there been problems at the Barr Farm, but the 2023 spring rains caused $1.5 million in damage to the Highway 47 stabilization work. The District has approved another project directly upstream of Highway 47 called Eagleridge in order to protect the Highway 47 work. Eagleridge cost estimates could increase to nearly $7 million if the Board opts to include a fix or better tie-in to the 47 work.

More damage occurred at the 8th Street Bridge project site where, in 2022, I went to check out the recently completed work only to find that the City of Pueblo had torn up part of the restoration work with a bulldozer in a vain attempt to rid the area of a homeless encampment. Unfortunately, that damage Pueblo caused weakened the District's work and the 2023 floodwaters began undermining the stabilization structures. The damage was minor, Schuch said, but in the Fountain, minor problems compound and grow.

Meanwhile, both above and below the Masciantonio Trust Bank property that had seen $2 million in restoration work in 2018, neighbors saw fresh erosion problems and wanted the District to help them. "Everyone is lining up asking us for help," Schuch said, "but we're out of money. All the upstream problems continue and the downstream damage keeps adding up."

Frustratingly, Pueblo County didn't get its act together to conduct a damage assessment after the 2023 floods, and was therefore unable to receive emergency funding from Washington as El Paso County did, foolishly leaving millions in potential restoration and stabilization money on the table.

Another strand in the complex web of watershed management is the continued threat of wildfires. Has so much time passed since the Waldo Canyon and Black Forest fires that most people in the watershed seem to have forgotten how damaging those blazes were and how badly they impact the Fountain and her tributaries? For catastrophic floods and fires, it is not if but when—especially in the age of climate change.

For the District, money is a serious problem. In the next few years, the initial $50 million for project work will be used up. Then what?

Initially, the District looked at a mill levy to raise funds. A mill levy is a type of property tax based on the property's assessed value. Many communities have mill levies supporting their regional watershed work (Mile High Flood District in Denver, City of Fort Collins, and others). The District, in its founding decree, has the ability to ask for a mill levy in both El Paso and Pueblo Counties, or it could carve out an appropriate area to tax such as anyone living or running a business within one thousand feet of the creek or something similar. As you can imagine, the idea of more taxes, no matter how important or how small, doesn't sit well with most Coloradoans, particularly in tax adverse Colorado Springs, and it seems to me that anyone living within the watershed should be responsible for such a tax, not just a few.

"I don't know, what will it take to wake people up?" Schuch asked me at one point. "Another flood? A disaster? It seems like it takes a flood to get people to change their behavior."

Another possibility is to return to the Brewshed Alliance and try a "One Percent for the Watershed" program. That is, beer drinkers would have the option of adding 1 percent to their bill at the point of sale to raise money for creek restoration and other District work. Eagle Valley Land Trust and Eagle River Watershed Council established a Land and Rivers Fund with the voluntary 1 percent that has proved enormously successful, reaching far beyond local breweries and not requiring approval from reluctant taxpayers. Such a 1 percent program would not, however, generate near the resources that are required for the District to be fully functional.

My preferred idea is an in lieu fee program that allows the District to collect money from developers. Essentially, for every acre of wetlands developers destroy, they are currently required to create an equal if not greater amount of wetlands elsewhere to offset the impacts of destroying a wetland for housing or parking lots. As of 2024, developers in the watershed are purchasing wetland credits for wetlands far *outside* the watershed—nearly in Kansas in many cases. This is nuts. Schuch wants to bring that money back to the watershed by creating a series of wetland "mitigation banks" in several parts of the watershed that will help pay for creek and wetland restoration along the Fountain and the tributaries. One big benefit of this is that it might allow the District to supply engineering support for restoration work higher in the watershed, in cash-strapped communities like Green Mountain Falls. It could also allow fresh collaboration opportunities with Palmer Land Conservancy and headwaters advocates like Mallett and Corday.

"It's not going to bring in $20 million a year like a mill levy would, but we could raise $5-10 million a year. That's not nothing," Schuch said. "And it's not a new tax, it wouldn't have to go to a vote. We just need Army Corps approval."

The hidden hydrologist had . . . thoughts.

"How is any of this restoration?" He asked, referring to the District's work.

I shrugged and ordered another round.

"Basically," he continued, "Rerouting and stabilization does not restore watershed processes. We need to restore the process of the creek, and that takes a watershed-wide commitment that isn't there yet."

He explained that erosion is not a problem unless you put something—a bridge, a dam, a levee—in the way. Erosion and sedimentation are natural processes with important purposes. Without sediment, rivers erode more. "For example, CSU doesn't like sedimentation because it fills up reservoirs that were not designed to pass sediment. Reservoirs are sediment traps. So, downstream of reservoirs, rivers erode because of a loss of sediment. And then you get ridiculous situations where the Bureau of Reclamation or the Army Corps spends billions to dredge sediments out of reservoirs and truck it below the dam to dump it." He twirled his index finger around his ears in the universal sign for insanity.

"We've got to remove large dams, remove levies, and restore natural riparian buffers to protect infrastructure. You can replace big dams with smaller dams in a series that can be opened fully to allow sediment transport. If you really want to store water efficiently, you've got to get rid of manmade dams entirely and store the water in the aquifer like nature intended."

Although well-intentioned, the District is spending millions of dollars and enormous energy to put Band-Aids on a cancer. Or, as Schuch put it, like eating a spaghetti sandwich. The first bite is great; the rest is all over the floor. We're not dealing with real issues in a comprehensive way. To do so, we'd have to think like a creek.

"At the end of the day," the hydrologist said, "water always wins. The river always wins. All the legal wrangling, restoration, stabilization, transfers, diversions . . . lipstick on a pig."

"So, what should we do instead?"

"In some ways it's pretty simple. Allow the Fountain to be what it is. Get out of the way. Work within the creek's boundaries, otherwise we will just keep fighting the inevitable. Our whole society is Sisyphus when it comes to rivers. But it doesn't have to be that way."

River restoration isn't simple. Not only are there the political, legal, and economic complexities, but rivers and wetlands are themselves . . . complicated (sorry again, Ilan), packed with connections and jammed with life. Water doesn't simply traverse the land; it interacts with the land. Water creates its own relationship with land as a river migrates back and forth across its floodplain, patterning swales and loops, oxbows and pools. A healthy creek will maintain itself through time via these relationships. Yet, when those relationships are damaged, as they are in much of the Fountain watershed, recreating them is incredibly difficult. For restoration to be truly effective, the water's relationship to land, aquifer, soils, microbes, trees, fish, and insects must be allowed to thrive.

Evolution never ends. Water is constantly shifting, changing, and moving. If we simply get out of the way and allow the Fountain to be what it is *without* removing all the excess water coming from Colorado Springs and the upper watershed, what does that mean, practically? For the creek itself, it means a two-hundred-year or more process of adjustment while the creek learns to manage all that new water. The creek will indeed learn, but it needs time. Erosion, floods, cutbanks, channel migration—eventually the system will stabilize.

"That's what we *should* do," said the hydrologist.

"*Should* do, but *won't* do, right?" I said.

"Well, here's where it gets even more complicated."

"People?"

"People."

We've seen our society's fractured relationship with water. We see it as both a life-giving—even holy—resource and a dumping ground. While we extol the gifts of water, we also see water as a nuisance and a thing to be controlled, owned, and exploited.

Rivers are our friend until our attempts to dominate water doesn't work. If we were smarter, we'd allow water to do its thing, to go where it wants to go, and to manage our relationship with water by stepping back, making space. Remember, there is no such thing as a natural disaster, only natural hazards and human created vulnerabilities. Allowing water the space it needs would prove an act of rebellion, a radical shift from our habit of repeating the same mistakes ad infinitum.

If we were to allow the Fountain the time and space it needed to adjust to the new flows, we'd see infrastructure and properties under threat. Possible bridge collapse, railroad tracks inundated or undermined by erosion, loss of homes and outbuildings, and crumbling roads. Both the Barr Farm and the Frost Ranch would lose hundreds of acres of productive farm and ranchland and possibly their barns and houses to erosion. Other homes and business might also wash away, such as those that are currently threatened along Southmoore Drive, which has been closed since 2019. Anything built in the historic floodplain (which is larger than the one-hundred-year floodplain) would be under threat. Lower Arkansas Valley farmers would have a fit, and understandably so, with intakes and irrigation ditches clogged with sediment. Still, in the long run, they too would be better off. Or their great grandchildren will be better off—and isn't that who matters more anyway?

The negative human impacts of allowing the Fountain to run free would be enormous in the short run. We are the architects of our own problems. In the long run however, a rewilded, free flowing, and naturally stabilized Fountain would benefit us all—including the creek.

At one point, I got into a conversation with Spencer Shaw, a brilliant geology student at Colorado College. I asked him what it might look like if we allowed the Fountain to run free. And, is the Fountain even the Fountain anymore with all the changes?

Cautious and wise with his answer, Shaw explained how he

had used old maps and aerial photos of the Fountain and, utilizing GIS software, mapped the migration of Fountain Creek back and forth across the floodplain going back to the 1940s. Flooding, he said, is the main driver of channel change in the Fountain. There is a flood, the channel blows out, the creek moves, new vegetation comes in, the channel narrows, and then a new flood comes along several years later, blowing out the channel and again moving the course of the water. Wash, rinse, repeat. This is simply the way the Fountain works, he said. And it's always been that way. "The new and unusual thing is, of course, the impact of urbanization which has only made the Fountain more itself."

"What do you mean?"

"The Fountain continues to act like the Fountain; it's just on steroids now. Urbanization has only accelerated and augmented natural processes."

"So what is the Fountain? A river? A creek? A canal?"

He was silent for nearly a full minute.

"The Fountain is the Fountain," he said. "Consistently inconsistent."

Across the country, there are hundreds of watershed restoration efforts underway. This is an undeniable good. Yet, to me, as we seek to heal watersheds, rivers, and creeks, it's vital to also heal relationships with ourselves and each other. Ecological restoration and human restoration cannot be separated. We must make whole to make right.

The thing about the Fountain restoration plans is that they are based on the assumption that the people experiencing homelessness who live next to the Fountain and along its tributaries must be evicted in one way or the other if the Fountain is ever going to be whole again. Uprooting those finding shelter along the creek is a given in most people's minds. Yet no one seems to have a place for where the thousands of homeless individuals and families might go, what might happen to them, and what would be the larger societal knock on effects of such a mass eviction.

In my mind, there is no restoration of the creek without restoration of our humanity. Simply booting the unhoused from the creek banks is not only bad policy, it is inhumane. Human beings are not trash to be pushed aside or ignored. People require homes. For some of them, the answer is relatively simple. Build housing, increase supply, lower prices. For others, the solution will prove more complex due to mental health and substance use challenges. These folks will require transitional housing, coaching, navigation, treatment, and other support services, as well as homes. "The true measure of society," Mahatma Gandhi said, "can be found in how it treats its most vulnerable members."

Housing the unhoused is itself ecological restoration. Conservationists and other creek lovers must join with housing advocates—and yes, developers—to create long-term, humane, suitable solutions for the housing crisis. Any true environmentalist will have to become a housing advocate also. Only when we take care of our whole community can we talk about real restoration. First we restore human beings, and then we can restore the creek.

Jay Frost told me that at his son's thirtieth birthday, the beers were flowing, the conversation went deep, and Jay grew melancholy, apologizing to his three children for bringing them into such a messed up world. "I told my kids I was sorry. I felt I owed them an apology, that they didn't deserve this, and that we'd ruined it all and it wasn't their fault. It's not that I don't love them or treasure them, just that I felt . . . guilty."

I told him that I'd been having a similar struggle. That I didn't think things would be like this, and that I worried almost endlessly about my children's future. "But here we are."

"Well," he shrugged, "They want to keep the ranch up. My kids aren't surrendering even though I wouldn't blame them if they did. They're actually pretty damn passionate about this land and our creek so . . ." He shrugged again.

It seemed to me that kids these days are far smarter than we give them credit for, and I told Jay that. He agreed.

"You know . . . I'm only borrowing this land," he said. "I don't own it. It belongs to the future and my job is just leaving it better than I found it. That's all."

"If you're kids understand that," I said, "then things might be okay."

He nodded. "The kids are alright."

THE FOUNTAIN

"... the river still chatted on ... a babbling procession of the best stories in the world, sent from the heart of the Earth to be told, at last, to the insatiable sea."

–Kenneth Grahame, The Wind in the Willows

Back in Pueblo, the Fountain trickled like a hush through the gravels. A killdeer skirted the edge of the flow, running, stopping, then racing forward again on toothpick legs. The alluvial plain spread wide and flat, stripped of trees and shrubs. The creek ran swift but shallow. There had not been rain in weeks. The only water in the Fountain came from Colorado Springs' effluent and the occasional trickling spring. It was August and August always feels like the end of something, and I knew this book would end with an August.

I'd been throwing things out. Jettisoning much of my past, clearing the shelves. I'd been thinking about what holds me back—possessions, collection, old ideas, bad habits ... habits in general, ways of being that kept me stuck. I was fifty-three years old, and my children were off, my daughter in college and my two boys about to graduate high school. My water-boy would have to serve in the Finnish military before long. At a time of renewed Russian warmongering, this worried me. But, Jay was right. The world was theirs. I'd made a mess of things, I thought. How could I possibly make it better? Without my kids at home, what value, if any, did I have in this world? At fifty-three, what came next?

I'd crashed my mountain bike that summer, tearing up my arm, ripping a muscle, and spraining my SI joint. Porting boxes of books drove stabs of pain across my hip. I felt vulnerable and maybe even a bit old. I was ready for something new.

Through my life, I'd collected thousands of volumes, stuffing my bookshelves at home and filling boxes that disappeared into my mother's garage. What was the point? Immortality? I went at the collection with a metaphorical scythe, mowing the assemblage by the hundreds, winnowing what remained. I delivered dozens of books to the Pueblo Library and hundreds more to the used book store that funds The Friends of the Library. I sold antiquarian publications on eBay, gave away dozens of volumes, and spread what remained—mostly trade paperbacks and old ethnologies—throughout the Little Free Libraries scattered across Pueblo, Colorado Springs, and northern New Mexico. I thinned my wardrobe to the essentials, shredded old work files, consolidated photo albums, and organized my journals.

The future, it seemed, required lightness, elasticity, and the capacity to adapt with speed.

Rasa, my wife, found value in my frenetic exfoliation, taking the opportunity to move on from baggage she too had ported about for decades. My mother likewise took up my enthusiasm. Somewhat. As I prepared plastic bags of old clothes to pass out at the soup kitchen, she turned up with wool blankets—army issue from the Second World War—socks and shoes that still passed muster. Still, she was reluctant to give up on her own clothes, even outfits she had not touched in years. She clung to the idea she might wear some of them again someday. When I asked her about a garage sale, she steered the conversation to the spate of murders plaguing the city, not yet ready to unload what she no longer needed. I understood. Letting go of the past, letting go of the familiar, letting go of what we think we know can be challenging to say the least—even if it offers a brighter future.

Down by the Fountain, smoke from fires half a continent away filled the sunburnt sky. To the north, the roof of the world was bleached white; The Peak, nowhere to be seen. South, the haze obscured the Greenhorns and the Huajatollas. I walked along the creek, sheltered from the sun by an umbrella. The walking helped my busted up hip, and with each step the pain receded. A light breeze rose. It was as if someone moved ahead of me, holding an electric hair dryer inches from my face. My smart phone over heated and shut down. The thermometer showed 108 degrees. A record. Every single day that week had seen temperature records broken. Shattered.

I explored the gravel bars, keeping my feet in the water. A beaver, dead, floated past. The fuzzy corpse bobbed in the flow, releasing miniature bubbles that streamed from the pelt, gathering near the surface, clinging to the tips of fur. For a minute, I worried if this was *my* beaver, the animal whose pond I'd grown so attached to. The beaver whose dam had been ripped apart by a human machine. I thought of how far the body would have had to come, dozens of miles, and I wondered when and where it would come to rest and what it all meant, or . . . maybe it didn't mean anything. This is the way the world works. Think like a creek. The Fountain came long before and the Fountain will long outlive.

The creek had become a friend. Maybe it always was. The Fountain was a messy friend. A chaotic, drama-filled companion, the type that calls you at midnight, a hot mess, flipping their lid about this or that flailing relationship, money problems, or a tear-jerking work spectacle. The type of friend that could, at the same time, serve a salve, a port in the midst of a storm.

Did it recognize me? Did it know me? At the moment at least, I felt as if it did.

Prints crisscrossed the gravel bars. Most of the tracks were human, but there were also imprints from dogs, geese, a single small deer, a coyote, and what I thought to be a very large cat. The cat print was the size of my hand, round with four toes and no claw marks. Unlike canines, cats retract their claws. The heel was somewhat of a stylized "M" and, cat or not, the animal had been heavy, sinking more than an inch into the gravel.

Instinctively, I scanned the back willows near the bike trail. With my binoculars, I examined the middle distance, then the high branches of far-off cottonwoods. Nothing. Still, adrenaline spiked my brain.

I have never come face to face with a mountain lion. I'd seen them in the distance while hiking or backpacking. Several times, I had woken after a night in the wilderness to find fresh tracks near my tent or sleeping bag. Once, while hiking with a long-ago girlfriend in New Mexico, I had sat on a log beneath a towering alligator juniper. We rested, drank water, snacked then moved on. A short time later, a man ran up the trail. "Did you see the cougar?" No, we told him, and he led us back down the trail. There, in the alligator juniper, maybe six feet above where we had sat, an impressive female mountain lion napped, sprawled across the branches.

The cat tracks led me up and down the creek bank, then back among the trash where unhoused people camped, then to a half-buried Target shopping cart. The wandering of the animal suggested a hunt, or perhaps, a search for a mate. Young male mountain lions, like wolves, will range over hundreds of miles in search of a female and uncontested territory. On the other hand, maybe the animal simply sought a safe place to cross the creek. A route to avoid the cars, the train, and the people camped along the Fountain. The tracks led north, arrived at the water's edge, and disappeared. I crossed the creek to the west side and sought out where the cat, if that is what it was, had emerged from the water. I found nothing. Big cats are much like ghosts.

Back on the eastern bank, I came to some of the restoration work the Flood Control and Greenway District had completed. There were young cottonwoods and willows planted in straight lines, perpendicular to the flow. They were seven to nine feet high, spindly, and bent from the heat. Many of the cottonwoods were dead. Perhaps 30 to 40 percent of them powered on. Upwards of 90 percent of the willows thrived.

The heat got the best of me and I made for the shade of a mature cottonwood. When I crossed the bike path, a man ambled past, his nose in a book. A couple flew by on electric scooters. Again, I scanned the branches for the big cat. Seeing nothing, no one, I leaned against the cottonwood elder and sucked down a liter of tepid water. There was not a single bird song or call. I closed my eyes, listening.

There were layers of sound. At the base was the ever-present hum of I-25 and the city streets. Above that, sirens, diesel engines, and motorcycles. There was what sounded like a giant vacuum cleaner, but I could never place exactly what it was or where it came from. The breeze in the leaves. The cicadas and when I walked, the crunch of my footsteps. Somewhere in there I could pick out the swish and gurgle of the creek, the ripple of water and the shifting of sediments.

I strolled the forest, staying clear of the encampments, sticking to shade. Just as the cat came and went like a ghost, seven Mississippi kites appeared, circling and calling above. They sailed on slender, pointed wings; pale gray, bleached like the sky. They came low, caught the thermals, and spiraled into the white above, sliding with ease, aloft in the currents. Then they were gone. Then they were low, over the water. They rose and disappeared. Again, they were above. The spectral hide-and-seek continued for nearly an hour, and I sat in the shade, back pressed against the cottonwood, watching. I could smell the smoke. It came like campfire, thick and acrid, settling over the Fountain. Is this the future, I wondered. Heat, homelessness, and blankets of smoke. Or was there something different? Evolution hasn't stopped, history hasn't ended, and the future requires flexibility. When does the future begin, I wondered, and who says what it will be?

The kites moved up towards the Belmont neighborhood. I followed, then made for the shade of a highway bypass spanning the Fountain. Three men and a woman sat there, poking needles into their arms. They looked at me, embarrassed. I apologized for the intrusion and made my way back south to Nick's Dairy. I sat in the shadows of the squat building and ate a cup of ice cream.

The Fountain hushed its way south through the heat.

SOURCES

ORIGINS

"Yellowstone Valley and the Great Flood." *Indigenous People's Literature*. http://www.indigenouspeople.net/yellowst.html.

"James Osnowitz Drowns." *Pueblo Chieftain*, June 21, 1965.

"Flood Hits Castle Rock, Denver." *Pueblo Chieftain*, June 16, 1965.

"Huge Flood Roars Through Pueblo." *Pueblo Chieftain*, June 18, 1965.

Vigil, Karen. "Memories of 1965 flood dredged up by dam rights." *Pueblo Chieftain*, July 1, 1988.

Snipes, R.J. et al. "Floods of June 1965 in Arkansas River Basin, Colorado, Kansas, and New Mexico The United States Geological Survey Water-Supply Paper 1850-D." US Department of the Interior, 1966.

Miller, Lone. "Ninety-Fifth Anniversary of the Eden Train Wreck." *Pueblo Lore* 24, no. 9 (1999).

Helmers, Dow. *Tragedy at Eden*. O'Brien Printing Company. Pueblo, Colorado, 1971.

Pueblo Chieftain, August 11, 1904.

"Additional Eden Train Wreck Information." *Pueblo Lore* 30, no. 8.

Korber, John. "Last Eden Train Wreck Suit Settled – *1929*." *Pueblo Lore* 30, no.8 (2005).

Follansbee, Robert and Sawyer, Leon R. "Floods in Colorado." United States Department of Interior, US Geological Survey,

Water Supply Paper 997, 1948.

Colorado Springs Gazette, June 27, 1874.

Colorado Springs Gazette, May 27, 1876.

Rocky Mountain News, May 20, 1878.

Pueblo Commercial Standard, June 28, 1884.

Denver Republican, June 1, 1894.

Colorado Springs Gazette, June 21, 1894.

Fry, Eleanor. "The Fountain River-1914." *Pueblo Lore* 21, no. 9 (1996).

Fry, Eleanor. 2005. "The 1965 Flood." *Pueblo Lore* 30, no. 8 (2005).

Pueblo Chieftain, July 30, 1932.

Colorado Springs Gazette, May 31, 1935.

Maroney, Dennis, Lange, Carol, Rhodes, Jane. *Flooding on the Fountain*. Fountain Valley Vision Task Force, 2007.

Pueblo Chieftain, June 26, 1965, p. 7A.

Pueblo Chieftain, June 27, 1965.

Cohen, Jonathan A. "A Social and Cultural History of the Great Pueblo Flood of 1921, Its Aftermath, and Its Legacy." Master's Thesis, Harvard Extension School, 2020.

Owen-Cooper, Teresa. *Colorado Springs Gazette Telegraph*, January 1, 1998, p.4.

U.S. Army Corps of Engineers. *Flood Plain Information-Fountain Creek-Pueblo Colorado*. Albuquerque: U.S. Army Corps of Engineers, 1968, p.28.

Curran, Terence. "1,000 Ordered To Vacate Homes." *Pueblo Chieftain*, June 18, 1965, 1A.

"Fountain Water Reaches Hudson." *Pueblo Chieftain*, June 18, 1965, 15A.

Snipes, R. J., et al. "Floods of June 1965 in Arkansas River Basin, Colorado, Kansas, and New Mexico." *Floods of 1965 in the United States*, Geological Survey Water-Supply Paper, 1850-D, US Department of the Interior.

Jansson, Tove. *The Moomins and the Great Flood*. 1945.

Kuusi, M., K. Bosley and M. Branch. *Finnish Folk Poetry Epic: An Anthology in Finnish and English*. Helsinki: Finnish Literary Society, 1977.

Ryan, W.B.F., Pitman., W. C., Major, C. O, and Yüce, H. "An abrupt drowning of the Black Sea shelf." *Marine Geology* 138, no. 1-2 (1997): 119-126.

Ryan, W.B.F. and W.C. Pitman. *Noah's Flood: The Scientific Discoveries About the Event that Changed History*. New York: Simon and Schuster, 1998.

Peev, P., R.H. Farr, V. Slavchev, M.J. Grant, J. Adams, and G. Bailey. "Bulgaria: Sea-Level Change and Submerged Settlements on the Black Sea." 2020. In: Bailey, G., N. Galanidou, H. Peeters, H. Jöns, and M. Mennenga, eds. *The Archaeology of Europe's Drowned Landscapes*. Coastal Research Library, vol 35. Springer, Cham. https://doi.org/10.1007/978-3-030-37367-2_20

"Black Sea Flood Theory Put to Test." *Science*. Accessed January 25, 2023. https://www.science.org/content/article/black-sea-flood-theory-put-test.

Clark, Ella E. *Indian Legends of the Pacific Northwest*. University of California Press: Berkeley, 1953, p. 225.

Gunther, Erna. "Klallam Folk Tales." *University of Washington Publications Anthropology* 1, no. 4 (1925): 113-170. Told by Joe Samson of Elwah, interpreted by Vera Ulmer.

Kramer, Samuel Noah. *In the World of Sumer – An Autobiography*. Wayne State University Press, 1986.

Upton, John. "Ancient Sea Rise Tale Told Accurately for 10,000 Years." *Scientific* American, 2015. Accessed December 15, 2022. https://www.scientificamerican.com/article/ancient-sea-rise-tale-told-accurately-for-10-000-years/.

Kaelin, Celinda Reynolds. *Ute Legends*. Idaho: Caxton Press, 2017.

Mayor, Adrienne. *The First Fossil Hunters and Fossil Legends of the First Americans*. Princeton University Press, 2007.

Least Heat-Moon, William. *River Horse: Across America by Boat.* Boston: Houghton, Mifflin and Co., 1999.

BONES

"Mastadon Found." *Weekly Pueblo Chieftain*, December 20, 1900 (As seen in April 13, 1981 issue of Pueblo County Historical Society newsletter).

Superfund Site: COLORADO SMELTER, PUEBLO, CO. Cleanup Activities. Accessed April 2021. https://cumulis.epa.gov/supercpad/SiteProfiles/index.cfm?fuseaction=second.cleanup&id=0802700.

"Relics of Pueblo's Earliest Building Are Unearthed by Exploration Society". *Pueblo Chieftain*, 1927 (As seen in *Pueblo Lore* 24, no. 9. August 1999).

Liang, Olivia. *To The River*. Edinburgh: Canongate Books, 2011.

Preston, Steve. "Our Rich History: The Journal of Jacob Fowler, a wandering squatter, founder, surveyor." *North Kentucky Tribune, 2015.* Accessed December 13, 2022 and February 13, 2023. https://www.nkytribune.com/2015/12/our-rich-history-the-journal-of-jacob-fowler-a-wandering-squatter-founder-surveyor/.

Hart, Stephen Harding and Archer Butler Hulbert, eds. *The Southwestern Journals of Zebulon Pike, 1806-1807.* University of New Mexico Press, 2006.

Fuller, M. Harlin and R. LeRoy Hafen, eds. *The Journal of Captain John R. Bell, Official Journalist for the Stephen H. Long Expedition to the Rocky Mountains, 1820.* 1973.

The Lemuel Ford Papers. Denver Public Library, Western History and Genealogy Repository. Accessed October 15, 2021 and March 13, 2023.

John Charles Frémont. *Report of the Exploring Expedition to the Rocky Mountains in the Year 1842, and to Oregon and North California in the Years 1843–44 by Brevet Captain J. C. Frémont of the Topographical Engineers.* Under the Order of Col. J. J. Abert, Chief of the Topographical Bureau. Washington, DC: Gales and Seaton, 1845.

Orsi, Jared. *Citizen Explorer. The Life of Zebulon Pike*. Oxford University Press, 2014.

Kennedy, Roger G. *Mr. Jefferson's Lost Cause: Land, Farmers, Slavery, and the Louisiana Purchase*. Oxford University Press, 2003.

Fenster, Julie M. *Jefferson's America: The President, The Purchase, and the Explorers Who Transformed a Nation*. New York: Crown Publishers, 2016.

Harris, M.L. and J.H. Buckley. *Zebulon Pike, Thomas Jefferson and the Opening of the American West*. University of Oklahoma Press, 2012.

Egan, P.J. and M. Mullin. "Turning personal experience into political attitudes: the effect of local weather on American's perceptions about global warming." *The Journal of Politics* 74 (2012): 796-809.

Mian, M.K., S.A. Sheth, S.R. Patel, K. Spiliopoulos, E.N. Eskandar, and Z.M. Williams. "Encoding of rules by neurons in the human dorsolateral prefrontal cortex." *Cereb Cortex* 3 (Mar. 24, 2014): 807-16. Accessed October 21, 2022 and February 27, 2023. https://www.ncbi.nlm.nih.gov/pmc/articles/PMC3920771/.

Barrett, Ted. "Inhofe brings snowball on Senate floor as evidence globe is not warming." CNN, 2015. Accessed February 27, 2023. https://www.cnn.com/2015/02/26/politics/james-inhofe-snowball-climate-change/index.html.

MacFarlane, Robert. *Underland*. New York: W.W. Norton & Co., 2019.

RIGHTS

Deakin, Roger. *Waterlog: A Swimmer's Journey Through Britain*. London: Vintage Press, 1999.

Solnit, Rebecca. *Wanderlust: A History of Walking*. Penguin

Books, 2001.

Goldfarb, Ben. "The Colorado Steam Case That Could Revolutionize River Access." *High Country News*, June 27, 2022. Accessed November 15, 2022. https://www.hcn.org/issues/54.7/south-rivers-lakes-the-colorado-stream-case-that-could-revolutionize-river-access.

Jolly-Ryan, Jennifer. "Don't Go Chasing Waterfalls: The Intrepid, Pioneering, Whitewater Paddler's Right to Stop on Private Land." *University of New Hampshire Law Review* 17 (2018) p. 129. Accessed August 2022, January 2023, March 2023. https://scholars.unh.edu/unh_lr/vol17/iss1/17/.

Obermesik, Larry and Daniel Jenks. *The Lost Gold Rush Journals of Daniel Jenks 1849-1865 Untold Tales of Gold Rush Adventure*. Larry Obermesik, 2021.

John Pollard, et al., Lessee, Plantiff in Error v John Hagan, et al., Defendants in Error. 1845. Accessed March 22, 2023. https://www.law.cornell.edu/supremecourt/text/44/212.

Randall, Cassidy. "Who owns water? The US landowners putting barbed wire across rivers." *The Guardian*, 2018. Accessed August 13, 2022, March 17, 2023. https://www.theguardian.com/environment/2018/mar/15/privatized-rivers-us-public-lands-waterways.

Beasley, Beau. "Who Owns a River?" *MidCurrent*, 2022. Accessed December 3, 2022, March 20, 2023. https://midcurrent.com/conservation/who-owns-a-river/.

Winkler, Adam. "Corporations Are People' Is Built on an Incredible 19th-Century Lie," *The Atlantic*, 2018. Accessed April 10, 2023. https://www.theatlantic.com/business/archive/2018/03/corporations-people-adam-winkler/554852/.

Golden, Amy. "Report: 101,000 acres of Colorado public land are corner-locked." *Longmont Leader*, 2022. Accessed April 1, 2023. https://www.longmontleader.com/outside/report-101000-acres-of-colorado-public-land-are-corner-locked-5399791.

Trust for Public Lands. "Millions of Acres Blocked by Private Property." 2020. Accessed April 1, 2023. https://www.tpl.org/blog/millions-acres-public-land-are-blocked-private-property-were-changing.

Polcastro, Riya Anne. "Offroad App OnX Shows How Access to Public Lands is Increasingly Blocked by Private Landowners" *Triple Pundit*, 2022. https://www.triplepundit.com/story/2022/public-lands-blocked-private-landowners/763171.

Goldfarb, Ben. "Colorado Supreme Court drowns public access to riverbeds." *High Country News*, June 16, 2023. https://www.hcn.org/articles/rivers-lakes-colorado-supreme-court-drowns-public-access-to-riverbeds.

MacFarlane, Robert. *The Wild Places*. Penguin, 2007.

Beng, Richard Fuller, Landrigan, Philip, Balakrishan, Kalpana, et al. "Pollution and health: a progress update." *The Lancet*, 2022. DOI:https://doi.org/10.1016/S2542-5196(22)00090-0.

Silva-Blayney, Fran. "Contamination of Fountain Creek needs transparency from EPA." *Denver Post, 2018*. Accessed April 7, 2023. https://www.denverpost.com/2018/06/08/contamination-of-fountain-creek-needs-transparency-from-epa/.

Bolstad, Erika, 2023. "Some States Want to Give You a Constitutional Right to a Clean Environment." *Pew Stateline*. Accessed April 11, 2023. https://www.pewtrusts.org/en/research-and-analysis/blogs/stateline/2023/04/06/some-states-want-to-give-you-a-constitutional-right-to-a-clean-environment.

Kirsten Williams. "Fundamental Environmental Rights: State Constitutions as a Vehicle of Change." *JURIST*, 2021. https://www.jurist.org/commentary/2021/11/kirsten-williams-environmental-rights-amendments/.

Tang, K. and O. Spijkers. "The Human Right to a Clean, Healthy and Sustainable Environment." *Chinese Journal of Envi-*

ronmental Law 6, no. 1 (2022): 87-107. doi: https://doi.org/10.1163/24686042-12340078.

Stone, Christopher D. "Should Trees Have Standing? – Towards Legal Rights for Natural Objects." *Southern California Law Review* 45 (1972): 450-501.

Stone, Christopher D. *Should Trees Have Standing: Law, Morality and the Environment.* Oxford University Press, 1974, 2010.

Cynthia F. Coveli et al. "Update to a Survey of State Instream Flow Programs in the Western United States." *U. Denv. Water L. Rev.* 20 (2017): 355. https://digitalcommons.du.edu/wlr/vol20/iss2/10/.

Colorado Water Conservation Board. "Instream Flow Program." https://cwcb.colorado.gov/focus-areas/ecosystem-health/instream-flow-program.

Kampf, Stephanie, et al. "Comment on Revised Definition of Waters of the United States (WOTUS)." 2019. chrome-extension://efaidnbmnnnibpcajpcglclefindmkaj/https://www.engr.colostate.edu/abhaskar/wp-content/uploads/2021/06/WOTUS-comment-CSU.pdf.

Balsam, Joe. "This wild river in Quebec is now considered a person. How will it help with conservation?" *The Globe and Mail*, 2021. Accessed April 12, 2023. https://www.theglobeandmail.com/canada/article-this-wild-river-in-quebec-is-now-considered-a-person-how-will-it-help/.

Surma, Katie. "Colorado Town Appoints Legal Guardians to Implement the Rights of a Creek and a Watershed." *Inside Climate News*, 2024. https://insideclimatenews.org/news/12012024/rights-of-nature-boulder-creek-colorado/.

Barkham, Patrick. "Should Rivers Have the Same Rights as People?" *The Guardian*, 2021. Accessed December 2022. https://www.theguardian.com/environment/2021/jul/25/rivers-around-the-world-rivers-are-gaining-the-same-legal-rights-as-people.

Das Gupta, Kaushik. "Once Upon a River." *The Indian Express*.

Accessed January 17, 2022. https://indianexpress.com/article/opinion/columns/once-upon-a-river-ganga-yamuna-legal-rights-uttarakhand-high-court-4651659/.

Kimmerer, Robin Wall. "Speaking of Nature." *Orion*, 2017. Accessed December 2018 and December 2023. https://orionmagazine.org/article/speaking-of-nature/.

Kimmerer, Robin Wall. *Braiding Sweetgrass: Indigenous Wisdom, Scientific Knowledge and the Teachings of Plants*. Milkweed Editions, 2013.

O'Donnell, Erin. "Rivers as living beings: rights in law, but no rights to water?" *Griffith Law Review* 29, no. 4 (2020): 643-668. DOI: 10.1080/10383441.2020.1881304.

Brown, Adrienne Maree. "The River." *Open Rivers: Rethinking Water, Place & Community*, no. 13 (2018). https://libpubsdss.lib.umn.edu/openrivers/article/the-river/ || DOI: https://doi.org/10.24926/2471190X.5342.

Borges, Jorge Luis. *The Book of Sand and Shakespeare's Memory*. Penguin Classics, 1975, 2007.

ALL TAPPED OUT

The Colorado Water Plan. https://engagecwcb.org/colorado-water-plan.

Report Card for America's infrastructure. Accessed March 27, 2023. https://infrastructurereportcard.org/cat-item/drinking-water-infrastructure/.

Shaper, David. "As Infrastructure Crumbles, Trillions Of Gallons Of Water Lost." *National Public Radio*, 2014. Accessed March 27, 2023. https://www.npr.org/2014/10/29/359875321/as-infrastructure-crumbles-trillions-of-gallons-of-water-lost.

"Amara Annexation Debate Continues." *Fountain Valley News*. Accessed March 24, 2023. https://www.epcan.com/story/2022/11/02/news/amara-annexation-debate-continues/13296.html.

Shinn, Mary. "Colorado Springs water rule that could block annexations approved." *Colorado Springs Gazette*, 2023. Accessed March 2023. https://gazette.com/news/government/colorado-springs-water-rule-that-could-block-annexations-approved/article_7543611a-910a-11ed-94e2-9387e7e341c0.html.

Shinn, Mary. "Norwood told Colorado Springs mayor it would go to voters with annexation blocking water rule." *Colorado Springs Gazette*, 2023. Accessed March 2023. https://gazette.com/government/norwood-told-colorado-springs-mayor-it-would-go-to-voters-with-annexation-blocking-water-rule/article_f8358e02-982d-11ed-aca2-b35123f194d0.html.

Lewis, Shanna. "Controversial Colorado Springs water service extension ordinance moves forward." *Colorado Public Radio*, 2023. Accessed February 2023. https://www.cpr.org/2023/01/26/controversial-colorado-springs-water-service-extension-ordinance-moves-forward/.

Harner, John. *Profiting from the Peak: Landscape and Liberty in Colorado Springs*. University Press of Colorado, 2021.

Summit Economics. *White Paper Exploring Potential Solutions to Regional Storm water Challenges*. 2012.

American Society of Civil Engineers. *Infrastructure Report Card for the Colorado Springs Area*. 2012.

Branch, John. "Urban Critics Question Aesthetic of Sprawlorado Springs." *Colorado Springs Gazette Telegraph*, January 12, 1997, p. 1.

Quillen, Ed. "Perhaps It's Time to Pretend That General Palmer Never Existed." *Denver Post*, May 11, 1999, p. 7B.

National Association of Realtors. "Community and Transportation Preference Survey." 2023. https://www.nar.realtor/reports/nar-community-and-transportation-preference-surveys.

Kunstler, James H. *The Geography of Nowhere: The Rise and*

Decline of America's Man-made Landscape. Simon and Schuster, 1993.

Kunstler, James, H. *Home from Nowhere: Remaking Our Everyday World for the 21st Century*. Simon and Schuster, 1996.

Kunstler, James, H. *Architecture*. TEDCulture, 2004. https://youtu.be/8jBMP7mjmno.

"Sierra Club v. Colorado Springs Utilities et al." No. 12005cv01994 - Document 353 (D. Colo. 2009).

Harrison, Scott,. "Cleanup and repairs continue in El Paso County after Monday's heavy rain, hail, flooding." KRDO, 2023. https://krdo.com/news/local-news/top-stories/2023/06/13/cleanup-and-repairs-continue-in-el-paso-county-after-mondays-heavy-rain-hail-flooding/.

Bryan, Maggie. "Flood damage eating away at property in Pueblo County near Fountain Creek." KOAA, 2023. https://www.koaa.com/news/covering-colorado/flood-damage-eating-away-at-property-in-pueblo-county-near-fountain-creek.

Shinn, Mary. "Colorado Springs has seen extraordinary population growth over the years. What does that mean for its water supply?" *The Gazette*, 2023. https://gazette.com/premium/colorado-springs-has-seen-extraordinary-population-growth-over-the-years-what-does-that-mean-for/article_d7be7298-6e14-11ee-958c-d7a44d961622.html.

Wilson, Sarah. "Fountain Creek watershed projects improve quality of life, but impact often goes unnoticed." *The Pueblo Chieftain*, September 10, 2021. https://www.chieftain.com/story/news/2021/09/10/fountain-creek-watershed-district-completes-major-projects-pueblo/8258276002/.

Boczkiewicz, Robert. "Major breakthrough reached in Fountain Creek case to settle clean water lawsuit." *The Pueblo Chieftain*, October 29, 2020. https://www.chieftain.com/story/lifestyle/2020/10/29/plan-could-settle-fountain-creek-lawsuit-and-improve-water-quality/6080013002/.

THE BIG STRAW

"Businessmen Dissatisfied with Hydro Settlement," *Colorado Springs Gazette*, June 18, 1906, p.5.

Sherow, James Earl. *Watering the Valley: Development Along the High Plains Arkansas River, 1870-1950*. University Press of Kansas, 1991, p. 60-61.

Harner, John. *Profiting from the Peak: Landscape and Liberty in Colorado Springs*. University Press of Colorado, 2021.

Reid, H.I. *Water Works Report*. Mentioned in *Colorado Springs Gazette*, May 1, 1888, p. 3. Submitted to John Himebaugh, chairman of the Committee on Water Works.

Lakes, Arthur. "The Pikes Peak and Colorado Springs Water Works." *Engineering Magazine* 10 (1896): 282–283. Retrieved January 15, 2015.

"Up Pike's Peak by Rail." *The Illustrated American*. Illustrated American Publishing Company, 1891, p. 165.

Worster, Donald. *Rivers of Empire: Water, Aridity, and the Growth of the American West*. New York Pantheon, 1985.

Fry, Eleanor. "Fountain Underflow." *Pueblo Lore* 26, no. 11 (November 2001).

"The Fountain Underflow Project." *Pueblo Chieftain*, December 31, 1905.

"Fountain Underflow." *The Pueblo Star-Journal*, August 31, 1905.

Aschermann, Aria. "Whatever Happened to the Fountain Underflow Project?" *Pueblo Lore* 32, no. 6 (June 2006).

Sawyer, Edwin. "Our Mountain Water System, The Present Water Supply of Colorado Springs." *Colorado Springs Gazette*, 1901.

McGlasson, W.J. "City Water Could Support 539,000." *Colorado Springs Gazette Telegraph*, 1977.

City Major Supplier of Region's Water Resources, *Colorado Springs Utilities*, "Water Historic Timeline."

Hobbs, Gregory J. jr., et al. *Citizen's Guide to Colorado Water Law, 5th edition*. Water Education Colorado, 2021.

Coleman, Caitlin. Citizen's *Guide to Colorado's Transbasin Diver-*

sions, Water Education Colorado, 2014.

Smythe, William Ellsworth. *The Conquest of Arid America.* New York: Harper & Brothers, 1900.

Runyon, Luke and Matt Bloom. "Water is Leaving Colorado Farmland for the City – But Will It Ever Return?" KUNC, 2018. https://www.kunc.org/environment/2018-06-13/water-is-leaving-colorado-farmland-for-the-city-but-will-it-ever-return.

Goodland, Marianne. "Buying and Drying: Water Lessons from Crowley County." *The Colorado Independent*, 2015. https://www.coloradoindependent.com/2015/07/09/buying-and-drying-water-lessons-from-crowley-county/.

Lower Arkansas Valley Water Conservation District. "Development of Land Fallowing - Water Leasing in the Lower Arkansas Valley (2002 through mid-2011): Report for the Colorado Water Conservation Board." 2011. chrome-extension://efaidnbmnnnibpcajpcglclefindmkaj/https://dnrweblink.state.co.us/cwcb/0/doc/195733/Electronic.aspx?searchid=4f5e7fce-e7a6-49ff-b28d-dbff0a5186ef.

Jenkins, Matt. "Water Warrior." *High Country News* 44, no. 5 (2012): 14-20.

Jenkins, Matt. "A Colorado newspaperman fights for his valley's water." *High Country News*, 2012. https://www.hcn.org/issues/44.5/a-colorado-newspaperman-fights-for-his-valleys-water.

Peterson, Brittany. "Colorado to Reuse Water for Drinking, New Supply." *Pueblo Chieftain*, October 23, 2022.

Kuta, Sarah. "Special Report: Just 53% of Colorado cities use permanent water restrictions, despite proven savings." Water Education Colorado, 2021. https://www.watereducationcolorado.org/fresh-water-news/special-report-just-53-of-colorado-cities-use-permanent-watering-restrictions-despite-proven-savings/.

Alliance for Water Efficiency. "Use and Effectiveness of Municipal Irrigation Restrictions During Drought." 2020. https://www.allianceforwaterefficiency.org/impact/our-work/use-and-effectiveness-municipal-irrigation-restrictions-during-drought.

Lewis, Shana. "A giant loop water system around El Paso County might help utilities plan for the future." KRCC Colorado Public Radio, 2022. https://www.cpr.org/2022/01/20/el-paso-county-water-supply-utilities/.

Shinn, Mary. "Colorado Springs has seen extraordinary population growth over the years. What does that mean for its water supply?" *The Gazette*, 2023. https://gazette.com/premium/colorado-springs-has-seen-extraordinary-population-growth-over-the-years-what-does-that-mean-for/article_d7be7298-6e14-11ee-958c-d7a44d961622.html.

Parched. The Boldest Idea of All (podcast). https://www.cpr.org/podcast-episode/the-boldest-idea-of-all/.

Wockner, Gary. *Boondoggle on the Colorado River*. 2023. https://writersontherange.org/boondoggle-on-the-colorado-river/.

Mullane, Shannon. "6 southern Colorado counties, facing drought and thirsty neighbors, move to block water exports." *Colorado Sun*, 2023., https://coloradosun.com/2023/07/03/colorado-san-luis-valley-water-plan/.

DARK WATERS

Nimmo, D.R., S.J. Herrmann, J.S. Carsella, C.M. McGarvy, H.P. Foutz, L.M. Herrmann-Hoesing, J.M. Gregorich, J.A. Turner, and B.D. Vanden Heuvel. "Mercury and selenium in fish of Fountain Creek, Colorado (USA): possible sources and implications." *Springerplus*, Apr 12, 2016.

McCauley, Josie. "Trash, Transients, and Trout: The State of Fountain Creek." *The Catalyst*, 2019. https://thecatalystnews.com/2019/05/07/trash-transients-and-trout-the-state-of-fountain-creek/.

Lindwall, Courtney and Molly Ginty. "'Forever Chemicals'

Called PFAS Show Up in Your Food, Clothes, and Home." *Natural Resources Defense Council*, 2023. https://www.nrdc.org/stories/forever-chemicals-called-pfas-show-your-food-clothes-and-home.

De La Garza, Alejandro. "*Dark Waters* Tells the True Story of the Lawyer Who Took DuPont to Court and Won. But Rob Bilott's Fight Is Far From Over." *Time*, 2019. https://time.com/5737451/dark-waters-true-story-rob-bilott/.

Smith, Jerd. "As the Fountain Valley Emerges from a Water Crisis, The Big Question is What Comes Next?" *Water Education Colorado*, 2018. https://www.watereducationcolorado.org/fresh-water-news/as-the-fountain-valley-emerges-from-a-water-crisis-the-next-big-question-is-what-comes-next/.

Smith, Logan. "Xcel plans to replace Colorado power plant in Pueblo with renewable energy battery system." CBS Colorado, 2023. https://www.cbsnews.com/colorado/news/xcel-colorado-pueblo-power-plant-renewable-energy-storage-ldes/.

Swanson, Conrad. "EPA's Proposed Changes on PFAS Limits Would Deem Dozen's of Colorado Water Sources Unsafe." *Fort Morgan Times*, 2023. https://www.fortmorgantimes.com/2023/03/14/epa-pfas-water-forever-chemicals-limit/.

Smith, Jerd. "Colorado Launches PFAS Takeback, Emergency Grant Programs." *Water Education Colorado*, 2021. https://www.watereducationcolorado.org/fresh-water-news/colorado-launches-pfas-takeback-emergency-grant-programs/.

Weis, Kati. "U.S. Air Force pays $9 million for cutting-edge water treatment in Fountain following PFAS contamination concerns." CBS Colorado, 2023. https://www.cbsnews.com/colorado/news/air-force-pays-9-million-water-treatment-fountain-pfas-contamination/.

"Elevated Levels Of 'Forever Chemicals' Found In Some Colorado Drinking Water Districts." CBS Colorado, 2021. https://www.cbsnews.com/colorado/news/chemicals-water-denver-colorado-pfas/.

Stoeckel, Donald. "Evaluation of fecal contamination by human and ruminant sources in upper Fountain Creek, Colorado, 2007-2008, by using multiple lines of evidence." U.S. Geological Survey, 2011.

TRIBUTARIES

MacFarlane, Robert. *The Wild Places*. Penguin, 2007.

Goldfarb, Ben. *Eager: The Surprising Life of Beavers and Why They Matter*. Chelsea Green, 2018.

Seaton, Ernest Thompson. *Lives of Game Animals*. Doubleday, 1929.

PATHWAYS

Schmitt, Angie. "How Windshield Perspective Shapes the Way We See the World." *StreetsBlogUSA*, 2014. https://usa.streetsblog.org/2014/01/07/how-windshield-perspective-shapes-the-way-we-see-the-world.

Pozzi, Paul M. "Speed Freaks: Tunnel Vision and Physiological Perception. *Introduction to Cognitive Psychology*, 2014. https://sites.psu.edu/psych256sp14/2014/01/30/speed-freaks-tunnel-vision-and-physiological-perception/.

DISCARDED

Hailey, Charlie. *The Porch: Meditations on the Edge of Nature*. University of Chicago Press, 2021.

Berry, Wendell. *Preserving Wilderness, Home Economics*. North Point Press, 1987, p. 151.

Jim O'Donnell's interviews with unhoused Fountain dwellers is online at www.aroundtheworldineightyyears.com.

FLOW

Rahel, F.J. and L.A. Thel. (2004, July 22). "Flathead Chub (Platygobio gracilis): a technical conservation assessment," USDA

Forest Service, Rocky Mountain Region. http://www.fs.fed.us/r2/projects/scp/ assessments/flatheadchub.pdf.

Roberts, J.J., J.F. Bruce, and R.E. Zuellig. "Changes in biological communities of the Fountain Creek Basin, Colorado, 2003–2016, in relation to antecedent streamflow, water quality, and habitat: U.S. Geological Survey Scientific Investigations Report." 2018. https://doi.org/10.3133/sir20175162.

David M. Walters, Robert E. Zuellig, Harry J. Crockett, James F. Bruce, Paul M. Lukacs and Ryan M. Fitzpatrick. "Barriers Impede Upstream Spawning Migration of Flathead Chub." Transactions of the American Fisheries Society 143, no. 1 (2014): 17-25. DOI: https://doi.org/10.1080/00028487.2013.824921.

"What Climate Change Means for Colorado." United States Environmental Protection Agency, 2016. https://19january2017snapshot.epa.gov/sites/production/files/2016-09/documents/climate-change-co.pdf.

Colorado State Climate Summaries. North Carolina Institute for Climate Studies, 2022. https://statesummaries.ncics.org/chapter/co/#::text=Temperatures%20in%20Colorado%20have%20risen,very%20hot%20days%20since%202000.

"Nearly Three Billion Birds Gone Since 1970." Cornell Lab of Ornithology. https://www.birds.cornell.edu/home/bring-birds-back/.

Elbien, Asher. *The Road Is an Ecological Trap: an Interview with Ben Goldfarb.* https://heat-death.ghost.io/the-road-is-an-ecological-trap-an-interview-with-ben-goldfarb/.

Goldfarb, Ben. *Crossings: How Road Ecology is Shaping the Future of Our Planet.* W.W. Norton and Company, 2023.

"CODEX Analysis-Apex, Keystone, Threatened, Endangered Species (Federal and State) and Applications to Fountain Creek." https://codex.cnhp.colostate.edu/content/map.

Fountain Creek Watershed Water and ISFs. https://maps.dnr-gis.state.co.us/dwr/Index.html?viewer=mapviewer.

"Black Footed Ferret Pueblo County Reintroduction." Colorado Parks and Wildlife, 2018. https://cpw.state.co.us/Documents/WildlifeSpecies/Mammals/BFF_InfoSheet_2018.pdf.

"Energy (Solar) Development and Wildlife in SE CO." Colorado Parks and Wildlife, 2017. https://cpw.state.co.us/Documents/Conservation-Resources/Energy-Mining/Solar-Energy-BMPs.pdf.

Bester, Seth. "'Once-in-a-generation' land mission begins between Colorado Springs military, conservation groups." *The Gazette*, 2023. https://gazette.com/premium/once-in-a-generation-land-mission-begins-between-colorado-springs-military-conservation-groups/article_b219ebfc-78f6-11ee-9910-ff99f582e0a9.html.

"Colorado Open Lands: Peaks to Prairies." https://coloradoopenlands.org/land-conservation/, https://www.codot.gov/projects/archived-project-sites/peaks-to-plains-trail.

"Palmer Land Trust, 2022-2027 Strategic Plan." https://www.palmerland.org/sites/default/files/2022-04/2022-2027_PLC_StrategicPlan-web.pdf.

PALIMPSESTS

Shaw, Dorothy Price. "The Craigin Collection." *Colorado Magazine* 25 (1948): 166-178.

Lecompte, Janet. "The Craigin Collection and Its Problems." A paper read before the Colorado Historical Society, 1952.

The Craigin Manuscripts. Colorado Springs Pioneer Museum. https://www.cspm.org/collections/manuscript-collections/cragin-manuscript/.

Walker, R.T. "Professor Francis, W. Craigin: An Appreciation." From a paper read before unknown, circa 1959.

Laing, Olivia. *To the River*. The Cannons Press, 2011.

Hailey, Charlie. *The Porch: Meditations on the Edge of Nature*. The University of Chicago Press, 2021.

Curtis C. Smith. "Frank Waters' Minorities: Romance and Realism." *MELUS* 11, no. 4 (December 1984):73–83. https://doi.org/10.2307/467199.

Wroth, William, ed. *Ute Indian Arts and Culture: From Prehistory to the New Millennium Paperback.* Published by the Taylor Museum of the Colorado Springs Fine Arts Center Distributed by University of New Mexico Press, 2000.

West, Elliott. *The Contested Plains: Indians, Goldseekers, and the Rush to Colorado*. University Press of Kansas, 1998.

Kaelin, Celinda. *Ute Legends*. Caxton Press, 2017.

Kaelin, Celinda. *American Indians of the Pike's Peak Region.* Arcadia Publishing, 2008.

Southern Ute Tribe History. https://www.southernute-nsn.gov/history/.

Smith, David P. *Ouray: Chief of the Utes*. Wayfinder Press 1986.

Ardelean, C. F., Becerra-Valdivia, L., Pedersen, M.W., et al. "Evidence of Human Occupation in Mexico Around the Last Glacial Maximum," *Nature* 584 (2002): 87-92.

Bennett, et al."Evidence of Humans in North America During the Last Glacial Maximum." *Science* 373 (2001): 1528-1531.

Bennett, M.R., David Bustos, Daniel Odess, Tommy M. Urban, Jens N. Lallensack, Marcin Budka, Vincent L. Santucci E., Patrick Martinez, Ashleigh L.A. Wiseman, and Sally C. Reynolds. "Walking in mud: Remarkable Pleistocene human trackways from White Sands National Park (New Mexico)." *Quaternary Science Reviews* 249 (2020).

Bustos, D., J. Jakeway, T. M. Urban, V. T. Holliday, B. Fenerty, D. A. Raichlen, M. Budka, S. C. Reynolds, B. D. Allen, D. W. Love, V. L. Santucci, D. Odess, P. Willey, H. G. McDonald, and M. R. Bennett. "Footprints preserve terminal Pleistocene hunt? Human-sloth interactions in North America." *Science Advances* (2018): 4.

Ghosen, Tia. "Fisherman Pulls Up Beastly Evidence of Early Americans." *Live Science*, 2014. Accessed January 23, 2023.

https://www.livescience.com/47289-mastodon-found-under-chesapeake-bay.html.

Madsen D.B., et al. "Comment on "Evidence of Humans in North America during the Last Glacial Maximum." *Science* 375 (2002).

Nichols, Johanna. "Linguistic Diversity and the First Settlement of the New World." *Language* 66, no. 3 (Sep. 1990): 475-521. Linguistic Society of America.

Oviatt, C.G., D.B. Madsen, D. Rhode, and L.G. Davis. "A Critical Assessment of Claims That Human Footprints in the Lake Otero Basin, New Mexico date to the Last Glacial Maximum." *Quaternary Research* (2002): 1-10.

Philippsen, B. "The freshwater reservoir effect in radiocarbon dating." *Heritage Science* 1, vol. 24 (2013).

Pigati, J.S., et al. "Response to Comment on 'Evidence of Humans in North America During the Last Glacial Maximum.'" *Science* (2022): 375.

Potter, Ben A., James C. Chatters, Anna Marie Prentiss, Stuart J. Fiedel, Gary Haynes, Robert L. Kelly, J. David Kilby, François Lanoë, Jacob Holland-Lulewicz, D. Shane Miller, Juliet E. Morrow, Angela R. Perri, Kurt M. Rademaker, Joshua D. Reuther, Brandon T. Ritchison, Guadalupe Sanchez, Ismael Sánchez-Morales, S. Margaret Spivey-Faulkner, Jesse W. Tune, and C. Vance Haynes. "Current Understanding of the Earliest Human Occupations in the Americas: Evaluation of Becerra-Valdivia and Higham (2020)." *PaleoAmerica*, 2020. https://doi.org/10.1080/20555563.2021.1978721.

Raff, Jennifer. "Finding the First Americans" 2002. Accessed January 3, 2023. https://aeon.co/essays/the-first-americans-a-story-of-wonderful-uncertain-science.

Raff, Jennifer. *Origin: A Genetic History of the Americas*. Twelve, 2022.

Steeves, Paulette. *The Indigenous Paleolithic of the Western Hemisphere*. University of Nebraska Press, 2021.

Emmitt, Robert. *The Last War Trail: The Utes and the Settlement of Colorado*. University Press of Colorado, 2000.

Marsh, Charles, S. *The Utes of Colorado: People of the Shining Mountains*. Pruitt Publishing, 1982.

Garcia-Simms, Charlene. "El Pueblo 1854 Christmas Tragedy." Pueblo: Fray Angélico Chávez, Hispanic Genealogical Society of Southern Colorado, 1998.

Johnson, Brian. "Ute Removal and The Hunt Treaty - The Agreement a Buffalo Makes When Pierced with Arrows." Denver Public Library, 2021. https://www.denverlibrary.org/blog/cultural-inclusivity-equity-research/dodie/ute-removal-and-hunt-treaty-agreement-buffalo-makes.

Carrol, Rick. "Pitkin County's namesake as questionable as Columbus Day?" *The Aspen Times*, 2017. https://www.aspentimes.com/news/is-pitkin-countys-namesake-as-questionable-as-columbus-day/.

Waters, Frank. *The Wild Earth's Nobility: Book I of the Pike's Peak Trilogy*. Swallow Press/Ohio University Press, 1971.

VISIONS

Lancaster, Brad. *Rainwater Harvesting for Drylands and Beyond (2nd edition)*, volumes 1 and 2. 2019.

Gies, Erica. *Water Always Wins: Thriving in an Age of Drought and Deluge*. University of Chicago Press, 2022.

Swanson, Conrad. "Colorado Springs violated stormwater regulations, judge rules in lawsuit over runoff." *The Gazette*, 2018. https://gazette.com/news/colorado-springs-violated-stormwater-regulations-judge-rules-in-lawsuit-over-runoff/article_ab1930c6-e498-11e8-a668-87b7a5c314e5.html.

May, Stephen J. *A Kingdom of Their Own: The Story of the Palmers of Glen Eyrie*. Glen Eyrie Press, 2017.

Harner, John. *Profiting from the Peak: Landscape and Liberty in Colorado Springs*. University Press of Colorado, 2021.

"Colorado Springs in 187." *Colorado Springs Gazette*, April 19,

1873.

Webb, Walter Prescott. *The Great Plains*. Ginn and Company, 1959: quoted in Harner.

Poulton, Curt, A. "A Historical Geographic Approach to the Study of the Institualization of the Doctrine of Prior Appropriations: The Emergence of Appropriative Water Rights in Colorado Springs, Colorado." PhD diss., University of Minnesota, 1989: quoted in Harner.

"Summer Tour No.1 – Fountain Valley." *Pueblo Lore* 15, no. 7 (July 1990).

"Fountain Lake Hotel." *Pueblo Daily Chieftain,* April 21, 1889.

Jent, Breeanna. "Colorado Springs Completing Restoration of North Douglas Creek, a Poster Child Project in Stormwater Progress." *The Gazette*, March 14, 2023. https://gazette.com/news/environment/colorado-springs-completing-restoration-of-north-douglas-creek-a-poster-child-project-in-stormwater-progress/article_7db905ae-c1d2-11ed-8fb4-2f1df9393646.html.

Boyce, Dan. "After Decades of Neglect, Fountain Creek Holds New Promise for Colorado Springs." *CPR News*, 2020. https://www.cpr.org/2020/07/24/after-decades-of-neglect-fountain-creek-holds-new-promise-for-colorado-springs/.

"Senator Salazar Sees Fountain Creek as Future 'Crown Jewel.'" Westside Pioneer, 2006. https://mail.westsidepioneer.com/Articles/092806/FountainCreek.html.

Shinn, Mary. "Colorado Springs Fishing Shop Aims to Clean Up Fountain Creek, Offer More Public Access." *The Gazette*, 2021. https://gazette.com/news/colorado-springs-fishing-shop-aims-to-clean-up-fountain-creek-offer-more-public-access/article_d2df4b30-c542-11eb-9c96-f351c51da9a7.html.

Shinn, Mary. "Kayaking Down Fountain Creek? It Could Be Part of the Reimagined Look for Colorado Springs Creeks." *The Gazette*, 2021. https://gazette.com/news/kayaking-down-fountain-creek-it-could-be-part-of-the-re-imagined-look-for-colorado/article_875852f6-625a-11eb-bce3-ffd12d046fe7.html.

Bzdek, Vince. "Can Restoration Make Fountain Creek Rise Again?" *The Gazette*, 2021. https://gazette.com/news/can-restoration-make-fountain-creek-rise-again-vince-bzdek/article_73bdcaea-ddc2-11ea-971f-6f54669df8eb.html.

Shinn, Mary. "New Vision Proposed for Monument and Fountain Creeks Includes Beaches for Tubing, Boating." *The Gazette*, 2022. https://gazette.com/news/local/new-vision-proposed-for-colorado-springs-creeks-includes-beaches-for-tubing-boating/article_8f3b05dc-dacb-11ec-9ca2-af2d-97ca8ef4.html.

"COS Creek Plan, Fountain Creeks Watershed Vision and Implementation Plan." 2022. https://coscreekplan.org/index.html.

HEALERS

Lawton, Rebecca. "The Healing Power of Nature." *Aeon*, 2017. https://aeon.co/essays/why-forests-and-rivers-are-the-most-potent-health-tonic-around.

Leopold, Aldo. *A Sand County Almanac*." Ballantine Books, 1949.

Hemingway, Ernest. *The Complete Short Stories of Ernest Hemingway: The Finca Vigia Edition*. 1998.

Liang, Olivia. *To the River: A Journey Beneath the Surface*. CannonGate Books, 2011.

Grahame, Kenneth. *The Wind in the Willows*. 1908.

Maclean, Norman. *A River Runs Through It*. University of Chicago Press, 1976.

Graves, John. *Goodbye to a River*. The Curtis Publishing Company, 1959.

Kart, Jeff. "The Gutter Bin Stops Trash Before It Gets Into Rivers And Lakes." *Forbes*, 2019. https://www.forbes.com/sites/jeffkart/2019/05/28/the-gutter-bin-stops-trash-before-it-gets-into-river-and-lakes/?sh=481026986574.

"USDA Forest Service, Rocky Mountain Bee Plant (*Cleome serrulata*)." https://www.fs.usda.gov/wildflowers/plant-of-the-week/cleome_serrulata.shtml.

RESTORATION

Corday, Jackie. "Restoring Western Headwater Streams with LowTech Process-Based Methods: A Review of the Science and Case Study Results, Challenges, and Opportunities." *American Rivers*, 2022. chrome-extension://efaidnbmnnnibpcajpcglclefindmkaj/https://static1.squarespace.com/static/5d838acc42e01b1dcc1d7668/t/6387ca575d-93dc60f4185e9c/1669843547769/FINAL_LTPBR+White+-Paper_Nov2022-SHARE%5B84%5D.pdf.

Section 404 of the Clean Water Act: Floodplain Management (Executive Order 11988). https://www.epa.gov/cwa-404/floodplain-management-executive-order-11988.

Mallett, Jerry and Sally Ranney. "Proposal to Protect the Holy Cross Wilderness Area and Homestake Creek Wetlands." *Colorado Headwaters*, 2022.

Smith, Jerd. "Proposal to shrink Holy Cross Wilderness, increase water storage draws hundreds of comments." *Colorado Sun*. https://coloradosun.com/2020/07/09/holy-cross-wilderness-reservoir-plan/.

Mallett, Jerry, Sally Ranney, Bill Dvorak, and Sherri Tippie. "Proposal to Enhance Colorado Water Resources Through Preservation and Restoration of Wetlands and Aquifers in Headwaters Regions." *Colorado Headwaters*, 2019. chrome-extension://efaidnbmnnnibpcajpcglclefindmkaj/https://coloradoheadwaters.org/wp-content/uploads/2019/10/Colorado-Headwaters-Proposal.pdf.

Smith, Jerd. "River ecologists are eager to show how beavers are critical to improving watersheds in the West." *The Colorado Sun*, 2021. https://coloradosun.com/2021/05/21/beavers-climate-colorado-river-health/.

"Enhancing Keystone Ecosystem Resiliency in the Fountain Creek Watershed." Keystone Ecosystems Initiative.

Clark, Moe. "Stream restoration evolves to include beaver imitation, gets boost from Colorado Legislature." *Water Education Colorado*, 2023. https://www.watereducationcolorado.org/fresh-water-news/stream-restoration-evolves-to-include-beaver-imitation-and-gets-a-boost-from-the-legislature/.

SUGGESTED READINGS

- *Notes for the Aurora Society: 1500 Miles on Foot Across Finland*, Jim O'Donnell, 2009, Infinity Publishing
- *River-Horse: The Logbook of a Boat Across America*, William Least Heat-Moon, 2001, Penguin Publishing Group
- *Citizen Explorer: The Life of Zebulon Pike*, Jared Orsi, 2014, Oxford University Press
- *Mr. Jefferson's Lost Cause: Land, Farmers, Slavery, and the Louisiana Purchase*, Roger Kennedy, 2003, Oxford University Press
- *The Wind in the Willows*, Kenneth Grahame, 1908
- *To The River: A Journey Beneath the Surface*, Olivia Laing, 2011, Cannongate
- *Underland: A Deep Time Journey*, Robert MacFarlane, 2019, W. W. Norton and Co.
- *Waterlog: A Swimmer's Journey Through Britain*, Roger Deakin, 1999, Vintage
- *The Lost Gold Rush Journals: Daniel Jenks 1849-1865*, Larry Obermesik & Daniel Jenks, 2021, Larry Obermesik
- *Eager: The Surprising, Secret Life of Beavers and Why They Matter*, Ben Goldfarb, 2018, Chelsea Green Publishing
- *Water Always Wins: Thriving in an Age of Drought and Deluge*, Erica Gies, 2022, University of Chicago Press
- *Profiting from the Peak: Landscape and Liberty in Colorado Springs*, John Harner, 2021, University Press of Colorado

- *The Contested Plains: Indians, Goldseekers, and the Rush to Colorado*, Elliott West, 1998, University Press of Kansas
- *Cadillac Desert: The American West and its Disappearing Water, Revised Edition*, Mark Reisner, 1993, Penguin Books
- *Rivers of Empire: Water, Aridity, and the Growth of the American West*, Donald Worster, 1985, Oxford University Press

ACKNOWLEDGEMENTS

Above all, my deepest gratitude goes to my wife, friend, and life partner Rasa Lila O'Donnell, who supported me emotionally and at times financially through this endeavor. I wake grateful for her every single day. Thank you to my children Isabella, Ilan O'Donnell, and Sky Prentice, and my parents Virginia and Jim O'Donnell.

Thank you also to my grandparents, long dead before this book was written but people of profound influence on the trajectory of my life: Florian J. "Bud" Siegle, Gertrude Siegle, Martha Bartlett and Richard Bartlett. I miss you all, still.

Thank you also to Sylvia O'Donnell, Bill, Barbara, and Justin Barr, Allison Schuch, Terry Hart, Margaret Ward-Masias, Judy McGinnis and the Pueblo Historical Society, Leah Davis Witherow, Kelly Murphy, Hillary Mannion and the Colorado Springs Pioneers Museum, David Burnham, Trout Unlimited, Alex Jouney, Jerry Cordova, Kellina Gilbreth, David Eick, John Harner, Mary Shinn, Bill Banks, Katherine Cline, Dr. David Kilby, Jerry Mallett, Theron Horton, Erin Elder, Jackie Corday, Larry Obermesik, Vera Campbell, Jamie Valdez, Celinda Kaelin, Amy Brautagin, Hannah Mooney, Susan Finzel, Richard Skorman, The Catamount Institute, Julie at the Catamount Institute, JoJo Trujillo, Chuck Finley, Nate Miller, John Harner, Anna Cordova, Lauren Rosenthal McManus, Bill Dvorak, Rachel Zancanella, Robert Zuluaga, Natalie Flowers, Dr. Brian Mihlbachler, Matt Hildner, Mitch Berg, Dr. Laura Hempel, Steve

Welchert, H. Wayne Brown, Judy McGinnis, Margret Ward-Masias, Anglers Covey, Summer LaJoie, Richard Mulledy, Ryan Bouton, Ferris Frost, Barbara at Pueblo Parks and Recreation, Alan Ward, Laura Paskus, Tim Dee, Helen Benevides, H. Wayne Brown, Theron Verna, Jay Frost, the kids of the Cheyenne Mountain Junior High Creek Club, Dr. William Fleming, Frank Winn Graves, Chyna Dixon, Steve Welchert, Mark D. Shea, Karin Hill, Angel at Econolodge Downtown, Longinos Gonzales, Jr., Jessica Mills, Kristy Milligan of WestsideCares, and Lauren Rosenthal McManus. An extra special thank you to Jay, Renee, Cindy, Jonny, Cheryl, Junior, Hope, Duffy, and the other unhoused Fountain Creek denizens who helped me understand their lives and what it was like to live next to the Fountain.

And a very special shout out to all the amazing people at Torrey House Press. Will Neville-Rehbehn, Kirsten Johanna Allen, Kathleen Metcalf, Gray Buck-Cockayne, Scout Invie, and Callie Stephenson.

There are so many people that made this book possible and I apologize if I missed anyone.

ABOUT THE AUTHOR

Author, photographer, and activist Jim O'Donnell began his career as a field archaeologist and historian working throughout the American Southwest, Mexico, Peru, and France. He is the author of *Notes for the Aurora Society: 1500 Miles on Foot Across Finland* and a collection of travel stories. His work has appeared in *Sierra Magazine*, *El Palacio*, *Sapiens*, *MM Magazine*, *Ensia*, and elsewhere. O'Donnell continues to work as a community conservation activist and wilderness advocate in the American Southwest where he works to protect and restore wetlands and watersheds. Born and raised in southern Colorado, O'Donnell lives in Taos, New Mexico.

TORREY HOUSE PRESS

Torrey House Press publishes books at the intersection of the literary arts and environmental advocacy. THP authors explore the diversity of human experiences and relationships with place. THP books create conversations about issues that concern the American West, landscape, literature, and the future of our ever-changing planet, inspiring action toward a more just world.

We believe that lively, contemporary literature is at the cutting edge of social change. We seek to inform, expand, and reshape the dialogue on environmental justice and stewardship for the natural world by elevating literary excellence from diverse voices.

Visit www.torreyhouse.org for reading group discussion guides, author interviews, and more.

As a 501(c)(3) nonprofit publisher, our work is made possible by generous donations from readers like you.

Torrey House Press is supported by The King's English Bookshop, Maria's Bookshop, the Jeffrey S. & Helen H. Cardon Foundation, the Sam & Diane Stewart Family Foundation, the Barker Foundation, the George S. and Dolores Doré Eccles Foundation, Diana Allison, Klaus Bielefeldt, Joe Breddan, Karen Edgley, Laurie Hilyer, Susan Markley, Marion S. Robinson, Kitty Swenson, Shelby Tisdale, Kirtly Parker Jones, Robert Aagard & Camille Bailey Aagard, Kif Augustine Adams & Stirling Adams, Rose Chilcoat & Mark Franklin, Jerome Cooney & Laura Storjohann, Linc Cornell & Lois Cornell, Susan Cushman & Charlie Quimby, Kathleen Metcalf & Peter Metcalf, Betsy Gaines Quammen & David Quammen, the Utah Division of Arts & Museums, Utah Humanities, the National Endowment for the Humanities, the National Endowment for the Arts, the Salt Lake City Arts Council, the Utah Governor's Office of Economic Development, and Salt Lake County Zoo, Arts & Parks. Our thanks to our readers, donors, members, and the Torrey House Press Board of Directors for their valued support.

www.ingramcontent.com/pod-product-compliance
Lightning Source LLC
Jackson TN
JSHW021307171224
75586JS00017B/111

* 9 7 9 8 8 9 0 9 2 0 1 1 9 *